HOPE
EMERGES

Joseph Macenka

ISBN: 1493635530
ISBN 13: 9781493635535

Library of Congress Control Number: 2013920488
CreateSpace Independent Publishing Platform
North Charleston, South Carolina

AUTHOR'S NOTE

When the call finally came just after Christmas 2011, I was prepared—or so I thought.

With well in excess of three decades in the news business, I had plenty of experience dealing with the federal government, and those experiences had, by and large, followed the same general rule: The higher you went up the ladder, the tighter the restrictions became. And in a post-9/11 world, media access got even tighter across the board.

I understood that backdrop of tightly controlled access when I approached federal officials in Washington in late 2011 with a proposal for a book: The US Department of Veterans Affairs, under fire for decades for failing to keep up with the overwhelming needs of the nation's service personnel, had ramped up its efforts in response to the wars in Iraq and Afghanistan. Part of that response included the establishment of a small group of so-called Polytrauma Rehabilitation Centers to take care of the worst of the worst, those with multiple types of traumatic injuries. In short, the polytrauma centers were a success. Patients were able to find a new normal, to return to their homes, their communities, their jobs, all because of dedicated teams of medical professionals who were ramping up patient care to new levels.

And not only was the polytrauma system working, but it was producing a superstar within its own ranks: The worst of the cases, especially those whose brain injuries had left them comatose, were winding up at the McGuire Veterans Affairs Medical Center in Richmond, Virginia, and the polytrauma staff, time after time, would come through for them. "Miracle" was a term that kept surfacing when patients discussed their care at McGuire's polytrauma unit. The staff of mostly young, all energetic, all very focused and innovative professionals was establishing new standards for success and quality of medical care in the VA health system, standards to which this overburdened bureaucracy had long aspired.

There was a story within the walls of McGuire's Polytrauma unit, a story of triumph, a story of hope, a story of success cultivated by a dedicated group of medical professionals working together for the common goal of doing everything possible for the nation's service members. But to tell the story, one would need unfiltered access to the staff, the patients, and their families. And the VA, quite simply, had never been particularly known to grant that type of carte blanche availability, especially in light of federal privacy laws and the growing veil of international distrust brought on by the war on terrorism.

The VA had an inspiring success story in its midst. Getting clearance to tell it, however, might be difficult, if not impossible.

The bid to get approval for a book led ultimately to the VA's headquarters in Washington, DC, where department spokeswoman Kerry Meeker listened patiently to the proposal, then advised that it would take some time for her to run it through the necessary channels.

With each passing day that followed, I assumed my chances for approval were diminishing. I figured the proposal would either be rejected outright or the VA would slap so many restrictions on it that it would become difficult, if not impossible, to put a human face on the project.

On the afternoon the face of my cell phone sprang to light and it showed Meeker was finally calling back, I braced for the worst possible news.

As it turns out, the VA had something else in mind.

"This is a story," Meeker said, "that deserves to be told."

She was right.

For roughly the next 18 months, I was a witness to the inner workings of Richmond's polytrauma unit staff as they worked their miracles on military personnel with all types of severe injuries caused by all manner of particularly violent traumatic events. The resolve displayed day in and day out by the staff, patients, and families was nothing short of heroic, and their willingness to share their experiences was just as impressive.

Dr. Ajit Pai, the unit's medical director, typically introduced me to the patients, telling them I was working on a book about the unit, telling them a bit about my background and telling them it was their choice if they wanted to speak with me. Never once did they refuse. Never once was I asked to leave a patient's room during an examination, therapy session, or what could sometimes become very delicate discussions between staff members, patients, and their loved ones.

All the subjects in this book agreed to allow their real names to be used with the sole exception of a patient who also happened to be a gastroenterologist at Walter Reed National Military Medical Center. That patient and his wife are referred to in the book as Bruce and Helen Wallace, at their request.

After receiving VA clearance for the project, the first person I interviewed at McGuire was Dr. Shane McNamee, the unit's first full-time medical director. It would be an understatement to say he paved the way for the success of this project, not only by asking the staff for their cooperation in telling the polytrauma story but by frequently pulling me aside in the hallways and introducing me to yet another person he felt I should meet.

McNamee's office door was always open for me, and the same was true for his successor, Pai, who was nothing short of tireless in his support. He would cheerfully block out his time for me, often in 90-minute chunks, to make sure I understood everything from intricate details of traumatic brain injury and various treatment options to the inner workings of the VA bureaucracy and the demands that life in the polytrauma unit can place on staff members' private lives.

The rest of the staff members were no less generous, giving me unrestricted access to therapy sessions, their expertise, and their frank observations. Monique Jones, one of the speech-language pathologists, even slipped into a role as a technical adviser of sorts, reviewing and offering suggestions for several chapters in which I had questions about whether I had accurately portrayed particular methods employed by staff members.

My gratitude isn't limited to the staff. It's one thing for the patients and their loved ones to have allowed me an unfiltered view of their lives. For them to have done it while trying to piece together a semblance of normalcy in the immediate aftermath of what will likely end up being the single most traumatic event of their lifetime represents a gift I can never repay.

And finally, I need to thank four women, starting with my wife, Jody, for her patience as I worked through this project while also making what frequently were poor efforts to balance a full-time newspaper job as well as my part-time passions as a football official and a baseball umpire. Darlene Edwards, the spokeswoman at McGuire, effortlessly displayed her prowess as an advocate. I cannot put into words the value of Anne Catlett's counsel and listening skills, and I can never adequately thank my very dear friend Linda Marie Painter. Every time I needed the perspective of an outside party, of someone who could be trusted to put all other factors aside and speak openly, she was there.

To all, my sincere gratitude. You helped show that hope does indeed emerge.

CHAPTER ONE

THE RIGHTING EFFECT

A worn, sad look on his face, the father shook his head slowly as he sat in an armchair at the foot of his son's hospital bed.

"He had it all—six-pack abs, thick neck, big arms, you name it. I almost didn't recognize him; he had gotten so big and strong," David McHenry said, before rattling off a list of the myriad injuries from an improvised explosive device (IED) in Afghanistan that left his son facing a long recovery, a road that had landed him in the Polytrauma Rehabilitation Center (PRC) at McGuire Veterans Affairs Medical Center in Richmond, Virginia.

It was eighty-one degrees outside, an unusually warm afternoon in late February, even by Southern standards, and a number of patients had gone out to the fourteen-thousand-square-foot rooftop garden that adjoins the polytrauma unit on the second floor of the hospital. The warm, healing sun, the gentle breezes, and the daffodils in the planter boxes standing at attention in full bloom seemed a perfect way for the patients to celebrate the imminent arrival of spring. US Army Spc. Jon McHenry was one of the lucky ones to get a room with a wall-to-wall window overlooking the rooftop garden, a professionally landscaped masterpiece of respite, complete with teak wood benches and a gurgling water fountain, sitting atop an otherwise drab, boxy hospital built with millions and millions of red bricks.

On this afternoon, however, Jon had the shades in the window of room 110 drawn almost completely closed, casting a dark gray shadow inside the room where he lay huddled in bed, his brown hair matted by long hours of sleeping in the same position and his spindly, pasty white, surgically scarred legs covered by a fleece blanket with an army camouflage print. It had been less than four years since those legs had carried him to high school basketball stardom in his native Newport, Pennsylvania, a small, tight-knit community where he built a reputation as a fierce competitor, tenacious point guard, and strong floor leader who scored nearly eight hundred points in two years as a starter.

Two days after Christmas 2011, the blast of an IED on a dark road in Afghanistan's Paktia province had taken the lives of three of his comrades and gravely wounded Jon as well as his commanding officer, Capt. Luis Avila, and Spc. Michael Crawford. In the blink of an eye, Jon, who was driving an armored troop transport vehicle when it went over a device packed with an estimated 400 pounds of explosives, went from being in the best shape of his life, a rock-solid, 170-pound military policeman, to a twenty-two-year-old soldier fighting for his life. He had fractured bones stretching from his neck to his feet, and his numerous internal wounds included traumatic brain injury (TBI), casting a pall of uncertainty over his ability to ever fully recover.

So on a day when other patients sat outside his window, drinking in the restorative late-winter sunshine and the beauty of the rooftop garden, Jon McHenry—whose new battles included one to keep his weight above 125 pounds—lay curled up in bed under a military blanket, struggling to keep warm.

Jon was less than sixty days into a recovery process that would be measured not in months but in years and would include treatment for injuries both seen and unseen. Like thousands of other members of America's military who had cheated death on the battlefields of Iraq and Afghanistan, he had come home and discovered he had even more demons to battle.

"It just devastates you as a parent to see your child go through this," explained his father, who had maintained an almost constant vigil beside his son since his return to the United States. Jon's wife, Jay, nearly seven months pregnant, smiled gently and adjusted a pillow as her husband shifted gingerly in an attempt to get comfortable, his movements limited by a full-torso, tortoise shell-like brace designed to protect his fractured vertebrae. A blue balloon emblazoned with "It's A Boy" danced in the air at the end of its lace tie anchored to the bed railing. A leather basketball, signed by the current members of the Newport High School basketball team, sat on a shelf above the bed. The window ledge was crowded with flowers, get-well cards, and a giant fruit basket, and scattered across the room were bags of Doritos, packages of Twinkies, and a giant box of Fruit Loops—all fair game for a patient who had orders to gain weight by any means necessary, even if that meant loading up on junk food in between the meals of healthy, albeit bland, hospital food.

Although getting a room overlooking the rooftop garden was a stroke of good fortune for Jon, it paled in comparison to the fact that he had been sent to Richmond for his rehabilitation. Richmond's PRC had quickly emerged as a leader in the field of caring for and rehabilitating service personnel with multiple types of traumatic injuries. Time and again, those with the very worst injuries found the very best care, their best chances of finding a new normal, in the hands of the staff at McGuire's polytrauma unit.

The long, winding path that led Richmond to prominence in the poly-trauma field actually began in Vietnam, the first war in which the United States used helicopters on a widespread basis to quickly evacuate the wounded from the battlefield and get them to field hospitals for stabilizing measures. That quickly translated into a marked increase in survival rates for those wounded in combat, but over the coming years, that also translated into an overwhelmed Department of Veterans Affairs (VA) healthcare system that was ill prepared for the legions of wounded service members returning to the United States and needing extended care, many of them for Posttraumatic Stress Disorder (PTSD).

As the United States began investing more dollars into veterans' health care, the nation became embroiled in new wars, first in Iraq and then in Afghanistan, where America's military hierarchy began noticing a new breed of injuries linked to the popularity of insurgents using IEDs. The relatively small land mines of the Vietnam era were giving way to larger, more complicated, more powerful devices that often were buried under road surfaces and frequently contained three hundred to four hundred pounds of explosives. With an increase in the size of the bombs came an increase in the amount of devastation. No longer were typical soldiers' injuries the kinds associated with gunshot wounds and small land mines. Many were losing more than one limb and suffering multiple fractures throughout their body, devastating blast-related damage in their groin and chest areas, and strokes associated with the rapid loss of blood.

Another trend also was emerging, a disturbing common bond with many of the wounded: The magnitude of the IED blasts was leaving them with significant brain trauma. Now, instead of coming back from Vietnam with PTSD, gunshot wounds, and land-mine injuries, America's warriors were returning home with all that plus massive internal injuries, numerous fractures, multiple amputations, and TBI, which is loosely defined as any damage to the brain caused by an external force. The US military's medical community, which had increased the rate of battlefield injury survivability in Vietnam, saw those rates continue to go up in Iraq and again in Afghanistan. US troops were overcoming life-threatening injuries on foreign battlefields only to come home to find themselves in equally significant fights—this time to figure out a way to move on from myriad injuries.

Just as the United States had improved its response in those critical first hours and days after its service members were injured in battle—the Department of Defense said the battlefield injury survival rate went from 78 percent in Vietnam to more than 95 percent in Afghanistan—it needed to get better in helping them once they got home and began the difficult journey of trying to become whole again, of trying to again become fathers, husbands, and soldiers. The VA, still stinging from criticism that it had not responded well to the waves of service members who were suffering from

PTSD and other long-term medical problems in the Vietnam era, would become the central player in the response to TBI.

Congress in 2004 passed two laws that led to the development of a program to meet the complex rehabilitation needs of America's injured military members. It became known as the Polytrauma System of Care (PSC), and it consisted of four components that would take advantage of the VA's vast healthcare network, which included more than 150 medical centers and more than 1,700 clinics and other satellite facilities. The most visible of the four components was the establishment of four Polytrauma Rehabilitation Centers, where the VA would set up specialized services for those with the most severe injuries. The system also initially included three lower levels of care for those with less severe injuries. Those three, in descending order, were twenty-two network sites, more than eighty support clinic teams, and doctors with polytrauma training at the remaining VA medical centers.

During Operation Iraqi Freedom, the typical path of an injured service member was to be flown from the site of the injury to the closest military field hospital to be stabilized, then to Landstuhl Regional Medical Center, a massive US military hospital near Ramstein Air Force Base in Germany, to be prepared for a flight home. In most cases, the first stop in the United States was Bethesda, Maryland, site of Walter Reed National Military Medical Center, where surgery and other acute care likely would determine the service member's next destination.

Before Iraq, that next destination would often be a military hospital that was close to either the injured service member's hometown or where their unit was based. With the establishment of the PSC, however, that question of where to send severely injured warriors was no longer governed primarily by convenience regarding proximity to either their home or their unit but by where they could get the best treatment they needed for their multiple injuries. The first four PRCs included one on the West Coast, in Palo Alto, California; one in the Upper Midwest, in Minneapolis, Minnesota; and one in the Southeast, in Tampa, Florida. The decision of where to put a PRC to serve the large population base along the East Coast and the Northeast became an easy one, in large part not only because the VA hospital in Richmond was barely a two-hour ride from Bethesda, but also because the McGuire VA Medical Center was already one of the largest facilities in the VA system. In addition, McGuire had been part of the VA's Defense and Veterans Head Injury Program since 1992, and the hospital had a well-established working relationship with the physical medicine and rehabilitation department at Virginia Commonwealth University's (VCU) medical school, about a ten-minute ride away in downtown Richmond.

So Richmond's VA hospital in 2005 began building what would become its polytrauma unit, and by the time Jon McHenry arrived in January 2012, it had grown from a few rooms on a single hallway to a twenty-bed, fourteen-thousand-square-foot facility with sixty-eight staff members. Two months after Jon got to Richmond, construction began on an $8.5 million, two-year makeover that would increase the size of the unit to thirty-four thousand square feet and make the operation even more efficient.

There was something else about Richmond that swelled over the years: its reputation.

Now that the US military healthcare system had made significant advances in figuring out how to help those injured on the battlefield survive, the VA's PRCs—including a fifth unit opened in San Antonio, Texas, in 2012—started making strides in helping them thrive.

The cornerstone of that effort was what Dr. Shane McNamee, the medical director who nurtured Richmond's polytrauma unit from its infancy, called *relationship-based medicine.* It was grounded in a simple principle for the unit's doctors, therapists, and other staff members: If you're going to help a patient, then your job starts by getting to know them, by listening to them as well as you can, so you can understand what their goals and desires are. No two brain injuries are alike, and that means it's unlikely that two patients will respond the same way to what might appear to be the same problem. Because of that, McNamee explained, each patient's therapy must not only be unique, but it must be flexible—and it must involve significant, continuing input from the patient and their loved ones.

McNamee realized that type of approach went against the grain of managed healthcare in the private sector, where insurers often dictate what kind of therapy a patient will receive and for how long. In the private sector, he said, brain-injury patients may not always get the most effective therapy or get it for a duration that will give them the best possible care. That is where the VA's tiered system of care can offer superior therapy for patients, starting with the inpatient setting at the PRCs and then working down to the less-structured environments of the lower three tiers, allowing patients to continue to have their needs addressed as the years pass.

McNamee smiled. "This isn't conveyor-belt therapy."

McNamee assembled a team of mostly young professionals who were highly energetic, dedicated, and worked well together for the common goal of taking the most severely wounded and getting them back to their homes, their families, and their units. Along the road to recovery, the staff was unceasingly patient and sensitive to the fact that the patients and their caregivers were going through what would likely be the darkest chapter of their lives, a chapter that often includes as its baggage divorce and other fractured personal relationships, career ambitions that are cut short and need to be reconfigured, and medical outcomes that are impossible to predict and can even include death. The team became particularly adept at making advances with patients with TBIs, including those who were in a coma when they came through the doors at Richmond. Time and again, the Richmond staff would work medical wonders with their TBI patients, and as a result, the word got out: If you were among the worst of the worst cases, your best chances for success were in Richmond.

"We are never happier than when the patient walks out of here," McNamee said. "When the last thing we see is their rear end go through the main doors of the unit, that's as gratifying as it gets."

The massive construction job that would expand and improve the unit had yet to begin as spring 2012 approached, but McNamee already knew how he wanted to finish it: by having a sign made for placement over the entrance to the unit, written in Latin, to say simply: "Turning patients into people."

One of the psychologists McNamee brought on board was Sherry Ceperich, who came to McGuire in 2008, when there were eight psychologists at the entire hospital, and she was the only on the polytrauma unit. Five years later, there were eighteen psychologists at McGuire and plans to hire more, and Ceperich, a counseling psychologist, was joined on the polytrauma unit by a neuropsychologist.

"It's progressive here," Ceperich said. "People believe that people are going to get better. It's a very hopeful place."

According to Ceperich, the recovery of the patients goes hand in hand with the camaraderie and enthusiasm of the staff for their shared mission of healing those who put their lives on the line for their country. That shared mission was enabled, in large part, by the fact that the staff knew the nation's military hierarchy was squarely behind the polytrauma rehabilitation program. It's one thing to want to do your best for someone; it's another to be given the right tools to do that job, to come to work every day knowing you're going to get the resources and support you need to help your patients achieve the best possible outcome.

"We call it the righting effect," she explained. "It's an attitude of, 'I'm a professional. This is my job. I need to make this right.'"

———

Jon McHenry had originally planned to go to college, with the hope of playing basketball, but as his 2008 graduation from Newport High approached, he found that no matter how tough he was on the court, no matter how proficient a floor leader he was, there was limited interest in a point guard who was only five feet, eight inches tall. His best option appeared to be Lock Haven University, a 4,700-student school in Lock Haven, Pennsylvania, about a two-hour drive northwest of Newport, but one thing led to another, and a delay in SAT scores resulted in him not getting the necessary paperwork completed in time to be considered for admission.

"He struggled with his future, he really did," recalled his grandmother, Janet McHenry, upon whom Jon relied for advice during his formative years, a period when he had a troubled relationship with his birth mother. "We'd have these long conversations, and he'd say, 'What am I going to do, Nan?'

He wanted to find something that would lead to a good career, to make a good decision about his future."

Jon eventually settled on the army, which he joined with an eye toward getting experience as a military policeman and parlaying that into a career in law enforcement. It helped that he had a friend who had become an MP.

"I had only heard good things about it," Jon said. "The more I looked into it, the more sense it made."

His plan produced a bonus early in his enlistment when he was stationed in South Korea for two years and had the opportunity to play basketball on a university-level team, with which he excelled. When that deployment ended, he returned to Fort Hood, Texas, to await his next assignment.

In early December 2011, his unit was sent to Afghanistan, where Jon was a member of a quick-reaction team that had primary responsibility for providing security for a colonel. On December 27, with no colonel to guard that day, the team received a call about 11 A.M. to respond to an area about one and one-half miles from their base. One of the US military's unmanned drones had gone down in a field in between villages, and Jon's team was told to go guard the aircraft until a decision could be made about what to do with it.

By the time the soldiers arrived to secure the plane and the scene, a crowd of villagers had already gathered to take in the spectacle. Jon and the rest of his unit spent hour after hour standing in the field, watching the downed drone—and in turn being watched by the Afghans.

"They had nothing better to do than just stand there and watch us all day, and they did," he recalled.

Finally, at about 5:30 P.M., the appropriate personnel arrived at the site, examined the plane, and decided that the missiles should be taken off and hauled away and the wrecked remains of the drone should be blown up—a process that kept the soldiers in the field well past sundown and provided some entertainment for the Afghans who had stood watching all day.

The road between the base and the downed aircraft had a reputation as a troubled, potentially dangerous route, but there had been no incidents on it since Jon's unit had arrived in Afghanistan on December 4, barely three weeks earlier. Nonetheless, a road-clearance team was dispatched to check it for potential explosives before the drone-guarding soldiers set out on their return to their base. Road-clearance units had become a routine—but not foolproof—way of life for the US military in Afghanistan, where the use of IEDs buried under road surfaces had become an increasingly popular weapon of choice by insurgents.

By the time the convoy of four armored-personnel vehicles set out for the trip back to base, an uneasy feeling had grown in the soldiers about their audience of villagers.

"They just stood there and watched us all day. They kept their eyes on us," Jon said. "They had plenty of time to figure out who the officers were, who the highest-ranking guys were, who had the most bars on their uniforms."

Two of those—the unit's commander, Capt. Luis Avila, and Jon's squad leader, Sgt. Noah M. Korte—got into the vehicle that Jon was driving. It was number three in the line of four vehicles, and per safety protocol, the vehicles kept a distance of fifty meters between themselves when they pulled away from the site.

That was the last thing Jon remembered of that day.

———

After the first two armored-personnel carriers began driving slowly away from the site without incident, Jon's thirty-four-thousand-pound vehicle went over top of what was later determined to be an IED packed with nearly four hundred pounds of explosives—the same bomb over which the first two vehicles in the convoy had passed without incident moments earlier. Jon later explained that he believed the IED was command detonated when his vehicle went over top of it because the insurgents knew his cargo included a captain and a sergeant.

The results were horrific.

The seventeen-ton truck, a so-called mine-resistant ambush-protected (MRAP) vehicle, was launched some fifty feet in the air, according to witness accounts, and then rolled when it landed. When the troops from the other three vehicles reached the remains of the smoldering MRAP, it no longer had any doors. Korte and two other men were killed. Avila had massive injuries and lost one leg. Crawford had back and leg fractures. Jon, his helmet still securely fastened atop his head, was still belted into his seat, which was found outside the MRAP, resting against the vehicle. He had a fractured left foot, a fractured right foot, a severely fractured right tibia that later required a long titanium rod, a fractured right fibula that later required numerous screws and wiring, a ruptured spleen, a tear in his colon, numerous fractured ribs, a punctured lung that later spawned a blood clot, a fractured right collarbone, a fractured scapula, three fractured vertebrae, a frontal brain lobe contusion and bleeding on his brain—evidence of what doctors called brain rollover damage.

Even with all these injuries, Jon, with his badly fractured right leg bent up near his head, was still exhibiting the traits of a tough little point guard on the basketball court.

"They said I kept trying to stand up and see what was going on, to check on everybody," he recalled months later, shaking his head.

A Blackhawk helicopter was dispatched to the scene to evacuate the wounded to the large US base in Bagram, Afghanistan, where doctors tried to stabilize Jon, Capt. Avila, and Sgt. Crawford for a trip to Landstuhl. While medical teams tended to the three injured soldiers, the army once again put its notification network into gear, starting the process of contacting the families of the dead and the wounded with the news from Afghanistan. The families of the wounded generally were delivered the news via a telephone call; the families of those killed received a knock on the door and the news delivered in person. Until all families were notified and briefed on what had occurred, the military would release precious little information to the public via the news media. Even after notifications had been made, the military kept its comments brief.

———

US Department of Defense News Release No. 1048-11 was distributed on December 29, 2011. Under the headline, "DOD Identifies Army Casualties," was the following text:

The Department of Defense announced today the deaths of three soldiers who were supporting Operation Enduring Freedom.

They died Dec. 27 in Paktia, Afghanistan, of wounds suffered when enemy forces attacked their unit with an improvised explosive device. They were assigned to the 720th Military Police Battalion, 89th Military Police Brigade, Fort Hood, Texas.

Killed were:

Sgt. Noah M. Korte, 29, of Lake Elsinore, Calif.,

Spc. Kurt W. Kern, 24, of McAllen, Texas, and

"Pfc. Justin M. Whitmire, 20, of Easley, S.C.

For more information related to this release, the media may visit http://www.forthoodpresscenter.com or contact the Fort Hood public affairs office at 254-287-9993 or 254-287-0106.

That represented the entire contents of the news release. There were no details about what had happened that night on the dark road in southeastern Afghanistan. There was no mention of anyone having been injured in the IED blast. There was no mention that Korte was on his fourth overseas tour of duty, had two young sons, and was making plans to take his wife, Kristi, on a second honeymoon. There was no mention that Kern, a gregarious young man, had gone to culinary school but set aside his plans to become a chef so he could instead serve his country. And there was no mention that Whitmire, barely a year out of high school, had become an army medic and hoped to parlay that into a career as a physician.

There were practical reasons for the Department of Defense to take a brief, no-frills, standardized approach to its releases about deadly occurrences in Afghanistan. The deaths of Korte, Kern, and Whitmire came at the end of a year in which 404 members of the US military died in Afghanistan, and less than nine months into 2012, US fatalities in Operation Enduring Freedom would surpass the two thousand mark, according to figures verified by The Associated Press. Even though US troops died in Afghanistan at the rate of more than one a day in 2011, the annual fatality total marked the end of a four-year span in which US deaths in Afghanistan had increased.

Injuries to US troops far outstripped fatalities. There were more than 160 US troops injured in December 2011 alone, capping a year that pushed the total number of US military personnel hurt in Operation Enduring Freedom to roughly 16,000. By becoming part of that group, Jon and Capt. Avila joined another population group: those with confirmed cases of TBI.

The US military didn't begin testing for TBI on the battlefield until 2007, so exact numbers of service personnel affected by it in Iraq and Afghanistan remain difficult to pinpoint. In addition, the National Institutes of Health said the military's battlefield TBI screening "relies on subjective recall of the events" and "may be affected by fatigue." However, the Department of Defense does keep track of medically diagnosed TBIs among its service members going back to 2000, reporting nearly 274,000 cases from 2000 to the summer of 2013. Nearly 77 percent were mild cases, and it estimated more than 80 percent had occurred in nondeployed settings such as vehicle crashes, falls, sports activities, and military training.

A Congressional Budget Office report in 2012 estimated there were nearly nine thousand diagnosed cases of TBI among US service members overseas in 2010, but it did not estimate how many of those were related to battlefield activities. Perhaps the most telling number about brain injuries in the military is that the Department of Defense estimated as many as 75 percent of the US casualties in Iraq and Afghanistan were from IED blasts, so it stands to reason that, with the number of US deaths in those two wars closing in on seven thousand as 2013 progressed, there would also be a significant number of TBIs as well.

Those numbers were not David McHenry's primary concern after he got the telephone call from the army informing him of his son's injuries in an IED blast. In the weeks and months following that call, David's concerns involved not only his son's broken bones and other visible injuries, but the TBI and how that might affect him over the course of the rest of his life.

Brain-injury research, although still evolving, particularly in the area of blast-related TBI and its long-term consequences, was starting to produce evidence that TBI patients might have a greater propensity for other problems later in life such as seizures, strokes, dementia, Parkinson's, amyotrophic lateral sclerosis, and other serious medical conditions.

"Jon's still a young man," his father explained. "He's got his whole life ahead of him. He's got a wife. He's got a son on the way. I want him to have a future. I want him to have hopes and dreams. I want him to be happy." David paused. "I want him to be healthy."

So far, the US military's medical system had helped Jon McHenry survive. Now the next step was to see if he could again thrive.

As far as the team at Richmond's polytrauma unit was concerned, Jon was exactly where he needed to be. He had discussed his goals and his dreams with them, and they were ready to help him work toward achieving them. They had the tools, the professional expertise, and time on their side, and from all indications, he had the will and the drive.

Jon was one of the 114 patients admitted to Richmond's polytrauma unit in 2012, and as McNamee pointed out, the staff wanted the same thing for all of them: to help them find a new normal and to be able to watch them walk out the doors and return to their lives.

"This," he said, "is a place where hope lives."

CHAPTER TWO

1201 BROAD ROCK BOULEVARD

McGuire VA Medical Center sits in almost the exact center of the second precinct, one of four geographical areas that the Richmond Police Department uses to divide Virginia's capital.

Although the four precincts were laid out in an attempt to provide equal representation across the city of some 210,000 residents, crime statistics show that the second is anything but equal when it comes to violence. In 2012, for example, there were forty-two homicides in the city. Thirty-eight percent of that total—sixteen—occurred in the second precinct. Armed robberies are also a problem in the second precinct, as are assaults. All told, the precinct had Richmond's highest percentage of police calls for violent crimes in 2012.

Crime statistics such as those can make the area seem a world away from the redevelopment and bustling nightlife in downtown Richmond, where the tens of thousands of state government workers who call Richmond home and the meteoric growth of VCU and its medical campus have helped fuel a center-city renaissance in the development of apartments, condominiums, and restaurants. The city has also earned a reputation as a recreation hub, thanks in large part to the James River, which literally splits Richmond almost in half. The river features challenging rapids and is surrounded on both banks by a world-class network of parks, and these have become major draws for kayakers, mountain bicyclists, and trail-running enthusiasts from up and down the East Coast. Richmond also has drawn rave reviews for national competitions held in and around the river.

A short car ride south of downtown and the parks, however, that enthusiasm doesn't spill over to the hardscrabble neighborhood that the VA hospital calls home, an area that municipal planners typically refer to as being "in transition."

Capt. Harvey S. Powers, a twenty-year member of the Richmond Police Department, is the commander of the second precinct, overseeing a working-class area of South Richmond defined largely by small Cape Cod-style homes and bungalows that were built eighty or more years ago.

"In many cases, the original owners have passed on," he explained, "and the properties have become rental properties. And in many cases, we're talking about absentee landlords who have allowed those properties to deteriorate over time. A lack of pride in ownership is very much an issue."

In addition to block after block of predominantly run-down houses, the second precinct is also home to the Communities at Southwood, a 1,200-unit apartment complex that has become popular with Richmond's burgeoning Latino community.

"We find as many as ten people at a time living in each unit," Powers said.

Because a significant number of the Southwood residents may be undocumented, they may not have the identification necessary to open a bank account. As a result, they tend to carry large amounts of cash, which in turn makes them vulnerable to armed robbers who frequently prey on the residents at Southwood, a few hundred yards northwest of the VA hospital property. A few hundred yards east, within sight of the main entrance to McGuire, is the intersection of Hull Street and Belt Boulevard, the crossroads of what used to be one of the more vibrant neighborhoods in Richmond but has gradually deteriorated into one of its grittiest. Three of the four corners of the intersection are occupied by 1950s-era strip malls whose tenants used to include the likes of Sears and J.C. Penney. Those prominent retailers are long gone, however, having given way to a lineup that now includes a variety of payday loan offices, hair-braiding and nail salons, rent-to-own appliance, electronics, and furniture outlets, discount clothing stores, a Goodwill thrift store, and an array of storefront churches.

Just as the homes and apartments in the area can be targets for criminals, the malls have their share of problems as well. In April 2010, for example, a gunman tried to pull off a daytime robbery at a state-run liquor store in the largest of the three malls, Southside Plaza, but was quickly disarmed by two employees who then slammed him to the floor and held him there until police arrived and arrested him.

The crime that exists around McGuire has prompted many restaurants and take-out establishments in and around the second precinct to stop delivering food to the VA hospital—not because their delivery drivers have been robbed at McGuire, but strictly because it is located in a ZIP code where so many armed robberies have occurred. To err on the side of caution, the establishments have stopped sending their delivery drivers to all addresses within the ZIP code, including 1201 Broad Rock Boulevard, the home of the hospital.

"If I'm a delivery driver," Powers explained, "I can't blame them. I don't know if it's worth it to deliver ten dollars' worth of Chinese food."

As rough-and-tumble as the area is, however, the fenced-in VA hospital property can be, by and large, immune from the crime problems that exist in the nearby neighborhoods.

"The problems in the community," Powers confirmed, "don't tend to bleed onto the property."

Indeed, while the area around it has deteriorated, the VA hospital has emerged as an ever-expanding gem on the site of a former racetrack.

Opened in 1946, the VA hospital was named after Hunter Holmes McGuire, who was the personal physician to Confederate Maj. Gen. Stonewall Jackson during the Civil War and later served as president of the American Medical Association. McGuire, who lived in the Bon Air area of suburban Richmond, died in 1900. The VA hospital, one of three in Virginia, underwent a major renovation and expansion in 1984 and has been steadily growing ever since, reaching in excess of 2.2 million square feet of space—more than one-third the size of the Pentagon—by late 2013, and there are plans for continued construction.

McGuire's main hospital building, a sprawling red brick structure with more than four hundred beds as well as outpatient clinics that logged nearly 518,000 patient visits in 2012, has amenities that include a cafeteria, coffee shop, barber shop, bowling alley, pharmacy, chapel, and a retail store laid out over nearly 7,000 square feet that sells everything from food, clothing, and toiletries to flat-screen televisions, jewelry, and Rachael Ray cookware.

The main hospital is surrounded by a number of smaller buildings and a vast network of parking lots that can accommodate more than 2,100 vehicles. Those lots provide the canvas for what becomes a peaceful, visual reminder of the hospital's mission as the activity in the clinics dissipates late each afternoon and the majority of McGuire's 2,600 employees go home. The exodus of the cars from the lots exposes an asphalt landscape littered with wheelchairs and more wheelchairs, all left behind by visitors on their way home. The hospital encourages outpatients who are leaving to use wheelchairs to get to their cars and to leave them there in the parking lots; hospital workers round them up at the end of the day and return them to the main building.

McGuire, situated on 112 acres that are surrounded by a black metal picket fence and patrolled by an armed federal police force, gained fame in the 1970s as the first hospital in the VA system to have a heart transplant program. With the passing of the Vietnam era, however, McGuire began gradually extending its reach into the fields of rehabilitation medicine and brain injuries. Those efforts were helped greatly by the presence a short drive to the north of VCU's medical school, where leaders found it to be beneficial to both institutions for the VA and VCU to work together.

Dr. David X. Cifu, who joined the VCU medical school faculty in 1991 and quickly rose to chairman of the Department of Physical Medicine & Rehabilitation (PM&R), was instrumental in nurturing the bond between the university and the VA. Cifu recognized that his students would be exposed to training opportunities at the VA that they might not get elsewhere, and that the VA in turn would benefit from being able to tap into the resources of a well-funded university. When the mandate came from Congress in 2004 to establish a polytrauma rehabilitation network within the VA healthcare system, Cifu was serving in the dual roles of head of the PM&R department at VCU and head of PM&R at McGuire.

McGuire's PRC began taking shape in 2005 on a small scale. Because it was a new venture within a federal bureaucracy that had historically been slow to react, Cifu said, local expectations were modest.

"We saw it as a place to do some training and research with some students, to do some good work with a few patients," he explained.

As the war in Afghanistan rolled into its fifth year, Cifu was asked in 2006 to take on a leadership role with McGuire's polytrauma unit. Casualties in Afghanistan were mounting, and wounded were coming home to the United States in need of specialized care for multiple trauma. The pressure was on the VA—and in turn, the hospitals—to do a better job.

The VA, continuing to absorb criticism for not adequately responding to the needs of US service members injured in the Vietnam War, was adamant about avoiding a repeat with Afghanistan. The PRC program, according to the word from Washington, had to succeed. Failure was unacceptable. Richmond's polytrauma unit needed a full-time leader.

Cifu found one within his own ranks.

———

Family history alone would seem to suggest Shane McNamee had little choice. Born into a household where the ranks of physicians included his father, brother, sister, and two uncles, McNamee nonetheless decided to attend Marquette University and major in social philosophy.

"I like people too much to be in medicine," he joked when asked why he seemed averse as a teenager to toeing the family line and pursuing a life as a physician. "Besides, I wanted to see the world."

So upon receiving his bachelor's degree in 1996, graduating magna cum laude after eight semesters on the dean's list, McNamee joined Americorps

National Civilian Community Corps, where he worked for a year first in Denver, Colorado, at a school for teenage mothers and then in Austin, Texas, building community parks. From there, it was back home to Ohio for a job as a corporate fundraiser for the United Way of Greater Cleveland.

McNamee, who also spent four months living in a tent in Alaska, was hitchhiking in Ireland when his mother called with the news that he had been offered a full academic scholarship to attend the Medical College of Ohio. So at age twenty-four, with a work history that also included stints as a ball-bearing inspector, a bartender, and an employee at a Chuck E. Cheese pizza restaurant, he shelved his world tour to join the family business.

Several years later, McNamee had just begun the process of setting up interviews for potential places to serve his residency, and he arranged to stop at VCU while he was traveling through Virginia. He made an immediate impression on Cifu, who more than a decade after that still vividly recalled an intense, hour-long discussion. The two conducted the interview while sitting on a couch because McNamee was using crutches while he recovered from knee surgery.

As impressed as Cifu was that day, McNamee left even more of a mark during his residency—so much so, in fact, that when it came time to choose a full-time medical director in 2006 for McGuire's fledgling polytrauma unit, the choice was a simple one: a thirty-two-year-old physician who had just completed his residency in PM&R at VCU.

"He moved into it because he was what we've got. He was fantastic, but that said, he was green," Cifu described. "But don't get me wrong. Sure, he was young, he was a new guy, but he had a lot of confidence, a lot of personal skills—a great human being."

McNamee needed to put those personal skills to immediate use. He sensed that national VA officials, feeling pressure to produce results they could show Congress, were not happy with Richmond's polytrauma unit and that McGuire's continued participation in the program might be in danger.

"It was a hot potato," McNamee said.

He worked on hiring people for several key positions, including a nursing leader and two psychologists, and concentrated on trying to change the polytrauma unit's culture. Although he had confidence in the staff members, he wasn't convinced they were taking the right approach, in part because of the basic fundamental concept that governs brain injuries: No two are alike.

Even though he had only been exposed to the VA healthcare system for a few years as a resident at VCU, it was long enough for McNamee to observe the dynamics of a federal bureaucracy that can often encounter problems with ineffectiveness. The tendencies of a bureaucracy to treat the masses in similar fashion were in direct conflict with the need to address each person's brain injury as a unique case. In short, what works for one patient may not necessarily work for another, and to avoid that, he wanted the staff to concentrate more on personalizing the care of each patient.

"It should be relationship-based medicine," he said. "That has to be at the core of everything we do."

He had them focus on a number of initiatives that helped determine a patient's needs and desires both just before and immediately after their arrival at McGuire, and they began using what they learned from those initiatives to drive their course of treatment for each patient.

The results were almost immediate.

"We pivoted on that place," McNamee explained, "in like six or seven weeks."

As the staff began to function more efficiently and respond to the patients' needs more effectively, the word began to spread north to Washington, to the VA and Department of Defense hierarchies and to Congress. Richmond's polytrauma unit, which started with ten beds in eight rooms on a single hallway on the second floor of the hospital, was producing success stories.

McNamee was three days past his thirty-third birthday and just a few months into his new job when, on March 8, 2007, he went before Congress to testify in front of a panel of the House Committee on Veterans Affairs. Richmond's polytrauma unit, which just months earlier had been the target of grave concern in Washington, had staged a rapid turnaround in demonstrating how to take especially difficult brain-injury patients and help them work their way back to independence.

"It is my firm belief," McNamee told the committee, "that this highly coordinated, effective system is unparalleled in this nation's medical system for those who have suffered a traumatic brain injury."

The system of transitioning patients from acute-care facilities to poly-trauma rehabilitation centers and then back into the community, according to McNamee, "is world class and has no equal for those suffering from TBI." That process begins with three keys that are already in place before the patient arrives at McGuire: managing records quickly and efficiently, building relationships with the patients, and involving the family and other caregivers in the process. All three keys are rooted in the kind of superior communication that so many people say is lacking all too often in modern medicine and that so many patients identify as the downfall of today's managed care systems. Those systems, they complain, are broken because poor communication results in the right hand not knowing what the left hand is doing, in patients getting conflicting and confusing information, in healthcare providers and insurers failing to work together in a manner that makes the needs of the patients a priority, and in patients being required to go from one facility to another and still another to get care because it is not available in one efficient location.

The first key for patients entering the polytrauma system involves one of the main complaints of those who have become frustrated with managed care in the private sector. The VA has made it a priority to provide seamless medical records access for every facility in the system that is treating polytrauma patients. In this case, seamless doesn't just mean those facilities can access the records easily; they access them quickly. In Richmond, for example, Pat Rudd, the polytrauma unit's clinical case manager, has become a wizard at screening potential patients for the facility and getting their records into the hands of key people at McGuire sometimes several days before the patient arrives. If Rudd cannot get the entire file in the hands of Richmond's doctors and other staff members, she uses her connections at Walter Reed to get enough material so that the doctors and therapists who need specific information about a patient will have it at least twenty-four hours before the patient arrives.

That process eliminates any potential anxieties from patients, their loved ones, or the staff members about perhaps having to delay treatment after the patient arrives because their records have yet to catch up with them. Instead, the Richmond polytrauma staff typically has had several days to review the patient's records and start working together to develop a therapy plan by the time the patient arrives in Richmond.

"We got very good at getting ready for people very fast back when we first got swept up in Afghanistan and things got busy," Rudd remembers. "We didn't have any choice. They were coming back so fast; we had to make it work. There was a real sense of mission, and everyone came together to do whatever we had to for the troops. They were putting their lives on the line for us over there. It was our job to make it right for them once they got back. It's easy to work together when you've got that kind of motivation."

The second key—a direct outgrowth of the first—is the importance of relationship-based medicine. By showing their willingness to get access to important records before the patient arrived, the staff hopes to demonstrate to the patient and their loved ones a willingness to establish a line of communication and trust, and now that the patient is on the premises, those efforts mushroom. The goals are to reduce fear of the unknown by the patient and their family and to show them that the staff is committed to forming a foundation for successful rehabilitation. For example, the staff typically tries to set up a video teleconference with the patient and their loved ones several days before they arrive in Richmond, giving everyone an opportunity to see each other, to put a name with a face, to speak with one another, and to begin building relationships and trust. In addition, the staff's offices are interspersed with the patient rooms throughout the polytrauma unit, which encourages interaction between the patients and the staff, and having the key team members there on the unit creates an environment akin to the healthcare version of one-stop shopping. In the outside world of managed care, the patients go see their therapists and specialists. On the polytrauma unit, the therapists and specialists come to the patients.

The third key is recognizing that the patient's loved ones are part of the equation and must be integrated into the care plan. At Richmond, that translates into Barbara Bauserman, who as the polytrauma unit's family education coordinator, makes it her job to keep families in the loop on literature and seminars that may improve their understanding of what can be complicated and intimidating medical terminology. It also translates into having social workers on a twenty-four-hour pager system in case there are emergencies with the family of a polytrauma patient, and it means having military liaisons stationed on the unit to provide immediate, face-to-face answers to questions that may affect the status of a patient and his unit or service branch.

Having those three keys in place frees up the patients and their caregivers to concentrate on rehabilitation and allows them to work with the psychologists, speech-language pathologists, physical therapists, occupational therapists, recreational therapists, and other staff members who have tailored their individual programs toward the single goal of restoring as much independence as possible.

McNamee went back before the same House Committee on Veterans Affairs panel in September 2007 to testify again. Not coincidentally, the polytrauma system in general—and the Richmond unit in particular—charted a steady growth in personnel and success stories in the years that followed.

"Once the watering started, it was just an amazing seed," Cifu described. "It just exploded in terms of greatness within three years once resources started pouring in. It really was a perfect storm."

He cited the leadership exhibited by McNamee, straight out of his residency and early in his tenure as the Richmond unit's medical director, as being vital to the success of the program.

"Meekness doesn't have a role when it comes to these kinds of programs," Cifu said. "But I'll tell you what. He's got great people around him. Shane may be the tip of the sword, but he's got a strong shaft and handle pushing him. But we also needed a sharp tip of the sword to make it happen."

"He was the perfect leader at the perfect time for this program," agreed Rudd, the unit's clinical case manager who joined the staff in 2006 and is one of its most senior members. "He made the people around him better and he made this whole program better."

McNamee said much of the reason for Richmond's success was due to a Washington hierarchy that was committed to doing the right thing for the nation's warriors and veterans and was committed to trusting the VA to accomplish the task. As for his own role, he said, many of his decisions were designed to merely do what is so infrequently done in the world of modern medicine.

"There's trust built," he explained. "And the way you build trust is by being trustworthy."

Establishing trust is not limited to such measures as improved medical records access and better communication with patients and their caregivers. Another step that the detail-oriented McNamee instituted was having the staff try to limit admissions to the unit to Mondays, Tuesdays, Wednesdays, and Thursdays.

"You've got forty-eight hours to establish trust with someone. That's the way I look at it," he said. "And that's part of the reason why we try not to admit people on Fridays. I want us to have a chance to see them, to work with them, to get to know them, and if we admit them on Friday and then leave for the weekend, then we're missing out on a vital window."

Cifu, who remained the head of the PM&R department at VCU and also later became national director of the VA's PM&R Program Office, credited McNamee with helping mold Richmond's polytrauma unit into "the envy of the nation in terms of the quality of personnel that are there, the caring qualities of the people and the abilities to take care of patients."

It's a long way from the program's infancy and from the time when some people weren't certain about its future.

"There were a lot of bad days," Cifu said. "There were angry people coming down on us and frustration and all that. But you know what? We've learned by taking care of people. We've learned by taking care of some very challenging patients. And now we've got every bell and whistle and every toy. And now I can proudly say that the people that are here are the best in the VA system."

Cifu paused.

"I've given a hundred lectures now on the PRC network and the greatness of Richmond, and every time I do, people are drooling," he said. "Nobody's got a team like the Richmond PRC. Nobody. And it's not arrogant if it's true."

At the center of that team was McNamee, who helped pave the way for a polytrauma program that steadily grew into three units at Richmond: 2-B, the inpatient unit on the second floor in the B-section of the main hospital, as well as a stand-alone building several hundred yards to the south. That building houses the Polytrauma Transitional Rehabilitation Program, which serves as a finishing school of sorts to help prepare patients to return to their families and the community, and the Servicemember Transitional Advanced Rehabilitation (STAR) program, which helps patients transition back into specific jobs or educational paths.

After four-plus years of devoting long hours to nurturing the polytrauma program into a thriving operation marked by numerous success stories, McNamee was promoted to an administrative position as the hospital's chief of PM&R. He was replaced as the polytrauma unit's medical director by Dr. Ajit Pai, another young, energetic physician who had come through the VCU pipeline and been groomed by Cifu and McNamee while completing his residency and a fellowship in Richmond. Because of his work with Cifu and McNamee, Pai was acutely aware of the state of the polytrauma unit that he was inheriting. He knew the unit was functioning well, enjoyed a solid reputation in Washington as a polished gem, and was getting plenty of support and resources.

Pai also was aware that the support, resources, and working environment on the polytrauma unit were not typical in the world of medicine in general, especially in the private sector.

"I know I don't live in any form of reality when I'm over here," he said, adding that McGuire has built a culture of "leadership that's willing to kick down doors for you."

A reminder of that comes every Monday at 8:30 A.M., when Pai begins his work week by leaving his office on the polytrauma unit and walking several hundred yards down two long corridors for a meeting in the hospital director's office with other key leaders at McGuire. Such executive-level meetings in a corporate or private setting might feature the top brass asking what those beneath them can do to make life easier for the leaders. At McGuire, that's far from the case.

"Every Monday morning," Pai stated, shaking his head, "they want to know what they can do for me."

He had to get used to the dynamics of having superiors who want to go to bat for him, instead of vice versa. Once he realized that McGuire's leadership team wasn't just paying him lip service, he got comfortable with telling them what the polytrauma unit needed to continue functioning at a high level.

"I have to ask, but I pretty much already know the answer," he said. "It's usually, 'Whatever you need.'"

On his way to and from those weekly meetings, Pai passes McGuire's human resources office, where a sign on the wall displays the VA's motto—words taken from Abraham Lincoln's second inaugural address.

The date was March 4, 1865, and it was a time of significant upheaval in the United States. Within weeks, the Civil War would end, and Lincoln would be assassinated. On that day, however, the president spoke of recovery and healing, calling on Americans "to bind up the nation's wounds, to care for him who shall have borne the battle and for his widow, and his orphan, to do all which may achieve and cherish a just and lasting peace among ourselves and with all nations."

Pai needed to read Lincoln's passage repeatedly before he was able to finally absorb its significance.

"I had no idea what it meant, what Lincoln's words meant," he said. "And now, I recognize the depth of it and how brilliant a man he was."

Pai paused for a few seconds and then leaned forward at his desk.

"This," he explained as a smile crossed his face, "is way cooler than traditional medicine."

CHAPTER THREE

NEWPORT, PENNSYLVANIA

It was just before 9 A.M. on a typical weekday morning, and the McDonald's just outside downtown Newport, Pennsylvania, was abuzz with activity. An employee with a floor-scrubbing machine was working her way deliberately, almost delicately, across the dining room, exercising care not to disturb the customers eating at tables and waiting in line for their food. Outside, another employee walked slowly down the drive-through lane, waving a wand from a power washer back and forth on the concrete surface as a steady stream of cars inched toward the pick-up window.

Cleanliness wasn't the only hallmark here. The grass was neatly trimmed, the shrubs carefully sculpted, the workers friendly and prideful. Like many small towns across America, the Perry County community of Newport, about a twenty-minute ride north of the state capital of Harrisburg, has been hit hard by tough economic times, but that hasn't dented the community's pride, sense of purpose, or values.

The signs of a troubled economy are plentiful. Empty storefronts, as is the case in so many small towns across America, seem to outnumber occupied ones along the downtown landscape. Men who are in their thirties and forties, men who in a more thriving economy might be hard at work, bide their time by sitting around on front stoops and watching the world go by. Even the churches feel the pinch. One former house of worship in Newport has found a second life as a law office.

Nevertheless, Newport, like many other rural communities across America, still embraces small-town values, values that make it continue to be an attractive option to serve in the military and defend your country. Leave the McDonald's, drive across the old-style steel girder bridge that crosses the Juniata River into town, just past the Hard Hat bar and grill, and you're met immediately by the intersection of Second and Market streets, the town square where flag poles stand sentry on either side of the street, one to hold the US flag and the other for the flag of Pennsylvania.

The US flag is a common theme in Newport. You'll find the Stars and Stripes, or the Newport High School Buffaloes flag—or both—mounted on brackets on many a front porch as you make your way through this community.

There's another large flag pole at the north end of Second Street in Newport, this one the centerpiece of the town's Veterans Memorial Park. The park includes two baseball fields, a tennis court, picnic shelter, playground, and a basketball court. To get to them, you must first walk past the memorial that salutes those from Newport who gave their lives in service to their country.

"Dedicated by a grateful people," the plaque at the base of the flag pole says in part.

Private William H. Saylor was the first, killed June 6, 1918, in France. A few blocks west of the memorial, the William H. Saylor Veterans of Foreign Wars Post No. 34 now stands in permanent recognition to his sacrifice.

Three other men joined Saylor as casualties from Newport before World War I ended.

Seven other sons of the community died in World War II, as did three more in the Korean War.

The memorial holds fourteen names in all, fourteen men from a community that seems too small to afford losing that many in the name of service.

The military, as is the case in so many small towns across America, is a popular option. Officials at Newport High School said the military was especially popular in the years immediately following the 9/11 terrorist attacks, but that interest quickly waned, and by the time Jon McHenry got out of Newport High in 2008, he was one of just two people in his graduating class of seventy-seven to go into the military.

Barely three hundred feet down Second Street from Veterans Memorial Park is the modest, well-maintained house that Janet and Bill McHenry have called home for nearly four decades. Bill McHenry, now retired from a long career in retail sales, and his wife have reached the stage of their lives where their main priority is doting on their twelve grandchildren. Janet McHenry smiled easily as she sat in an armchair in the front parlor and chatted with a visitor. To her right was a sign on the wall that says, "I CAN AT GRANDMA'S."

She grew especially close to one of her grandsons, Jon. He had a difficult childhood with his birth mother, and by the time he graduated from high school, his parents were divorced, and he was no longer on speaking terms with his mother. Jon looked to his grandmother to play an important supporting role in his life, and she embraced the responsibility.

As a young child, Jon spent time playing on the basketball court at Veterans Memorial Park, within shouting distance from his grandparents' home. As he grew older and matured, it seemed no conversation was off-limits with the woman he came to trust, the woman he knew as "Nan."

"He was an absolute delight," she said.

Making their relationship all the more special was the fact that in late May 2012, Jon and his wife, Jay, were due to present Janet and Bill McHenry their first great-grandchild.

Then on December 27, 2011, Jon's father, David McHenry, showed up at his parents' kitchen with tears in his eyes. Janet and Bill had every reason to fear that Jon might end up becoming the fifteenth name on the plaque of the war memorial just up the block.

"Jon's been injured," Janet recalled her son saying, the pained, wounded tone of his voice confirming that the news from Afghanistan was grave.

As David began detailing what he knew of Jon's injuries, Janet struggled to come to terms with what had happened and the rush of emotions overwhelming her.

"We were just sitting around the kitchen table, and I didn't know what to do. So I just started in prayer out loud," she said.

Janet paused, shook her head and exhaled slowly.

"I don't ever want to go through a morning like that ever again. Not being able to get to him, not knowing what was happening, all the unknowns—it was very difficult. It was very difficult on all of us."

––––––

David McHenry was at work when he got the call. Still recovering from shoulder surgery the previous September, he was limited to light duty and was working in a rear office at AmeriGas, a Harrisburg propane gas company, when the call from the army came through.

"I was just sitting in the back room," he said. "It was such a nightmare when they tell you. I had to get my supervisor and put him on the phone for me because I couldn't concentrate. He had to write down contact numbers and all that. It was the worst feeling.

"I sure wouldn't want to take that phone call if nobody was around me."

The army officer detailed what he knew of the IED blast and Jon's injuries. David was told that his son had undergone emergency surgery at a military hospital in Afghanistan, where, among other things, his spleen had been removed and his badly fractured right leg stabilized for a flight to the US military hospital in Landstuhl, Germany.

David wanted to see his son. The army told him the goal was to get Jon back to the United States as soon as possible, depending on whether he could be stabilized for the long flight. Before that could happen, the first priority was to see how Jon did on the flight from Kandahar, Afghanistan, to Germany and immediately after arrival at Landstuhl. His injuries were myriad, and there were no guarantees at this early stage about his continued stability, let alone his long-term prospects. As with many service men and women injured in battle, especially with percussion-related blasts, it could sometimes take days, weeks or even months to realize the full nature of the damage to the body.

The army told David that it was making back-up arrangements to get him to his son's bedside in Germany as fast as possible, if needed.

"I was on standby to go to Germany if he took a turn," he explained. "I was on notice to go to an airport that wouldn't be more than two hours away."

The next few days were agonizing, with David's worries being eased only by the fact that the military gave him contact numbers for staff in Landstuhl to provide him with up-to-the-minute updates about his son's condition. He took full advantage of those contacts, calling Germany several times daily to see how his son was doing.

"I have to say they were very good," he recalled. "I talked to them quite often, and I always felt like they were being as helpful as they could be."

Less fruitful were the repeated attempts to speak with his son, although it was not related to any shortcomings of any of the hospital staff members in Germany. Instead, every time David called and tried to arrange a talk with Jon, his son was either in surgery, in surgical recovery, sleeping, or sedated so heavily that he was unable to talk. Fate, it seemed, was conspiring against David McHenry. His son was getting extensive, around-the-clock care in Germany, including multiple surgeries, in an effort to stabilize him for a planned trip back to the United States, but a return home was no certainty at this point, and from David's perspective, not only couldn't he get to Germany to see his son, but he couldn't even seem to set up a brief phone conversation—just a quick chat to tell him how much his friends and family back in Pennsylvania loved him, were thinking of him, and were praying for him.

David's frustration reached a head on New Year's Eve.

Before the IED blast, David and his girlfriend, Barb, had already gotten tickets to welcome in the new year at the fire hall in nearby Millerstown, where the evening's entertainment was Last Call, a band featuring one of David's buddies. Those New Year's Eve plans went out the window with the IED blast. Yet Jon didn't appear to be going anywhere any time soon, and his father remained on standby to be flown over to see him. So with everything

seemingly at a standstill, Barb persuaded David to try to put aside the traumatic events of recent days for just a few hours and relax at the New Year's
Eve party. The spirit of Christmas was still fresh, and a new year was upon
them, so why not at least try to be upbeat? She encouraged him to celebrate
the fact that, despite the severity of his injuries, despite all the uncertainty
about his future, despite the fact that three of his comrades had died in the
horrific explosion, Jon McHenry was still alive, still fighting, still hanging
in there.

So, with the best of intentions, off to the fire hall they went.

David tried to relax and get in the spirit of celebrating the arrival of 2012,
but he was understandably overwhelmed by thoughts of his son's struggle in
a hospital bed in Germany, safely away from the dangers of Afghanistan but
also far from the United States, where his family could do little but wait,
wonder, hope, and pray. He excused himself from Barb, got up from the
table, and walked to the men's room, where he found it empty and relatively
quiet. Its walls served as a buffer from the now-distant sounds of revelers
welcoming in 2012 to the sounds of Last Call. David's thoughts again turned
to his son, and it wasn't long before he surrendered to the waves of emotions
rolling over him.

"I was pretty upset," he said. "I was crying a little bit trying to cope with
all this, and it was a lot. It was hard. Very hard."

At that moment, however, the restroom door swung open, letting in the
sounds of celebration—as well as another man.

Seeing David crying, the man inquired about his well-being. David, not
wanting to unduly burden this gentleman who was kind enough to demonstrate concern at a New Year's Eve party about the emotional state of someone
he didn't know, tried to briefly explain what had just happened to his son
in Afghanistan. Yet he found that the more he told the gentleman, the more
engaged the stranger became, and the more questions he asked.

Thus David McHenry spent part of New Year's Eve in the men's room of
the fire hall in Millerstown, Pennsylvania, unburdening himself to a stranger about how the atrocities of war had torn his son apart and turned the
McHenry family's world upside down.

"He showed compassion," David remembered. "We talked a little bit. Okay, maybe more than a little bit. We actually hugged. And then we both left, and we both went back to see the band."

Except that wasn't the end of it. David didn't know it at the time, but it would not be long before he would see this compassionate stranger again, and the next time, it would not be a chance encounter in a men's room.

The next time, it would not be an accident at all.

———

New Year's Day 2012 brought David McHenry a telephone call that changed circumstances seemingly in an instant. All the frustrations, all the uncertainties of recent days were about to be replaced by action.

Swift action.

Jon was coming home.

The army called David to say doctors at the hospital in Landstuhl felt Jon might be capable of handling a flight back to the United States. The plan was to fly him to Washington and transport him by ambulance to Walter Reed in nearby Bethesda, Maryland. Walter Reed has developed a well-deserved reputation as the military's top destination for specialty surgery, and the doctors in Landstuhl felt Jon would be best served by going to Bethesda for surgery on his badly fractured right leg.

David was taken aback by the news. One day earlier, his life was literally on standby, waiting for a hastily arranged flight to go Germany to see his son. Now, his son would instead be coming to him, and, in what amounted to an unintended bonus, the trip to Bethesda in the northwest suburbs of the nation's capital was less than a three-hour drive from the family's hometown of Newport, Pennsylvania.

Although the doctors in Landstuhl wanted to try to fly Jon back to the United States, they nonetheless had concerns about his ability to withstand the lengthy flight on a military cargo plane, a craft not built primarily for carrying humans, let alone those with multiple fractures and numerous other internal injuries. So they asked David for permission to give his son an epidural injection of a powerful painkiller to hopefully make the flight easier for him. David himself months earlier had been given six epidural injections during his recovery from neck injuries suffered in an automobile accident and knew that the procedure could be risky because it involved a needle being inserted between two vertebrae. Yet he also knew firsthand the painkilling benefits of the injections. So he gave his consent for the doctors to give his son an epidural and put him on a flight home.

While he was on the phone with the Landstuhl staff, David decided to try again. He asked if he could speak with his son before they gave him the epidural and sent him home. He was told to wait on the line while they checked to see if Jon was conscious. He had been through this wait numerous times in recent days, all without the desired outcome, and he was prepared for a similar result this time. Instead, it wasn't long before he heard a faint but familiar voice on the other end of the line—a voice that, days earlier, he wasn't sure he would ever hear again.

"It may not have even been two or three minutes we talked, but I was so grateful just to hear his voice," David described. "I just remember asking him how he's doing, and he said he wasn't doing real good. He had a lot of pain. I proceeded to tell him they were going to give him an epidural. I said, 'They're going to give you a shot, Jon. It's going to make you feel much better.' I explained to him real quick it was the same kind I had with my neck injury.

"He said, 'When am I going to see you, Dad?' Just from his voice, I don't think he really understood where he was at."

The longer the conversation went on, the more apparent it became to David that his son, the tough little warrior who always relished proving to people that they shouldn't underestimate him merely because of his relatively small stature, had been left confused and badly shaken by what happened on that dark road in Afghanistan.

"He kept telling me, 'I'm going to be okay,'" David said. "And I kept telling him, 'Keep fighting. Be strong.'

"And you know what? That's what he's done ever since."

———

While the military's decision to send Jon McHenry from Germany to Bethesda was welcome news to his father, the hasty nature of the travel arrangements made by the staff in Landstuhl didn't leave David McHenry much time to make the trip from Newport down to Walter Reed. After making phone calls to his employer to arrange for some time off, packing clothes, and taking care of various other details, it was dark by the time David got in his car to leave. It was past 10 P.M. when he finally made his way into Maryland and onto Interstate 495, also known as the Capital Beltway, which encircles Washington, DC and its immediate suburbs, including Bethesda and the sprawling Walter Reed hospital complex.

David was growing anxious, thoughts of his injured son racing in his head as he drew within about a mile of the beltway exit for Walter Reed. In an instant, something else immediately diverted his attention—from his son, from Afghanistan, from everything military.

Looming immediately in front of him as he made his way down a hilly, winding stretch of the beltway were the massive spires of the largest cathedral David had ever seen. On New Year's Day 2012, the cathedral was illuminated to offer a presence to travelers that was equal parts majestic, powerful, comforting, stunning, and peaceful. He didn't know it at the time, but he was driving past the Washington, DC Temple of the Church of Jesus Christ of Latter Day Saints.

Built along the beltway in Kensington, Maryland and dedicated in 1974, the temple has spires that reach 288 feet high, making it the tallest temple in the United States. It is illuminated nightly, making it visible to travelers on the beltway, but the Mormon Church adds even more lights for the holidays, adding to its prominence when David drove past it that night.

"I remember coming over the crest of a hill, and it looked like these rockets with lights beaming from them," he described. "You're just so damn scared to begin with, and not knowing and all the uncertainty with Jon, and then you see something beautiful like that.

37

"I don't know what it was, but it just made me think that maybe it was going to be okay. Maybe it was a sign that things would work out."

Minutes later, David pulled into the Walter Reed complex and was directed to the building where he would wait to finally be reunited with his son once Jon arrived from Germany. Much to his surprise, he was told a short time later that not only had Jon's flight arrived in Washington, but an ambulance also had already delivered him to Walter Reed some ninety minutes before David got there. It was 10:30 P.M. on New Year's Day, and David McHenry felt bad. He had very much wanted to be at Walter Reed to make sure his son had a familiar face to welcome him home when he first got to the hospital.

As it turned out, that wouldn't have been possible, even if he had arrived earlier.

"When he first got there, they made him get through admissions and all that first," David explained. "So I wouldn't have been able to see him there any sooner anyway."

When the staff at Walter Reed finally got Jon processed and into a bed, his father was led in to see him.

Months later, David still shook his head when he recalled his initial reaction to what he saw in his son, who five days earlier had weighed nearly 170 pounds of well-defined muscle, the result of long sessions in the weight room, and was in what he felt was the best shape of his life. In a matter of days, Jon McHenry had gone from a proud, chiseled military policeman to a pale, gaunt young man in a body full of broken bones and internal injuries. Compounding his appearance was the fact that his weight had dropped precipitously, and at one point not long after the IED blast, it had reached a low of 132 pounds.

"I'll tell you what I wasn't prepared for was the amount of muscle he had lost," David recalled. "I remember what he looked like before. He was ripped. And in just that short amount of time, he was gone. He was just skin and bones."

He paused, took a deep breath and exhaled slowly.

"It almost made me think that if he was that weak right now..."

His voice trailed off, and he didn't finish his thought.

"It was one of those slap-you-in-the-face feelings," he said later. "When I first laid eyes on him, I was glad to see him just because he was alive. But it was discouraging—amazing, really—to see how fast someone can deteriorate.

"But at the same time, I was encouraged by the fact that he was built up enough, so he had something to live off of. That's where all those lifting weights helped him."

————

January 1 marked the start of an eighteen-day stay for Jon McHenry at Walter Reed, much of it devoted to surgical and orthopedic needs. Jon's spleen had been removed in Afghanistan, and he had a chest tube inserted in Germany. Soon after he arrived at Walter Reed, surgeons there discovered he had blood clotting in one lung, so that needed to be addressed. Doctors operated to insert a stent. Surgeons also set his badly fractured lower right leg and implanted a long titanium rod that was secured with several screws. His fractured left foot was placed in a cast. A tear in Jon's colon also had to be surgically repaired. Finally, he needed to be fitted with a large tortoise shell-like brace that encased his torso to help promote stability and set the stage for the healing of his three fractured vertebrae, multiple broken ribs, and fractured collarbone and scapula.

Not surprisingly, with all the surgeries and related procedures, Jon was given frequent painkillers. Doctors even equipped his intravenous line with a device that let him increase the dosage if the pain became too severe.

"He'd use it, too," his father said. "He'd click that button on the IV line, and usually within ten minutes, he'd be asleep."

Because of Jon's generous amount of painkillers, David assigned little significance to the fact that his son's focus wasn't always sharp.

"He'd be in and out, sure," David recalled. "But they had him on a lot of drugs. I figured it was just the medication."

The staff at Walter Reed had a different perspective.

Immediately after the IED blast, doctors had told David that his son likely had the mildest form of TBI, the result of what was described as rollover damage associated with the fact that the vehicle Jon had been driving was launched airborne and ended up on one side. Jon had scalp lacerations on his forehead and what doctors described as a contusion in the same area.

Again, his father figured the initial diagnosis of mild TBI was accurate, and that as doctors backed off on Jon's painkillers, his cognitive functions would return to normal. That wasn't necessarily the case, however. David admitted that as the days at Bethesda wore on, Jon would occasionally seem a bit more anxious than usual, a bit more agitated, and a bit less patient.

Twelve days into his son's stay at Bethesda, David was told that Walter Reed's neurologists now felt Jon's TBI was more severe than initially believed. Instead of mild, it was now being called moderate.

In David's eyes, the whole picture changed.

Broken bones, punctured lungs, blood clots, torn colons—surgeons could fix all those, but a damaged brain? How do you fix a brain that can no longer process like it used to? How do you make a damaged brain whole again? How can you be certain that this twenty-two-year-old man won't face a life of diminished brain capacity and function?

David McHenry was not prepared to hear the doctors at Walter Reed say they wanted to move his son some two hours south to Richmond, Virginia, home of the McGuire VA Medical Center. Five facilities in the vast system of VA hospitals had been designated polytrauma centers, designed specifically to handle multiple injuries that typified the modern war wounded. All five had distinguished themselves in different areas. In Richmond's case, the hospital's PRC had rapidly emerged as a haven for rehabilitating severe brain injuries, including those that left patients comatose for extended periods. Richmond was getting the most difficult cases, and time after time, the staff would get the patients back to the point where they could walk out the door and back into productive lives.

Now David was being told that if you had moderate to severe TBI, your best chances of recovery were in the hands of the staff at Richmond—and that his son needed to be there.

"I was so thankful to see him alive. Deep down, I kept telling myself that bones can be repaired. Bones can be fixed and will heal. But the brain injury—that really concerned me," he said. "All of a sudden, I find he's being moved to Virginia for brain trauma, and that upset me. It really concerned me. I was afraid for him, for his future."

On January 19, less than four weeks after the blast that forever changed him, Jon McHenry was put in an ambulance for the two-hour drive down Interstate 95 to Richmond, a road of uncertainty to begin the next chapter of his life.

CHAPTER FOUR

AJIT PAI

It was late 2007, and one of the patients at the PRC in McGuire VA Medical Center was dying.

The physical limitations of the man's spinal cord injury were being exacerbated by end-stage cancer that was slowly, relentlessly attacking his body. With no family around, he lay in bed, alone in his thoughts, as the hours turned into days.

One of the physicians on the unit, a young resident who was pondering a career with spinal cord injury patients, realized through conversations with the patient that he was alone in his final days, and that as the man took stock of his life, he was unfulfilled. As he approached seventy, the man wasn't pleased with how his life had turned out, and it left him sad. Now, to make matters worse, he was alone as death drew near.

So the physician, barely two years out of medical school, used the opportunity to do something that—to him, at least—seemed natural, seemed like nothing more than simply doing the right thing, just treating a patient, another human being, the way you might like to be treated. As the years passed, however, and his career advanced, he came to realize that what he did for that dying man helped frame what he would come to view as basic standards of patient care, as part of the formula for practicing what he called the art of medicine.

Whereas many physicians might have limited their contact with the dying patient to addressing his medical needs, to doing what would be clinically prudent for his spinal cord injury and his cancer, the young resident saw another part to the equation: the spiritual component.

Medicine, he came to believe, has to be about more than such factors as the latest in diagnostic equipment, surgical techniques, advances in physical therapy, and improved painkillers. Medicine has to not only tend to a person's body, but also to their emotional well-being. It's not about religion, per se, but about whether they are well-rounded, whether they are at peace with where they are in their lives, whether they believe they are the best person they can be, whether they have achieved balance.

Accordingly, the young physician, in addition to addressing the medical issues related to the dying patient's spinal cord injury and cancer, sat down at the man's bedside, and the two of them talked. Day after day, they spent time together, taking turns talking, taking turns listening, but both of them growing—the old man in his final days and the young resident just starting life as a physician.

The resident added something else to the mix of his care for the dying patient. As the end approached, the young physician began reading to the man. He chose excerpts from *Many Lives, Many Masters* by Brian L. Weiss, a physician and psychotherapist whose research and writing topics include reincarnation, Hinduism, and survival of the soul after death. Some of those passages include

> "Everything comes when it must come. A life cannot be rushed...we must accept what comes to us at a given time... life is endless...we just pass through different phases. There is no end. Time is not as we see time, but rather in lessons that are learned."

"Our task is to learn, to become God-like through knowledge. We know so little.... By knowledge, we approach God, and then we can rest. Then we come back to teach and help others."

"There are many gods, for God is in each of us."

"Wisdom is achieved very slowly. This is because intellectual knowledge, easily acquired, must be transformed into 'emotional,' or subconscious, knowledge. Once transformed, the imprint is permanent. Behavioral practice is the necessary catalyst of this reaction. Without action, the concept will wither and fade. Theoretical knowledge without practical application is not enough."

The physician kept talking with the dying patient, kept listening to him, kept reading to him, kept trying to address his spiritual healing as well as his medical needs, up to the man's death.

Less than three years later, that physician, Ajit Pai, was named the medical director of Richmond's polytrauma unit. Pai was thirty years old.

———

On March 19, 2003, US troops, joined by forces from the United Kingdom, Australia, and Poland, began streaming into Iraq for what US President George W. Bush called a hunt for weapons of mass destruction. It marked the start of what became the Iraq War and led to the birth—not long after that—of the US military's PSC.

The US military hierarchy was still stinging from decades of criticism that not enough had been done to address the medical needs of troops returning from the Vietnam War, needs that included PTSD and left legions of men and women voicing their disapproval and frustration for decades afterward at what they said was an ineffective and overloaded system of healthcare in the Department of Veterans Affairs. Now that the Iraq War—and its new weapon of choice, the IED—was producing waves of troops with multiple fractures, massive internal injuries, amputations, and TBI, the military responded by creating a series of so-called PRCs, where the most complicated cases could receive the concentrated care they needed.

This time, there was a solid commitment from the Department of Defense and the VA to offer a superior standard of care, to learn from the shortcomings of the Vietnam era and target more money, more facilities, more people, and a more focused, coordinated effort to taking better care of our nation's war wounded.

On the late winter day in 2003 that the coalition troops rolled into Iraq, the day that ultimately led to the establishment of the PSC, Ajit Pai was in Philadelphia, where he was nearing the end of his second year of medical school at Drexel University College of Medicine. His days were consumed largely by sitting in lecture halls, and like many med students, his world was largely confined to his studies. He had little time for such interests as current affairs, either in the United States or abroad.

Pai wasn't sure what career track he would find himself on after medical school, but at that stage of med school, the war—and taking care of the war wounded—were not on his radar screen. His radar screen, in fact, was not cluttered at all.

"I was not thinking about anything," he said, "other than myself."

Born in Flushing, New York, in 1979, Pai was the son of a nuclear engineer whose job led to him moving his family to New Hampshire when Ajit was still a baby, then to Knoxville, Tennessee, and later to Chattanooga, Tennessee, before the family settled in Cherry Hill, New Jersey, where Pai graduated from high school.

While in high school, Pai participated in a volunteer program that sent students to (among other places) a nursing home, where he got a chance to speak with patients on an extended basis. It was there that he began to embrace the idea of becoming a physician.

Pai stayed in New Jersey for college, enrolling at Rutgers University, where he got a bachelor's degree in 2001 after majoring in biology with a psychology minor—and made time to become a rabid fan of the Scarlet Knights' football program, a passion he continued to embrace even after settling professionally in Virginia.

A job in the military healthcare system still wasn't on Pai's radar in the summer of 2005 when, fresh out of Drexel, he arrived in Richmond to begin an internship in internal medicine at Virginia Commonwealth University. After that internship ended the following June, he stayed in Richmond and at VCU, this time for a three-year residency in PM&R. It was during this period that he fell under the wide nets cast by Drs. David Cifu and Shane McNamee.

Taking advantage of the leadership of Cifu, McNamee, and others, Pai flourished, and he was named chief resident in VCU's Department of PM&R in April 2008.

Because of the collaboration Cifu had cultivated between VCU and McGuire, Pai spent more and more time at the VA hospital, and when his residency ended in June 2009, he began a fellowship in spinal cord injury medicine at McGuire the following month. As the one-year fellowship progressed, he thought he had finally found his calling as a spinal injury specialist, so when the end of his fellowship approached the following summer, Pai—by then married and with an infant daughter—looked for jobs in the spinal injury rehabilitation field. He found one in the private sector at a rehabilitation hospital back in New Jersey, and he signed a contract.

The move made sense on a number of levels. Not only had he been unable to find a full-time job that seemed to be a good fit in Richmond, but his wife, Amie Miklavcic, an obstetrician/gynecologist (OB/GYN) whom he had met in med school at Drexel, had to drive a considerable distance each day on traffic-choked Interstate 95 to a job south of Richmond, and her contract at that job was about to expire. By moving back to New Jersey, they would both be able to raise their daughter closer to their families, Ajit would have a full-time permanent job, and Amie was confidently hopeful that she could find one in the OB/GYN field.

That perspective changed early one morning when Pai walked into McGuire and was met in a hallway by McNamee, who delivered some stunning news. After more than four years of tirelessly nurturing the poly-trauma unit from its infancy into a world-class rehabilitation facility, one that was drawing rave reviews from patients and officials throughout the US military hierarchy and had established itself as a jewel in the VA's system of advanced care for multiple traumas, McNamee had hit the wall.

Still relatively young himself, he wanted to spend more time with his family, and he felt the time was right for a new professional challenge as well. He had been a devoted advocate in the start-up of the polytrauma unit, and his work had resulted in countless success stories of patients being able to literally walk out the doors of 2-B and back to a semblance of independent living. In short, his motto, "Turning patients into people," was working.

Now he wanted a change, and he was taking a promotion as chief of the hospital's PM&R service. His job, he told Pai, was open.

Pai knew McNamee couldn't officially name him his successor, but he also nonetheless knew the implications of what McNamee was telling him: If Pai wanted the job, the work he had already done in his time at VCU and McGuire would earn him the backing of Cifu and McNamee. That backing, in turn, would go a long way in determining the choice to be the new head of the polytrauma unit.

Pai, immediately intrigued by what he later would call the one job that could keep him in Richmond, was also mortified by the quandary he faced: Not only were people at the rehabilitation hospital back in New Jersey waiting for him to start, but he had already signed a contract to work there.

Years later, Miklavcic chuckled as she recalled the morning she was in heavy traffic on I-95, driving to work, and her cell phone rang. On the other end was her normally mild-mannered husband, and he was struggling to remain calm as he broke the news that McNamee had just shared with him.

"Um, honey, I'm on 95. I don't think I can have this conversation right now," she recalled telling him. "But I knew. I knew when I hung up that phone that he was going to take that job. I don't think he ever had a doubt that he would take the job."

The people at the rehabilitation hospital in New Jersey understood, and they let Pai out of his contract. Pai took over as medical director of the polytrauma unit in August 2010, and that fall, his wife joined the staff of the Virginia Women's Center, a practice in Richmond's northeast suburbs that has more than two dozen OB/GYNs and other physicians.

———

The rhythm of the polytrauma unit can create some long, trying winters. The nature of the war in Afghanistan was such that the heaviest fighting would occur each summer, then taper off as the typically harsh winters would settle over the nation.

In Richmond, a somewhat typical pattern was for the unit to be at or near capacity in the summer and fall months with a mix of those wounded during heavy periods of fighting as well as those injured in car crashes or summer-related activities such as swimming pool accidents. As fall would slip into winter and inch toward spring, most of those patients would complete their rehabilitation and move on. The patient population might begin to fall off a bit. During those periods, service members injured in Afghanistan might find themselves on 2-B with a significant number of patients who had already been there for months and were still struggling in their rehabilitation. These were the tough cases, and the staff spent long hours over a long period of time trying to help them down the road to recovery. Often times, the patients still on the unit as the winter drags on become frustrated. Their loved ones become frustrated. And the staff could become frustrated as well. Everybody involved in the equation wants to see improvement, and when that improvement doesn't always materialize in a speedy fashion, it can be difficult.

In addition, because many of those patients spend months at a time on the unit, and their caregivers are with them as well, there is a tendency for them to regard the polytrauma unit as their temporary home of sorts and to view the staff as their temporary family. Everyone spends a lot of time together in relatively close quarters, and everyone is working toward the common goal of improvement by the patient.

Combine those dynamics with the fact that in the winter it might still have been dark when employees arrived for work in the morning, or when loved ones arrived to begin the day with the patients, and it might already be dark again when those people started to go home at night.

Add it all up, and it can make for some understandably frustrating times.

It was with this in mind that Dr. Ajit Pai, then in his third year as the medical director of the polytrauma unit, sent an e-mail to the sixty-eight members of the staff on February 13, 2013. The subject of the e-mail was "Civility," and he opened the e-mail by addressing the staff as "Team," as was his practice.

"Please continue working hard at the extremely difficult duties before you," he wrote in part. "You are making a real difference in people's lives. Let's take it one step farther and make certain our patients, families, visitors, and own team members feel we're considering them, not just ourselves."

The e-mail came with an attachment of an article about behaving in a civil manner, and the article included ways to know your triggers for anger, assess your own behavior, be considerate of others, and empty your "bitter bag" and forgive others.

It was, as Pai said later, another example of the type of administrative duties not covered in medical school but that are nonetheless an important part of the job. Although technically responsible for job-performance reviews of only the physicians, fellows, and residents on the unit, he is looked at to provide leadership for the entire staff.

"When I took this job," he explained, "I was a little worried about everything that came with the administrative and leadership functions. Shane had done such an incredible job of getting the unit performing at such a high level, and I didn't know if it could get any better. I really didn't want to mess that up."

Instead, Pai grew into the leadership role, and he added his own personal touches along the way, especially in the area of putting a premium on patient care. Nowhere is that more evident than when he goes into a patient's room—where he often sits down so he can literally be on the same level with those for whom he is caring—and when patients are given a weekend pass.

As patients progress in their rehabilitation, one of the gauges they and the staff can use is to see how they can function outside the hospital walls. For that reason, the staff is fond of issuing so-called weekend passes to patients. They could be used simply to go stay at a nearby hotel for the weekend with their loved ones, providing them with an environment other than the polytrauma unit, or they could be to attend such events as a relative's anniversary party, a wedding, or a graduation.

Whatever the reason, before patients leave 2-B, Pai gives them his business card with his personal cell phone number on it. If there are any medical issues while they are out in the community, he tells them, they are to call him first.

"After all they've been through," he explained, "how can you trust these guys to somebody else? We know them best. They've generally been with us for months, so it just makes sense."

He claimed he gives out his number to only about 5 percent of the polytrauma unit's patients. His wife and others think the percentage is higher than that—perhaps significantly so.

"It's not unusual for him to get calls from a family member who just needs somebody to listen to," Miklavcic said. "That's how he needs to be. That's how he wants to make things okay."

Pai doesn't view giving patients 24/7 access to him via his cell phone as doing anything special for them.

"He thinks it's all in a day's work," his wife explained.

Pai's style leaves an impression on patients, their caregivers, and his peers.

David McHenry shook his head when asked about the compassion Pai had shown for his son, Jon, after he was severely injured in Afghanistan.

"I've probably been given a thousand business cards since Jon was first injured," David said. "Dr. Pai's is at the top of that stack. He listens. He helps. He makes sure you understand. If you're confused about something, he'll stay with you and talk you through it. He's very calm about it, too.

"Some people just tell you everything will be okay. You get the sense it's almost like they don't have time for you and they just want to move on. He doesn't do that. He wants you to know you're not alone. If you don't have an answer, he'll get you one. That means a lot to people. A whole lot."

That straightforward approach can work in other ways as well. Barbara Bauserman, who oversees the polytrauma unit's family education program, described a scene that helped illustrate not only Pai's demeanor with patients and their caregivers, but the depth of his caring. Bauserman recalled a meeting in which the wife of an injured serviceman expressed her frustration about her husband's slow progress.

Pai, in patient, even tones, was explaining to her why the staff was employing certain treatments, detailing how those treatments had produced progress, and telling her how the staff planned to proceed to keep her husband on a path of improvement. All the while, the wife listened, but she clearly wasn't impressed. Like so many caregivers who can become frustrated while watching a loved one's long-term struggles, she wanted her husband back to his old self, and she wanted it sooner rather than later. She wanted him to tell her something other than what she was hearing.

Finally, she could contain herself no more, and she cut off Pai in midsentence.

"But what are you going to *do?*" she blurted in a tone that suggested desperation and protest.

Pai responded in the same soft, reassuring, nonoffensive tone he had been using.

"What I can tell you I do," he said, "is that I start every day by praying for our patients."

With that, the woman apologized.

———

In the juggling act of overseeing patients and staff, Pai said he found a comfort zone much faster in his role as a physician. Part of that, he said, could have to do with the fact that so many members of the staff are more experienced than him and have been there longer than him. Quite simply, he said, they were already good at their jobs before he came along, and they don't need much direction.

In fact, when asked to name some of his mentors, Pai offered seven names, and five of those were staff members on the polytrauma unit.

"It really is incredible how much they bring, individually and as a group," he explained.

Regardless, as he neared the end of his third year on the job, he needed to do a better job of making himself available to the staff.

"I really feel I've taken for granted the leadership experience I've had," he said. "I need to develop a better appreciation and understanding that leading the team has a lot to do with just being a respectful person and being a good communicator. And by respect, I mean I need to respect their perspective, I need to respect their work ethic and I need to respect their expertise."

The members of the staff, because they are experienced and committed to working together to achieve the goal of patient improvement, get along well, a dynamic that might not be prevalent amid what can often be the significant restraints of a large federal bureaucracy. The staff members have semiannual team-building exercises that include bowling, laser tag, miniature golf, and scavenger hunts, not to mention the more frequent and popular post-work happy hour gatherings at O'Toole's, an Irish pub about a five-minute drive north of the hospital.

"We lean on each other a lot," said Monique Jones, one of the speech-language pathologists. "And sometimes it goes beyond just trying to pick each other up, to give someone an outlet to vent. Sometimes it comes down to saying, 'Hey, can you treat this guy today for me? I just can't do it. I need a break.'"

That kind of cooperation and support is what makes Pai proud of the work of the team, as is what he called a collective commitment to make the polytrauma experience better, both for the patients and the staff.

"You get different people on the team who want to do different things and take on more than what they were hired for," he explained. "That's what makes it so special. There's a real spirit of, 'What else can I do?' that's happening, and that's only going to make things better."

Alison B. Conley, one of the occupational therapists on the unit, said the spirit of teamwork, cooperation, and commitment that flows from the top down is a key reason why turnover among polytrauma staff is rare.

"There's not really a reason to leave," Conley said. She added that Pai, in a relatively short period of time, established a reputation for making sound decisions.

"He is not judgmental and he has expectations of professionalism. And I don't think those two qualities will get you in trouble."

With twenty available beds, Richmond's polytrauma unit had 114 patient admissions in the 2012 calendar year. Whereas the unit was often at capacity in late summer and early fall, Pai explained that the rest of the year, it probably averaged ten to twelve patients at any given time. Numbers like that make it easier for him and the rest of the staff to devote large doses of one-on-one time to patients.

Numbers like that, as Pai and the rest of the staff know, also don't typically exist beyond the walls of 2-B.

For example, Pai's wife stated that at her practice, it's not all that unusual for her to see as many as thirty-five patients in a day. Assuming she spends eight hours each day seeing patients, that would work out to more than four patients per hour.

"That is unfathomable with him," Miklavcic said. "It's very different in terms of our day-to-day jobs. But that's one of the things that he loves so much about what he does. And to tell the truth, I'm kind of envious of what he does on certain days. He loves the clinical side of things, but he loves that it's not cookie cutter."

Evidence of that came when Pai, then still just a resident, was able to spend so much time with his dying patient, to help him, to comfort him, to read to him, and to get him to consider the spiritual aspects of life as he prepared for death.

"Death doesn't really matter," Pai said later. "It's part of who we are. It's part of the process." He paused. "Every one of our patients who comes in here, I want to provide hope for the future."

That hope is not just limited to a patient's medical needs in the complicated world of polytrauma care.

"What about the spiritual? What about that end?" he asked. "And we're not just talking about religion. We're talking about your being, about what kind of person you want to be, about what kind of person you *can* be."

That spiritual component is something he is trying pass along to the residents and fellows who pass through 2-B. That's because the man, who still counts many of his own mentors among members of the polytrauma staff he oversees, has also become a mentor himself.

The list of people who regard Pai as a mentor includes McNamee, even though he is older and more experienced.

"He's a doctor's doctor," McNamee said. "What does that mean? That means he's a doctor that other doctors go to to ask doctor questions."

Pai was named assistant director of the residency program at VCU's Department of PM&R in August 2010, when he began the job as the medical director of the polytrauma unit, and he was named an assistant professor, also in VCU's PM&R Department, in October 2010, and given the primary responsibilities of teaching VCU fellows and fourth-year residents. Asked about his long-term plans, he mentioned the possibility of teaching and getting into administration. Clinical care is probably not something he can do for his entire career.

Any change in career paths, however, was not on his list of immediate plans. He was getting far too much satisfaction being part of a team that enjoyed good internal cooperation and excellent support, both from the hospital administration and the federal hierarchy in Washington. That support, in turn, helped lay the groundwork for what he called "as close as you can come to a perfect environment" for practicing rehabilitation medicine.

"I want to be here," he said. "I feel like I'm making a difference."

"I feel that my biggest job here," he explained, "is to manipulate all this so that it fits together like a Tetris model, so that when it's time for discharge, we're ready to roll."

To get there, though, Pai insists that medical needs alone not be the sole factor in the rehabilitation process.

"Be a human. Don't just be a healthcare provider."

CHAPTER FIVE

NEW PATIENT

Jon McHenry's transition from Walter Reed National Military Medical Center to the PRC at McGuire VA Medical Center began even before he made the trip down Interstate 95 from the suburbs of Washington, DC, to Richmond, Virginia.

A few days before Jon's arrival, several key members of the polytrauma unit staff gathered in room 142—which features a long conference table ringed by twelve chairs, with another eight seats along the walls of the room, and a videoconferencing hookup complete with a large, flat-screen television—and began mapping out a course of action for their latest patient.

The staff refers to these events as VTELs—short for video teleconferences—that are set up to allow incoming patients to meet their new care team before arriving in Richmond. In this case, the videoconferencing equipment connected Richmond and Walter Reed, where Jon McHenry was preparing to leave. It is a procedure that the polytrauma unit staff repeats for each new patient, and it is designed to set the stage for the best possible treatment, one that helps improve their odds for success in both the healing and rehabilitation process while at the Richmond facility.

The reasoning is simple: If the patient and his or her loved ones are able to see the new doctors and other caregivers, speak with them, ask them questions, and start a dialogue, it starts the formation of an important bond before those patients even come through the doors at Richmond.

"We want them to be able to put a face with a name, a face with a voice, to see that we're here for them and we're ready to start working on their behalf," said Dr. Pai. "So when they get here, everyone feels like we're already a step ahead, like we're already moving in the right direction."

The procedure for each VTEL is generally the same: to outline what services the patient can expect at McGuire and to enable the patient and the staff members to start connecting with each other. The staff will discuss short-term goals and their relation to long-term goals, and the patients and their family will be invited to talk about their goals as well.

"The long-term goal," Pai declared, "is pretty much the same for all patients: as functionally independent as possible."

Every patient can expect certain services, and other services are arranged depending on the nature of their injuries. For example, all patients who come to McGuire's polytrauma unit are assigned a social worker, whose duties include but are not limited to such tasks as helping them coordinate communications with liaisons to their military units, getting loved ones answers to questions about the patient's care, or helping them arrange child care or other outside services. All patients also are assigned a counseling psychologist, physical therapist, kinesiotherapist, occupational therapist, and recreational therapist.

The counseling psychologist helps the patient and his or her family adjust to the emotional challenges that a traumatic injury can present. The physical therapist coordinates the portion of rehabilitation aimed at movement and its relationship to their physical independence. The kinesiotherapist focuses on muscle strength and cardiovascular endurance. The occupational therapist works with such issues as whether the patient needs help with eating, grooming, bathing, and so on. The recreational therapist concentrates on how well adjusted the patient is becoming to his or her previous lifestyle.

The rehabilitation regimen expands if a patient has a TBI. If there is indication of a cognitive deficit, the patient will be evaluated by a neuropsychologist and a speech therapist, and an ophthalmologist and an optometrist will conduct examinations as well.

The polytrauma unit staff also has a patient education specialist who works with patients—and especially their loved ones—to try to simplify what can be a complicated tangle of technical language and an overwhelming course of therapy, medical appointments, and treatments. In addition, each patient is assigned a lead therapist, someone who is designated to help coordinate the work of the staff, serve as a point of contact if the patient has concerns, and act in general as a lead advocate/confidant for the patient. The staff tries to tailor the selection of the lead therapist to an individual patient's injuries, needs, and personality. For example, a patient with multiple fractures who will spend much of his therapy concentrating on rebuilding his or her strength might be assigned a physical therapist or kinesiotherapist as the lead therapist. Someone who has severe cognitive deficits might be assigned a speech therapist, and someone with significant psychological or emotional difficulties might be assigned a neuropsychologist as lead therapist.

Coordinating therapy sessions—most are scheduled to last one hour each—and other medical appointments is no small feat. Each patient's daily schedule is charted on a large board at the nurses' station in the polytrauma unit that is broken into one-hour increments. The schedule board starts at 8 A.M. and goes to 5 P.M., and the only blocked time is noon to 1 P.M., which is reserved each day for lunch. Other than that one sacred hour, it is unusual to look at the board and find any more than one free hour on a patient's daily schedule.

Yet no matter how many therapists or doctors a patient is scheduled to see on a given day, the key, according to Pai, is to get the rehabilitation process started as soon as possible. The easiest way to do that is to establish trust as soon as possible, because the sooner the patient believes in the staff and the staff's mission, the sooner the patient will buy in and become a willing part of that endeavor.

That's why the polytrauma unit staff not only starts the process with a VTEL before the patient arrives, but also why Pai wants to be kept abreast of the exact arrival time of a new patient in Richmond. He wants the patients to see—first on a videoconference screen, then in person when they arrive—that the staff is committed to being an advocate on their behalf, and that the level of commitment begins at the top, with the unit's medical director.

"I'm in that room, hopefully, within ten to fifteen minutes of when they first get there," Pai said. "They honestly don't trust us. Let's face it: They don't know us. So if we can help as soon as they get here and start building a good relationship within the first twenty-four hours, then that helps us, too, not only with the lines of communication, but with the trust."

In many cases, the East Coast's most notorious major highway actually provides an unwitting assist to the unit's staff in their bid to quickly establish a rapport with a new patient.

A large portion of the unit's patients come Richmond directly from Walter Reed, and many are still in the early stages of recovery from numerous surgeries and multiple fractures. Quite simply, they're still typically in a great deal of pain, and that pain can often be exacerbated by Interstate 95. What is supposed to be a two-hour ride down the interstate from the Washington suburbs to Richmond can often turn into an odyssey that is significantly longer, and it's not unusual for patients to arrive at the unit feeling worn out and more than a little beat up from the starts and stops and bumps and angst of a morning on I-95 that turned into a morning and an afternoon on I-95.

Thus when the ambulance that transported them from Walter Reed finally pulls up to the front entrance at McGuire, and they're wheeled back into the hospital, up an elevator, down a second-floor hallway to their new room and transferred from the gurney into their bed in 2-B, Pai finds his job relatively easy when he walks in a few minutes later to check on them.

He doesn't wait long to ask them a simple question: "Can I get you anything?"

More often than not, the response is: "Can you get me something for the pain?"

With that, Pai delivers a simple act—administering a dose of a pain-killer—that doubles as an early dose of trust, a building block in the long process of rehabilitation that will involve many people working toward a common goal.

———

One of 114 patients admitted to Richmond's polytrauma unit in 2012, Jon McHenry was in many ways typical. Seventy-two of those 114 had been diag-nosed with a TBI as a result of blast injuries, gunshot wounds, motor vehicle collisions, motorcycle crashes, or falls. After TBIs, the reason for patients being admitted to the polytrauma unit in 2012 were most often stroke (thir-teen), amputations not related to combat or motor vehicle collisions (nine) and neurological damage related to brain tumors, brain infections, or other brain surgeries (seven).

The Richmond unit's admissions figures for the year, however, also pro-vide a glimpse of how many people in the military can have a TBI away from the battlefield. Just twenty-six of the polytrauma unit's admissions, or slightly less than 23 percent of the 114, were a result of combat injuries.

Soon after Jon McHenry's arrival at McGuire on January 19, the staff found evidence that he had what was classified as moderate TBI, deflating David McHenry's hopes that his son's occasional slow responses, loss of focus, and moments of agitation were due primarily to all the painkillers he was getting for his numerous fractured bones, internal injuries, and surgeries. Instead, a magnetic resonance imaging (MRI) scan showed that Jon had what is called a *diffuse axonal injury* in his brain. Unlike a concussion, in which the brain typically bangs against the wall of the skull and then bounces back, causing a bruise, a diffuse axonal injury is what occurs when there is more of a violent, high-speed twisting or torqueing motion in the brain, resulting in large-scale damage to white-cell tissue. Diffuse axonal injuries are often explained as being similar to an especially violent case of shaken baby syn-drome, and they are common in vehicle rollovers, in which a person can often be twisted or thrown in several different directions in a violent fashion and in a very concentrated time frame.

Such injuries are not unusual in people who have survived IED blasts, especially the more powerful ones. Jon's IED blast, which featured an estimated three hundred to four hundred pounds of explosives that launched his armored personnel carrier airborne, certainly fit that bill. A testament to the power of the blast was that Jon, still strapped in the driver's seat with his helmet still secured on his head, was found outside the vehicle.

In the most severe diffuse axonal injuries, patients will end up comatose, and many will never regain consciousness. Jon's case was not that severe, which was especially fortunate given that there is no foolproof treatment for these injuries other than what is standard with many brain injuries: Try to limit the swelling and pressure inside the brain, and try to keep the patient stable.

Pai and his staff also based their diagnosis of moderate TBI in part on Jon's scores from the Glasgow Coma Scale, a standardized test aimed at assessing brain impairment and injury based on how the patient scores in three areas: the response of his eyes to various commands and other stimuli; motor response or movement, again to various commands and stimuli; and his verbal responses, both in terms of their accuracy and social acceptability. Results from the three test areas are added together, with the cumulative score ranging from a high of thirteen to fifteen points, signifying mild brain injury, to a low of three, which indicates severe injury. Jon's Glasgow score was a ten, which put him solidly in the moderate brain injury range of nine to twelve points.

Severe brain injury is often associated with patients who lose a great deal of blood, suffer strokes, have significant open-head wounds, have swelling on the brain, and experience seizures. Jon had none of these problems. Another indication of the moderate nature of his TBI was his experience in speech therapy while at the polytrauma unit. Patients with severe TBI may initially be unable to speak and have difficulty swallowing, and it is not unusual for them to spend five days a week for months on end with speech therapists as they struggle to regain control of their swallowing and speaking.

Jon, on the other hand, saw a speech therapist five times total, with many of his appointments devoted to exercises designed to determine whether his memory and other cognitive abilities had been significantly impacted by the TBI. Once the staff was satisfied that those abilities had not been severely affected, he was no longer scheduled for speech therapy appointments.

That's not to say that there were no bumps in the road on the TBI front for him.

According to David McHenry, his son would become easily agitated while at Walter Reed, and those seemingly unprovoked incidents continued at McGuire.

"I'd be with him for hours on end, for days on end sometimes, and when I'd have to go out for a while to take care of something, he'd get really annoyed, and I mean really annoyed to the point of being unreasonable," the elder McHenry recalled. "He'd be like, 'Where are you going? When are you coming back?' And as soon as I'd get back, he'd start right back in on me again. 'Where have you been? I need you here.'

"He wasn't like that before. Sure, he had a little bit of a temper like most teenagers, I guess, but never anything like that."

The polytrauma unit staff noticed it, too.

One night, Jon was struggling to get in a comfortable resting position in his bed, and he used the handheld remote intercom device at his bedside to call the nursing station and ask if one of the nurses could come to his room and help him. It's a common request for patients who are suffering from multiple fractures to their extremities, and Jon had the added burden of trying to shift while his torso was restricted by a cervical-thoracic-lumbo-sacral orthosis—a CTLSO, for short. In layman's terms, it's a hard, molded plastic back brace with a neck extension that leaves the patient looking as though he's been encased from waist to chin in a tortoise shell. Although the CTLSO is effective for promoting the healing of fractured vertebra, it doesn't exactly promote anything resembling freedom of movement.

For Jon, the bottom line was that not only wasn't he always comfortable when he first arrived at McGuire, but he wasn't particularly mobile, either.

On this night, however, a nurse didn't respond to Jon's room in what he felt was a reasonable amount of time. So he got back on the intercom and called the nursing station again, and this time he implored them to "get your ass in here!"

Jon later acknowledged that his second call on the intercom had not only been out of line, but he said it was out of character for him. The outburst, he explained, was one example of the "tweaks" he occasionally experienced in the aftermath of being diagnosed with moderate TBI. The "tweaks" would occur without warning, and he felt powerless to stop them. As time passed, however, they happened with less frequency.

"It's hard to explain them," he said. "Sometimes you lose control just like that. It's not like you want to do it. It just happens."

On some occasions, his father noted with a chuckle, what might seem like his son being agitated could just be a case of Jon simply being Jon. David recalled one of the doctors at Richmond explaining that the most significant damage in Jon's brain was in the frontal lobe area that controls, among other things, socially appropriate responses. The doctor told them that because of the damage, they might see what could seem to them to be a change in Jon's personality.

"I remember the doctor said, 'The best way I can explain it to you is that he's going to be very up front with you. There's no filter there. Whatever he's thinking, it's going to come out,' David recalled. "And I remember telling this lady, 'So it's going to be worse than it was? Because he's been like that his whole life.'"

Pai, asked later to speak generally about socially inappropriate outbursts by patients, said the staff reviews each event to try to determine such factors as what may have caused it, in what context it occurred, and whether it may be indicative of another problem. For example, frustration could be a natural reaction from a patient who may have hit a plateau in his or her rehabilitation and is struggling to improve, or has experienced a particularly difficult day, pain-wise. On the other hand, a seemingly unprovoked outburst of verbal abuse could be a sign that TBI very much remains an issue.

"We understand that people get frustrated. That's a natural part of the healing and rehabilitation process. We expect that. People are here because they want to get better," Pai explained. "If you weren't frustrated, we'd be worried.

"Now, that said, frustration cannot include abuse."

The intercom call was not indicative of any pattern of verbal abuse by Jon, who by and large had established a reputation as a diligent patient, particularly in the area of physical therapy and kinesiotherapy. He clearly wanted to get better, and once his fractured bones and internal injuries began to heal, he focused on regaining weight and strength.

Jon also had something else in his favor that the polytrauma unit staff cites as one key to a patient's recovery: a strong family support system. His wife, Jay, was staying at the Fisher House, a well-appointed, all-expenses-paid, extended-stay lodge for patients' families that is a short walk across one of the parking lots at McGuire from the main hospital building, and she was able to spend as much time as she wanted by her husband's side. David also took off large chunks of time from his job at AmeriGas and spent as many days as he could with his son. Because the McHenrys' hometown was only about a five-hour ride from Richmond, relatives and friends were able to drive from Newport to visit Jon, especially on weekends.

With plenty of family behind him, Jon adapted well to his rehabilitation stint at the polytrauma unit. As his fractures and internal injuries began to heal and his TBI "tweaks" gradually declined in frequency, he was able to shift his focus to regaining his weight, strength, and mobility. Given his status as a military policeman, his youth, his rich athletic background, and his passion for physical fitness, motivating him for his physical therapy and kinesiotherapy sessions was not an issue, as is the case with many young active-duty personnel. In fact, the only thing that seemed to hold him back on those fronts was pain associated with his myriad fractures and internal injuries, and the passage of time helped greatly in those areas.

What proved more challenging was another area of his newfound status as a war-wounded soldier: basic functions. How do you use the bathroom when your mobility is severely limited by various fractures in numerous areas of your body? How do you bathe? How do you dress?

Enter Alison B. Conley, one of the occupational therapists on the unit.

"In a word, she was great," Jon said.

Conley, who like so many staff members came to the polytrauma unit shortly after college and quickly found a comfort zone with the sense of camaraderie, teamwork, and purpose that the team displayed in helping the nation's service members, spent many an hour with Jon, helping him help himself with common-sense solutions to basic problems.

She said he was understandably in a significant amount of pain when he first arrived in Richmond, was not allowed to put any weight on his fractured legs, and was unable to move his right arm due to his fractured clavicle and scapula on that side.

"His spirits started to improve after about two weeks," she recalled. "I think getting to know the staff helped, and getting out of the bed was very beneficial."

Therapy, Conley said, helped Jon "prove to himself what he'd be able to do—that life was not over, and it didn't even really have to be on hold—proof that he could still do things; he'd just have to do them differently."

After his first week in Richmond, during which he had to stay in bed while he groomed himself, bathed, and used the bathroom, progress became evident. For Jon that progress began with two words, two simple words that helped start him down the path to regaining his independence, two words for which he will eternally be grateful to Conley.

"Velcro pants," he said, shaking his head and making no effort to suppress a sheepish grin.

The pants were part of a clothing line that comes from Sew Much Comfort, a Burnsville, Minnesota-based nonprofit established in 2004 to provide adaptive clothes for injured service members. With survival rates soaring for US troops injured in Iraq and Afghanistan, the charity saw a burgeoning need for clothing that would help injured service members who had limited mobility.

Sew Much Comfort organized an army of volunteers to begin designing, sewing, and distributing—at no cost to the troops—adaptive clothing aimed at eliminating the need for recovering service members to wear skimpy, undignified hospital gowns by replacing them with more functional regular clothing—or at least what appeared to be regular clothing. In fact, the charity's volunteer seamstresses were so skilled that most people had to look closely to see that the shirts and pants actually relied on strategic placement of well-disguised Velcro strips to accommodate prosthetic devices, casts, and braces.

The reasoning behind the use of Velcro was simple: It goes a long way in helping make up for a lack of mobility.

For example, if a patient was in a back brace and couldn't bend over to pull up a pair of pants, and the patient had leg fractures and casts on both legs, then a regular pair of pants wouldn't do much good. For starters, the back brace may prevent the patient from reaching down to pull on the pants, and even if he or she could, the pants might not fit over the casts on his/her legs. If, however, the patient had a so-called reacher—those metal arms that have become popular to help reach items in kitchens, featuring a claw-like clamp on one end of a rod and a trigger handle grip on the other to help govern the opening and closing of the clamp—then he or she could put on a pair of Velcro pants. Sew Much Comfort also designed the pants with extra wide legs to accommodate leg casts and/or braces. So all a patient has to do is use the reacher to slide the pants up and then use his or her hands to begin closing the Velcro seam downward before finishing off the closing of the seam with the reacher. With limited practice and instruction from an occupational therapist, a patient can quickly learn to dress using this method.

Adding to the ease of the process, Sew Much Comfort has clothing for pretty much any occasion. The selection of pants alone includes underwear, sweat pants, pajama bottoms, denim jeans, and dress pants.

Once Conley showed Jon how to dress himself, other functions quickly followed. It wasn't long before she had him transferring himself to a special stretcher that would allow him to shower himself. Barely a month after his arrival in Richmond, he was cleared to remove his back brace, and soon he was dressing himself completely, showering on a seated plastic tub bench, and using the bathroom by himself. His bed in Room 110 was no longer his 24/7 home; now it was reduced to something he used only for resting and sleeping.

However, just as Jon's struggles with TBI "tweaks" remained ongoing, his therapy sessions were not without occasional bumps in the road. The staff at the polytrauma unit is fond of reminding visitors that their patients have just experienced what is likely to be the most traumatic event that will occur in their lives, and their road to recovery and rehabilitation is not always straight and smooth.

"He was a fun guy to work with," Conley said. "Some days we didn't work because he was in pain. I'd get him a drink, somehow try to make him more comfortable or just let him be. Some days we didn't work because he was feeling down. Those days, we just talked. It's always a balance between pushing people and letting them recover, tough love versus being a cheerleader, physically as much as mentally."

As January passed and stretched into February and then March, the unit staff continued to work with Jon, and he continued to regain weight, strength, mobility, and independence. With the realization that he was recovering came the need to start considering his next move. He could remain in the military, or he could opt to leave the service via the so-called Med Board process, in which his medical condition would be considered by a military panel that would then determine a percentage of disability and, accordingly, a disability payment.

It was unlikely he would remain in the service, given that he had already been severely injured once and that his complete recovery seemed, at that point at least, in doubt. That left the question of what to do, and Jon admitted he was uncertain. Perhaps he would move to Florida or Arizona to start a new life with his wife and son. Whether that new life would involve finding a job or first going to college remained in question.

David, meantime, remained in his role as a concerned father, watching and waiting, pleased that his son's fractured bones and internal injuries seemed to be healing but concerned nonetheless about the TBI and what effects it might have on his young son, both in the short term and for the rest of his life.

"There's so much we don't know," he explained. "The brain is so complicated, and this whole TBI thing is still new. I worry about how this might affect Jon. I worry about what it might do to him when he's in his forties, fifties, or sixties. Will he be okay? Will there be things happening that we can't predict? We need more studies to see what TBI can do, because right now, we just don't know. The military doesn't know. The doctors don't know.

"And as a father, that scares me. It really does."

CHAPTER SIX

GOING HOME

While the PRC staff in Richmond worked to get Jon McHenry progressing on the road to recovery, help was forming in other areas as well.

One of those initiatives had already taken root back in Jon's native Perry County, Pennsylvania, and included a number of people who had never even met the young soldier. That effort began quite by accident, less than two hours into 2012, at a New Year's Eve party in the Millerstown fire hall.

Last Call, the group playing at the fire hall that night, had been a fixture on the area scene for years, and as a result they had acquired a solid, loyal following. The booking of Last Call helped organizers sell an estimated 250 tickets for the New Year's party at the fire hall.

"The place was packed," recalled Pat Whitmyer, a longtime friend of the group's lead singer. "They're a perfect band for a New Year's gig. Everybody was having a good time."

Last Call was wrapping up its final set about 1 A.M., and Pat and the friends at his table were talking about calling it a night as well. Pat needed to go to the men's room before they left, so he walked across the hall to the restroom and went inside. There was a middle-aged man near the sink, and Pat noticed immediately that he was clearly upset.

"I could see he had been crying," Pat said. "I just said, 'Bud, are you okay?' And he grabbed me and just sort of hugged me and started to cry some more."

He asked again what was wrong, and David McHenry began to let it all out.

"My son was in a bombing in Afghanistan," Pat recalled David saying.

This stranger kept apologizing, kept insisting his son was fine, kept saying he was coming home and everything would be okay. Yet Pat could tell by the man's demeanor that his son was anything but fine, that what had happened in Afghanistan was serious and had rattled his father to the core. So Pat tried to be a good listener, a comforter. He kept asking questions and letting David talk, letting him vent what had clearly been bottled up inside.

"I'm not the type of person to just walk by someone and just let them there crying," he explained. "We talked for a while. I think I got him calmed down. Then I went back out."

That was where the close-knit nature of Newport and Perry County began to manifest itself, and one by one, the local dominos began to fall.

"I got back to my table," Pat said, "and I told everybody about this guy I had just met in the men's room and how he was telling me about his son getting blown up by an IED and everything."

By that point, four days had passed since the IED blast, and word was starting to spread in Newport that one of the community's own had been injured. The fact that Pat Whitmyer and the elder McHenry both had friends who played in Last Call had helped them meet. Now, that initial connection would serve as a bridge to future encounters, including one that quickly grew into an exercise in community pride.

Pat's job as a regional operations manager for Cumberland Truck Company kept him on the road for long stretches, overseeing five of the company's branches, and it made him particularly appreciative of his limited amount of spare time. More often than not, when he had some free time, he would spend it on a motorcycle, frequently joining friends for long, relaxing rides on the back roads of Pennsylvania and elsewhere. He had a brother-in-law who was a correctional officer at the Dauphin County Prison who rode with a group called the Guardian Knights, an organization of motorcycle enthusiasts who shared the common bond of being in the law-enforcement field. Even though Pat himself had no connection to law enforcement, he was invited to begin riding with the Guardian Knights.

Pat found that he got along well with the group and was especially drawn by the nonprofit organization's mission to support law enforcement, first responders, and the US military. It wasn't long before the Guardian Knights made Pat Whitmyer, who had never worn a badge or served in the armed forces, an associate member.

"They're some of the greatest people I've ever met," he said. "My family comes first. My job comes second. And that club comes third."

"We just want to establish a reputation as being go-to people and do everything we can to take care of our military, our police officers and first responders," explained Rick Cagno, the Guardian Knights' president. Cagno is one of several members of the Guardian Knights who also works as a correctional officer at the prison in Dauphin County, home to the state capital of Harrisburg.

"We clean up pretty good when we're in uniform, but when we're off duty and on the road, we look pretty much like the rest of them. We're bikers. We're bikers first," Cagno stated. "But we're not bad-ass bikers. We're just bikers. We're softies. We're pushovers. We're teddy bears."

That became apparent when the Guardian Knights—because of Pat's and David's mutual connections with members of Last Call—found out almost two months into Jon McHenry's stay in Richmond that he was progressing in his rehabilitation to the point where McGuire's doctors were considering the possibility of allowing him to go home to Newport for a few days.

Jon and his father set an ambitious target: to get him home for a church service and celebration of his grandparents' fiftieth wedding anniversary on March 18. Jon was still encased in the hard torso brace to protect his fractured vertebrae, and he was still using a wheelchair because of his fractured legs. Yet no matter how much pain he was in, Jon seemed to especially perk up when his beloved "Nan" would come to visit him in Richmond, and he spoke optimistically of being able to walk through her front door to surprise her for her fiftieth. It was a goal, and it was a perfect one for Jon, who even though he was only in his early twenties had already become single-mindedly proficient at proving people wrong when they doubted the abilities of this compact warrior.

When the Guardian Knights found out about the possibility of Jon coming home, they reached out to his father with an offer. The club, still in its relative infancy, had organized a riding escort in 2011, gathering as many members as possible to get on their motorcycles and welcome home a wounded soldier by ushering him the final miles to his hometown. It was an immediate hit—with the soldier, his family, the community, and the Guardian Knights. Now the club wanted to organize an escort into Newport for Jon McHenry, to give him a hero's welcome home.

"This is way more than we ever even considered when it was five or six of us just getting together for a lunch run," said Cagno, whose club also became quickly adept at fundraising on behalf of needy beneficiaries.

Pat recalled David's reaction when he was told the Guardian Knights wanted to escort Jon back to Newport.

"He was just amazed that we would do that," Pat recalled. "And I said, 'That's what we are. That's what we do.'"

The final hurdle, of course, was whether McGuire's doctors would clear Jon for the roughly five-hour ride back to Pennsylvania. That, in turn, made it difficult for the members of the Guardian Knights to plan their escort. The club had about 170 members and supporters on an e-mail blast list and 300 or so "friends" on Facebook, but as Cagno pointed out, the less notice the Guardian Knights were given about when Jon would be cleared to come home, the greater the likelihood of it translating into a small turnout for the escort ride.

"A lot of people have to take off work to do it. They don't even hesitate to burn a vacation day to do it," Cagno said. "That's what impresses me about our people. This is a great group of people. But with Jon, we weren't sure how far in advance we'd learn about his travel plans—or even if he'd be able to travel."

The Guardian Knights learned several days ahead of time that Jon would be cleared to go home for a long weekend, but that didn't make it much easier to work out the logistics of where they would meet him to begin the escort—or at what time.

"We probably knew specifically about twenty-four hours in advance," Cagno said. "And as soon as we knew he was coming home, it was on, believe me. It was on."

In a perfect world, Cagno would have preferred that the Guardian Knights had traveled the entire distance to Richmond—roughly 250 miles from Newport—and escorted Jon all the way from the hospital to his family's home. Yet Cagno also knew that because Jon would be traveling on a Friday, a round trip of some 500 miles would not be feasible for his club members, especially considering that they would have to contend in both directions with the notoriously bad weekday traffic in Washington, DC.

"We try to get them as early in the trip as we can," explained Cagno. The group arranged to meet up with David's van, carrying Jon and Jay, his now seven-months-pregnant wife, a little more than an hour north of Washington. The site was an exit ramp of US 11/15 in Gettysburg, Pennsylvania, just north of the Maryland state line.

———

Friday, March 16, brought sun-splashed, unseasonably warm late-winter weather—a beautiful day for a motorcycle escort—when some forty members of the Guardian Knights set out for Gettysburg.

They reached their destination, roughly sixty-five miles south of Newport, then circled down the agreed-up exit ramp, pulled onto the shoulder and waited. Meantime, heading in the opposite direction, working his way up Interstate 95 from Richmond, David McHenry was doing his part to keep the surprise a secret.

"We got past DC," Jon recalled, "and I remember he started saying he might need to make a pit stop to go to the bathroom. The farther we went, the worse it got. By the time we got to the Pennsylvania state line, he said there was no way he was going to make it all the way home."

So David, approaching an exit on US 11/15, slowed and pulled onto the ramp.

What came next was something no one had anticipated. Instead, it was another reminder of the unpredictable nature of TBI and the lingering fallout associated with it.

During his stay at McGuire, Jon had experienced what he called "tweaks"—incidents where he would, by his own admission, lose his temper without explanation and become agitated with staff members to the point where he would unleash a string of profanity. David had also expressed concern about his son becoming unusually agitated with him on occasion and demonstrating some curiously fearful qualities.

Now, as David pulled off US 11/15 in Gettysburg on what should have been a day for nothing but celebration, joy, and pleasant surprises, another troubling episode of agitation was about to unfold.

Jon and David had significantly differing recollections of what happened.

Jon's take was that as his father reduced his speed, turned off US 11/15, and made his way down the exit ramp, he slowed even more when he approached a group of several dozen motorcycle riders who were waiting alongside their bikes.

"I remember joking with my dad and saying, 'Geez, this sure is a horrible place for the Hell's Angels to meet and have a convention,'" Jon said. "And then he said, 'No, Jon, they're here for you. This is not the Hell's Angels. These are the Guardian Knights. They're law-enforcement officers, and they're here to escort you home, to give you a hero's welcome in Newport.'"

Jon was overcome with emotions by the positive gesture.

"Nobody ever did anything like that for me," he said.

David McHenry had a different, darker take about what transpired on the exit ramp.

He said that as he drove down the ramp and slowed when he approached the Guardian Knights, his son took one look at the several dozen rough-looking motorcycle riders, many outfitted in leather chaps and riding custom bikes, and immediately went into a state of panic.

"I remember him saying, 'What's going on? Who are these guys? What's happening?'" David recalled. "Jon had this hunting knife that he would wear sometimes, and he had it strapped on, and he began reaching for it. And he couldn't get to it fast enough, and I was slowing down, and he just kept saying, 'What's going on? What's going on?'

"And I finally got him calmed down. I kept saying, 'It's okay, Jon. It's okay. They're here for you. Everything's fine. They're going to take you home.'"

——

Newport had actually turned out en masse once before to salute its young wounded warrior.

Shawn Lesh, Newport High School's athletic director, and the Newport Athletic Booster Club had teamed to organize a benefit night for Jon. Tri-Valley League rival Upper Dauphin High School was coming to town January 19 for a basketball game, and the communities rallied to the occasion. Students painted entry boards at the Newport gym to honor Jon, and a color guard welcomed spectators. Veterans were granted free admission, and quite a few—many of them in uniform—took advantage of the offer. All concession stand revenue went to a fund to help the McHenrys defray travel expenses for their hospital visits. In all, about $2,000 was raised by the seven hundred or so in attendance that night.

"We just thought it would be a great way to honor Jon," Lesh explained. "It wasn't about a Newport basketball game. For two or three hours, everybody forgot their issues and just concentrated on the McHenry family."

The speakers at halftime included David McHenry.

"He gave a real heartfelt speech," Lesh said. "There weren't too many dry eyes in the house."

Less than two months later, word got out on a Wednesday night that Jon was coming home in less than forty-eight hours, and once again, Newport sprang into action.

The mayor arranged for Newport's fire department and ambulance crew to join in the festivities when the Guardian Knights escorted Jon into town. Someone rounded up several hundred small American flags that were handed out to people along the route to wave as the procession made its way past.

Lesh recalled that anyone still inside the Newport High building came out to join in the parade.

Police stopped traffic to make sure no one interrupted the caravan when, shortly after 3 P.M., the Guardian Knights rumbled across the rusty steel girder bridge that crosses the Juniata River and leads into downtown Newport, kicking up swirling clouds of dust as they delivered Jon back to his grandparents in time for their fiftieth wedding anniversary.

"I could hear the thunder coming down Fourth Street even before I could see them," Lesh recalled several months later. "I still get goose bumps thinking about it.

"It was a pretty big deal for this community."

A crowd of about four hundred people lined the streets to cheer and wave as Jon McHenry—who not too long ago had been a high school basketball hero in Newport, a fierce competitor for the Buffaloes—returned to town underweight, in a leg cast, and requiring crutches to walk, this time as a war hero on the mend. The Harrisburg *Patriot-News* and the *Newport News-Sun* each sent a reporter and a photographer to chronicle the event. WHTM, the local ABC television affiliate, also sent a crew whose video footage helped generate plenty of positive media attention for the Guardian Knights.

"So we gave an afternoon of our time. Big deal. What we get out of it is so much more," said Cagno, the club president. "We do it because it needs to be done. It's not because we're looking for anything. Jon deserves it. They all do.

"But it's funny how when you do the right things for the right reason, other things come from it. For months and months after that, people kept coming up to us and telling us they saw us on TV that day, and they thanked us for doing that for Jon. That helped us grow as a club."

Jon appeared reluctant when he was interviewed upon his arrival home.

"I'm just not a big attention kind of guy," he said later. "I just don't like surprises like that."

It's not that he didn't appreciate all that the Guardian Knights and others did for him. It's just that he had been led to believe that Americans took for granted those who volunteered to serve in the armed forces.

"It just seems like people forget about them," he explained. "I never expected anything like that. Holy hell, it was amazing."

His grandmother used another word to describe the day Jon came home.

"Perfect," Janet McHenry said. "Everything about that day was just perfect."

Once the reporters and cameras retreated and the family was free to relax, Jon spent the rest of the weekend trying to stay in the background and focusing on making sure the limelight was on Bill and Janet McHenry and their landmark occasion.

First, however, Newport's war hero took some time Friday night to enjoy one of his favorite meals, one that he jokingly referred to as a Newport delicacy: fried chicken wings, appropriately from the local VFW post, the one named after William H. Saylor, who in World War I became the first son of Newport to give his life fighting for his country.

Pat Whitmyer, whose New Year's Eve chance encounter with a distraught stranger in a men's room several months earlier had set the stage for the sun-splashed day on which Newport turned out to welcome Jon, recalled going home after the escort and allowing himself to appreciate the work of the Guardian Knights.

"It still raises the hair on the back of my neck, even months later," he said. "These guys are true heroes. They all deserve whatever we can do for them. I just wish we could do more."

CHAPTER SEVEN

EMERGING CONSCIOUSNESS

Webster's Dictionary defines *coma* as "a state of profound unconsciousness caused by disease, injury or poison."

Although the definition is straightforward and simple, getting someone to emerge back into a state of consciousness is anything but.

The PRC at McGuire VA Medical Center has an emerging consciousness program designed for patients with TBIs. Whether they are comatose as a result of being wounded in the battlefield, by stroke, by car crash, or some other way, they all arrive at Richmond with one thing in common: They need the best possible help as they face an uncertain future. Not only is there a question of if they will regain consciousness, but also of what kind of brain function they will have if they do.

New patients are given a baseline assessment, a meticulous set of tests that will be used to determine not only their state of injury but also how the staff will start treating them. From there, doctors and therapists launch into a rigorous regimen of treatments that is constantly evaluated and adjusted with one succinct goal in mind: improvement.

To reach that goal, the staff engages in communication and collaboration to such an extent that it is not unusual, for example, for a speech therapist to sit in on a patient's physical therapy session to see if the patient is displaying a particular behavior that may provide beneficial information to the speech therapist's work. For instance, if a patient groans while the physical therapist is stretching him, can the staff determine if the groan is related to the stretch? Can the physical therapist get the patient to repeat the sound with a different stretch? Can the speech therapist do something later without a stretch and produce the same result? Are there other actions that the staff is taking that can result in repeating behaviors by the patient? What works? What doesn't work?

"The cross-over here is tremendous," said Michael Dardozzi, one of the unit's speech-language pathologists. "I mean, it's one thing to have good teamwork. But we're really taking that teamwork and trying to squeeze the most out of it, and it benefits the patient in the long run. And that's what makes it all worth it."

One of the cornerstones of Richmond's "EC program," as the staff calls it, is a multifaceted approach that includes but is not limited to intensive work by the staff to stimulate patients in the areas of touch, voice, and smell. The program is so rigorous that in addition to hourly therapy sessions that take up a good part of each day, nurses and other staff members who are walking the halls of the unit make it their practice to drop in and briefly visit with EC patients and simply tell them a story, tell them about their day, ask them questions, touch them on an arm or a leg. In short, the staff members try to familiarize the patient with their voices and hope that familiarity helps produce results down the road.

When patients don't have therapy sessions scheduled, it's not unusual for the staff to wheel them out to the front of the polytrauma unit's nurses' station during busy times of the day, simply to expose them to the stimuli that can be provided by familiar voices, computer keyboard tapping, ringing telephones—anything to try to keep challenging their senses, keep trying to add what the staff hopes will be another brick in a foundation that will eventually result in the patient regaining consciousness.

The teamwork approach doesn't end with the staff. The patients' loved ones are enlisted as well. Family members are encouraged to try such tactics as putting headphones on the patients to play their favorite music, read them a book, or play their favorite movie—or just sit by their bedside and talk with them and touch them.

Add up all the teamwork, and Richmond's EC program boasts a figure of 76 percent of its patients regaining consciousness within ninety days of their arrival.

"It takes a village. It really does," explained Dr. Pai. "You never know what might finally trigger it. No two brain injuries are alike, so we try not to limit our approach here. We want to involve as many people as we can. And let's face it: The families know the patient better than we do. So if they think something might work, something might be a trigger, go ahead and try it."

In Richmond, all that effort and collaboration pays off more than three out of four times with the patients opening their eyes again, responding to commands, talking, moving their arms and legs—in short, demonstrating purposeful actions.

"There is," Dardozzi declared, "no better feeling."

Not only is there elation, gratitude, and relief by the family to have their loved one conscious again, but having a patient emerge also literally opens up a whole new world for the staff. No longer do the therapists and other staff members have to focus their efforts on getting the patient to emerge. Now the stage has been set for healing. Now they can concentrate on helping the patient get better.

"There's no turning back," Dardozzi said. "This is when rehab starts, when it truly begins."

Using ninety days as the measuring stick for whether a patient emerges is no accident. That's because ninety days also happens to be the length of the program.

Pai makes that point clear to the families when new patients arrive. Pai assures them that he and his staff will work hard and work together to do the best they can for the patients, but he also tells the families that the staff has established the ninety-day figure as a reasonable amount of time for determining recovery and progress to that point as well as a reasonable course of future action.

"I probably tell them ten times in the initial meeting that it's a ninety-day program," he said, "and I spend plenty of time talking about progress and how we will review progress and how we will do it at regular intervals."

Pai meets formally with the families at the outset, again at the midway point, and in the late stages of the program to talk with them about their loved one's progress. The individual therapists set goals for the patient at the start of each week and try to see how many they can reach, and they also set individual goals in each therapy session, constantly adjusting the goals in an effort to do what works for the patient while also trying to maximize progress. There are weekly "team" meetings as well, sessions held by therapists and other staff members to analyze what has worked, what hasn't, and where they might be headed in the days ahead.

It can be a roller-coaster ride, in large part because recovery from TBI is not typically a straight-line process. There can be all-too-brief peaks followed by sobering valleys, and they can be especially frustrating for the family to watch. Family members are already devastated by seeing a loved one in a coma, and now they have to agonize through what can be a lengthy process of the patient not being able to communicate in a way that might suggest recovery is imminent.

There are several options if a patient doesn't emerge within the ninety days, including sending them to a long-term care facility, either within the VA system or in a private setting. Perhaps the family may seek to try another recovery program. If there are indications that the brain is healing and that the patient may emerge somewhere in the future, the patient could be moved elsewhere for a period of time with the goal of eventually returning to McGuire's EC program. The family also could opt to care for the patient at home.

Pai isn't the only one who reminds the families of the potential difficulties ahead when dealing with a patient who is comatose as a result of a TBI.

Dr. McNamee, whose jurisdiction as the hospital's chief of PM&R includes the polytrauma unit, also tries to reinforce Pai's message. McNamee meets with the families of new EC patients and delivers a straightforward analysis of what lies ahead.

"I tell them it's not on us from here on out, and it's not on them," McNamee said. "It's on their loved one and their loved one's brain. It's on their injury. So much of it comes down to whether the brain can heal. Sometimes, it can't."

It was into this environment that US Air Force Airman Bryce Powers arrived on November 26, 2012—four days after Thanksgiving—with his family hoping and praying that he could join the ranks of the 76 percent who emerge. They needed a miracle, and everyone told them McGuire's EC program represented their best chance.

———

Stationed at Misawa Air Base in northern Japan, home to the 35th Fighter Wing, Bryce Powers was off duty and out for a drive on Saturday, October 13, 2012. He and Kamee Mayfield, a fellow airman from Phoenix, Arizona, had been to Bible study the night before, so the budding friends decided to take advantage of nice weather and go out for a Saturday afternoon drive.

Bryce was at the wheel of a Cappuccino, a small, two-seater convertible roadster manufactured by Suzuki, when it went out of control, left the roadway, and struck a concrete pole. He and Mayfield both lost consciousness in the crash. Emergency responders initially believed Mayfield to be the more seriously injured of the two, and she was rushed to a hospital. Bryce was transported by ambulance first to a walk-in clinic, a Japanese version of the "Patient First" type of treatment centers so popular in the United States, where no appointments are needed and patients are generally treated for such nonemergencies as colds, sore throats, and the like.

After it was determined his injuries were far too severe to be treated at such a clinic, Bryce was eventually transported to a hospital. Tests showed he had contusions on his lungs, and he was later found to have ligament damage in his left foot as well.

The worst news, however, involved his head, which had struck the steering wheel with such force that it broke the wheel. Bryce had so many skull fractures that doctors later told his family they could not count them all. The result was that he wound up with not one significant brain injury, but four. Any one of them alone would have been enough to either kill him or leave him permanently comatose.

Cathy Powers was at the family's home in Monroe, North Carolina, when she got the telephone call from the air force about her son. It wasn't long before she was on a plane to Japan.

Her mind raced the entire trip, flashing through the sea of memories from her son's first twenty-plus years. Cathy's husband, Jim, was an air force veteran, and Bryce had wanted to join the service branch from an early age.

Bryce had joined the air force via its delayed entry program, committing as a seventeen-year-old junior at Piedmont High School, where he had been active in the Junior ROTC and had received the Union County Patriot Award in 2009, the year before his graduation. The air force quickly became everything he hoped it would be. He was learning and he was preparing for what he planned would be a long military career. He was, as his mother noted, happy and content, secure that he had made the right decision. He took his job and his responsibilities seriously—so much so, that before he went overseas, he crafted a living will, gave his mother power of attorney in case something happened to him, and took her to the bank and signed paperwork that would give her access to his account.

All this was flashing through Cathy's mind when she arrived in Japan and was led to a room at a hospital with two air force doctors who were using technical terms to tell her that her son's injuries were devastating and that he would not recover.

Then they pushed a legal form in front of her and told her that if she signed it, they could take him off the respirator, starting the process of permitting him to pass away.

"I had barely gotten off the plane and they're telling me to let my son die?" she recounted months later. "What mother would do that? What kind of mother?"

So Cathy decided to do everything she could to give her son every possible chance to recover.

Bryce and Kamee Mayfield both wound up returning to the United States, where Mayfield—although also suffering from significant brain injuries—charted a course of steady improvement. By the time the new year rolled around, she was well on her way to recovery.

Bryce, on the other hand, continued to struggle in an environment defined by more questions than answers. That included the matter of what had happened that afternoon on the road in Japan.

According to Cathy, there were several theories about what may have caused the crash, including the possibility that her son was driving carelessly, but no definitive conclusions were reached. First responders said both were wearing seat belts at the time of the crash. The car did not have air bags.

"Bryce was a very safe person," his mother said. "He didn't even like roller-coasters. He didn't like feeling out of control."

Jim Powers was not surprised to hear that blood tests had found no evidence of alcohol or drugs in Bryce at the time of the crash.

"I knew they wouldn't find anything," he said. "That boy had more opportunities in high school, and he never touched the stuff."

The bigger questions, however, centered on Bryce's extensive brain injuries.

The TBI, ranked as severe, involved the left side of his brain, which controls motor and sensory functions for the right side of the body. The upper left quadrant of the front of his skull struck the steering wheel with such force that it not only broke the wheel, but also caused one massive skull fracture and smaller fractures that were literally too numerous to count. He also had a diffuse axonal injury, also ranked as severe. Some studies have shown that roughly 90 percent of comatose patients with severe diffuse axonal injuries do not regain consciousness.

In addition, Bryce had an anoxic injury, meaning his brain had been deprived of oxygen for an extended period. Doctors were uncertain of the precise length of oxygen deprivation, but it was believed to have been more than five minutes. When oxygen levels are lowered significantly for more than four minutes, brain-cell death occurs, and the damage is permanent.

The fourth type of brain injury Bryce sustained was a direct result of his severe TBI. Not long after the crash, he developed hydrocephalus in his brain, or swelling of the ventricles. The resulting pressure buildup inside the already severely fractured skull also caused additional damage to the brain tissue.

Even with the diverse and widespread damage, Cathy pressed forward in her bid to see if her son could be saved. She immersed herself in the study of brain injuries, and the more she investigated, the more it became apparent to her that Bryce's best chance was in Richmond, roughly a five-hour ride from the family's home in southern North Carolina.

First, she had to get him out of Japan, a journey that began with a flight to a military hospital in Hawaii. From there, on November 26, it was on to Richmond International Airport, and then a short ambulance ride to McGuire.

"His injuries," recalled Pai, "were significant."

The staff had worked with patients with significant brain injuries before, however, and they knew better than to rule out anything, for the simple reason that it's difficult to predict outcomes with brain injuries.

So everyone banded together to see if they could make Bryce Powers part of the 76 percent.

CHAPTER EIGHT

NEW NORMAL

Landing in the PRC at McGuire VA Medical Center means that not only has something tragic happened to a patient, but their loved ones also have had their worlds turned upside down.

The patient's family and friends are thrust into new roles as caregivers, and it can be a daunting proposition, especially given that there is literally no adjustment period and that they are entering a world—that of TBI—full of complicated terminology, a roller-coaster ride of lows and highs, and a great deal of uncertainty.

Along the way, the families will get plenty of help from the polytrauma unit staff—help that starts before the patients even get to Richmond and continues after their arrival. The unit's extensive support system includes everything from social workers and psychologists to an exhaustive program of family education tailored according to the needs of each patient and his or her loved ones.

"We know this is likely to be the most difficult time of their lives, and we also know that this is a time when they need to concentrate on healing, on rehab," said Pat Rudd, the unit's clinical case manager. "So we try to ease the burden on them and let them focus on the important things."

Rudd works with the other facilities in the military healthcare system to screen prospective patients, help to determine who would be a good fit for Richmond's polytrauma unit, and to see that the staff is prepared to start meeting the patient's needs immediately upon arrival. The Richmond staff doesn't want the families of new patients to have to spend valuable time upon arrival explaining the patient's medical history and how other facilities treated the patient. Instead, Rudd coordinates with other facilities to obtain as much information as possible about the patients, including specifics about the nature of their injuries, treatments, therapies, and medications.

Just as Rudd serves as a gatekeeper of sorts for the polytrauma unit, making sure people and information get channeled in the proper direction, so do the Richmond unit's social workers. Each new patient is assigned a social worker, and that person will remain with the patient and their families throughout their stay on the unit, serving as an advocate for their needs.

Keneshia T. Thornton, who came to McGuire in November 2005, said her no-nonsense approach makes her a good fit as a social worker in the unit, especially for young service members who may lack experience in dealing with a military bureaucracy that can be complicated and intimidating.

"It's easy for me because of my personality," Thornton explained. "I've always stood up for the quiet child. I've always rooted for the underdog."

Thornton, who has a bachelor's degree in biology from Morgan State University and a master's in social work from Virginia Commonwealth University, spent several years working in hospice care before coming to McGuire.

"I got to meet people at the end of their lives who were able to take you on their journey with them," she said. "You learned different family dynamics."

She called the dynamics within the polytrauma unit "almost like a wheel. I'm in the middle with all these spokes."

Those spokes may include everything from navigating the complexities of the various military care facilities, to insurance questions for veterans, to coordinating information with an active-duty service member's superiors, to cutting through paperwork that will get injured patients adaptive wheelchairs and adaptive cars. On a more basic level, Thornton may be called on to help a patient's family members line up a room at the Fisher House, the small hotel on the grounds of McGuire that provides free lodging for loved ones, or at a nearby hotel if the Fisher House has no space available, or she may have to help the wife of an young injured service member line up day care for the couple's child so the wife can stay with her husband as much as possible.

Thornton welcomes all the challenges.

"You are the parent, when you get right down to it," she said. "You manage people's lives when they are here. I consider the patient and the family to be the rubber of the tire. Their job is not to worry about the spokes. I'll take care of the spokes for them. That's my job. Their job is to recover and just go along for the ride."

Because she has been with the polytrauma unit operation since its days of infancy, Thornton has seen plenty of success stories, a testament to the system constantly being tweaked and refined with an eye toward improving the experience for the patient and their caregivers. The ultimate goal is for the patients and their families to be able to take advantage of all the resources offered on the unit and for the patients to be able to recover and rehabilitate to the point where they are as functionally independent as possible and can get on with their lives.

"It's almost like the before and after shots," Thornton said. "It's shown me that if you get it right, this is what it could be."

However, because of the immense stress that can wash over families as they try to deal with such tragic occurrences as TBI, loss of limbs, comas, multiple fractures, speech impairment, and the possible long-term consequences of all of those, Thornton also has seen the dark side of people— marital strain that can lead to divorce, stress between siblings, stress between parents and their children, stress between in-laws and even stress between a service member's wife and his girlfriend. All have come into play within the walls of the polytrauma unit. As a result, the staff members on occasion have had to alter the dynamics in a way that brings the focus back to the patient's recovery and rehabilitation.

"It can go downhill real quick," Thornton said.

She noted that, in many cases, young service members who are on the verge of being shipped to Afghanistan will first have hastily arranged weddings in the weeks or perhaps just days before they leave, creating a scenario where in-laws may not be able to attend the ceremonies. That, in turn, can lead to some awkward moments on the halls of the unit.

"A lot of times we have families meeting each other for the first time on this unit," she explained.

In addition, those families may not always agree on what is best for the patient—or even on whether the marriage was a prudent move for the couple—and those discussions may not always be conducted in a manner considered appropriate for a hospital setting.

"As a team, we're stuck right in the middle of it. We've actually had to set up family schedules. We'll tell them they can't be on the unit at the same time. As mature adults, you can't be doing that."

It doesn't end there. Because of federal privacy rules, there are limits to what kind and how much information about a patient can be given over the phone and to whom it can be given, and family feuds can lead to someone who has been cut out of the visitation loop trying to coerce information from staff members by calling the nurses' station on the unit.

"Sometimes we have to put in a password for people to use when they call in to get patient information," Thornton said, shaking her head. Even more disheartening is how some people can try to exploit the injuries of a child for their own financial gain. Depending on the severity of the injury, a US service member who is hurt in combat may be eligible for a significant payment from the government as well as long-term disability benefits, and when word of those funds begins to spread, it has been known to produce an increase in the number of relatives visiting a patient on the polytrauma unit.

"Say I get injured in the war," Thornton explained, "and all of a sudden, here comes Absentee Dad. And his son doesn't want him around. He wasn't around for years, so why is he now all of a sudden here? Because his son's in line for some money. Very sad."

Even with all the stress that traumatic injuries can place on patients, families, and in turn, the unit staff, Thornton and the rest of the staff know they are privileged to be able to work where they do.

"This is living history in the making," Thornton said. "These guys have the strength of warriors."

The patients and their families may be highly skilled in the ways of war, but they are not always proficient in the complicated world of understanding traumatic injuries, modern medical techniques, and often mind-boggling jargon.

That's where Barbara Bauserman enters the picture.

———

Bauserman, who oversees the family education program on the polytrauma unit, calls it simply "the book." Some caregivers think that's an understatement. They refer to it instead as "the big book."

Its actual title is, *Traumatic Brain Injury: A Guide for Caregivers of Service Members and Veterans.* If that sounds imposing, it looks even more intimidating. It is a series of five books, bound together in a three-ring binder that is three inches thick. It is 453 pages long, printed on heavy-stock paper, weighs more than eight pounds, and is so bulky that when Bauserman gives it to patients, it comes with its own backpack to make it easier to carry.

The publication, put together through a joint effort of the US Department of Defense and the Department of Veterans Affairs, is designed to be a bible of sorts for caregivers of patients with TBIs. Although it is packed with useful information, Bauserman appreciates that someone who has just suddenly found themselves dropped into the world of polytrauma caregivers can already be feeling like they're facing a daunting task, and they may feel overwhelmed by the prospect of trying to delve into the book. The last of the five modules in the binder, for example, is titled, "Navigating Services and Benefits," and is 161 pages long by itself.

"Not everyone is ready for it right away," Bauserman said. "Some people may never be ready for it."

So Bauserman treats each caregiver individually, watching and listening to gauge what they want in terms of information and adjusting her efforts accordingly.

"Some are like sponges. They can't get enough," she explained. "Some need to move slowly. It's a hard process for some people."

The book devotes thirty-eight pages to its "Welcome" module alone, and the "Introduction to Traumatic Brain Injury" section is another fifty-two pages. It covers such topics as the basics of TBI, the causes and types, diagnosis and treatment, potential complications, and the recovery process. It is here that caregivers can get explanations for such terms as subarachnoid hemorrhage, cerebrospinal fluid, parietal lobes, coup-contrecoup injury, and other examples of the language of TBI. They learn the harsh reality that there is no established, consistent, guaranteed treatment for TBI. Once medical professionals have accomplished such needed measures as stopping bleeding in the brain, controlling pressure, and removing blood clots, subsequent treatment depends on a variety of factors, including the severity of the injuries and where in the brain they occurred. The brain, by and large, heals itself—if possible—and humans, in turn, can do little more than try to assist that process.

A ninety-four-page section follows on understanding the effects of TBI and how caregivers can help. It introduces caregivers to TBI effects they should watch for, ranging from sleep changes and attention problems to compensation strategies and less effective social skills, and tells them how they can help. From there it's on to a 108-page section that specifically addresses the role of caregivers, providing advice on how to take care of themselves, work on relationships with the patient and their families, and address long-term legal issues that may include guardianship, power of attorney, and wills.

In addition to the main, five-module book, a smaller three-ring binder is included in the backpack, called the "Caregiver's Companion." At twenty-five pages long, this publication contains an eight-page glossary of brain-related terms that TBI caregivers are likely to encounter as well as forms and other tools designed to help a caregiver organize care.

Whether the caregivers get "the book" and its companion right away or later in the process, Bauserman finds plenty of ways to work education into the caregivers' stay on the polytrauma unit. Pretty much every Tuesday through Friday, either in the late mornings or the early afternoons, she arranges a family education seminar designed specifically for caregivers of unit patients. The one-hour sessions, scheduled to accommodate the caregivers' schedules, cover such topics as amputee care, brain injury education, communication and swallowing problems, stroke prevention, and integrating back into the community. Some days, she will schedule what is called a "Caregiver Support Group," which is simply a session for caregivers to sit around and discuss their experiences, concerns, and fears.

On one particular weekday afternoon, Bauserman had arranged a family education session on the social work journey. Five caregivers gathered in what the staff refers to alternately as the unit's "couch room" or "quiet room," a visitors' lounge whose walls are lined with large, comfortable leather couches. One wall has high windows that overlook the rooftop garden. She brought the caregivers there to spend an hour behind closed doors talking frankly about the role of the social workers and how the caregivers can take advantage of their services.

It became quickly apparent that the caregivers were pleased with the assistance they were receiving from the social workers and that they were more interested in other topics. So the conversation shifted to the need for caregivers to show patience—with the patient, with themselves, and with the rehabilitation process. In many cases, those patience issues center on the possibility that a return to normal, as the patient and their family knew it, may not occur. Fractures and other injuries may have been so severe that the patient may never fully recover. Cognitive functions may not completely return. Brain damage could take years to heal. Instead of focusing on a return to what they once regarded as normal, the patients and their caregivers now need to concentrate on finding a *new* normal.

"What is realistic?" Bauserman began the session by asking the caregivers.

"He's dependent," one caregiver said of her injured husband.

"He may never be the same," another spouse said.

"What have you learned about hope?" Bauserman asked.

"It comes and goes," one wife answered.

"Emergencies are not planned," explained Thornton, one of three staff members to speak at the session. "There's no rule book, so you've got to go easy on yourself."

Caregivers also were told over and over to make time for their own personal needs—and to recognize when stress is gaining an advantage on them as they try to put the needs of the patient first and their own needs second.

"We're not expecting you to be a super person," Thornton told them. "If you burn out in the beginning, who's going to be able to take care of your loved one? You have to learn to take care of yourself."

To support her point that the caregivers can't do it alone, she asked them to take a few seconds and think about their patient's daily routine on the polytrauma unit—and specifically how many staff members come in contact with their patient.

"Look around," she said. "Count how many people it took in one day to care for your loved one. Now think about that. And remember that the next time things start adding up on you. You can't do it alone. We're all on this journey with you."

The session ended with the caregivers asking a few questions about specific issues related to communication within the bureaucracy and scheduling matters, and after the staff members in the room responded to their concerns, the hour was up and the caregivers returned to their loved ones.

"The simplicity of coming in here and closing the door makes it easy for people to open up," Thornton explained later. "Through these meetings, you see growth. Who you were the day you walked in to 2-B is not who you're walking out as."

The key to that caregiver growth, according to Bauserman, is for the staff to keep communicating, keep educating, keep listening, and keep being patient with the caregivers as they adjust to this new role into which they've been thrust. Through that comes trust.

"All you can do sometimes is keep the lines open, keep working," she explained, "and hope and wait for them to come around."

Bauserman, because of her easygoing nature, her superior listening skills, and her reputation for being a tireless advocate for patients and their caregivers, often becomes the staff's point person when caregivers have a problem they don't feel comfortable sharing with anyone else. Caregiver after caregiver can offer personal accounts about how she went the extra mile for them through simple acts of human decency that helped ease their road to a new normal. Some will tell of how Bauserman took extraordinary amounts of time to listen to them vent about their frustrations, and how she helped them work through their concerns. Others recall how she patiently broke down complicated medical topics and presented them in a manner that helped them finally gain a measure of clarity that they had not previously enjoyed.

Cathy Powers, who didn't have a car in Richmond while her son, Bryce Powers, spent five difficult months at McGuire, recalled how she tried without success to find a church that would pick her up on Sunday mornings and drive her to services. When Bauserman learned that Cathy had been turned down by all three churches she had called, Bauserman told her to be ready the next Sunday morning at a specific time at Fisher House, where Cathy was staying. Bauserman picked her up and drove her to the Presbyterian church in Richmond's West End where Bauserman herself regularly worships.

It didn't end there. The two ended up also going to an Episcopal church in a different neighborhood of Richmond to attend Sunday evening Celtic healing services.

"We call it the God spa," Cathy said. "You feel like you sat in a Jacuzzi and got your hair and nails done and got a massage—like you could make it one more week."

She paused.

"Barbara is an amazing person. She's a living angel."

Dr. Pai smiles and nods knowingly as he is told stories about the lengths to which Bauserman goes to help caregivers and patients.

"She is the glue that keeps this place together," he said. "This place would not function without her—literally."

A Thursday afternoon in March 2013 brought a group of caregivers—all either mothers or wives—to the polytrauma unit's couch room for a "Caregiver Support Group" session led by Bauserman.

Instead of following a rigid agenda, the participants were encouraged to use the one-hour session to bring up any issue concerning them, to air any topics they wanted, and see if the other caregivers or Bauserman could add a perspective that helped them on their journey to a new normal.

Much of the session was devoted to the stresses and uncertainties of being a caregiver.

"It wasn't just his life that was broken," one of the women explained. "It was mine, too."

"It's a feeling of dread—just dread," another said.

"I never realized grief was so physical," yet another added. "It takes so much out of you. It hurts."

Bauserman allowed the conversation to work its way around the room, then eventually started speaking.

"It makes you realize how vulnerable you are," she said.

As the women nodded in agreement, Bauserman went on to talk about *ambiguous loss,* a term that describes when there has been a loss that is difficult to define. As opposed to death, which can bring a sense of closure, there is no certainty that someone with a TBI will return to their previous form. That uncertainty can freeze the grief process, leaving the caregiver feeling effectively paralyzed from grief and unable to resolve his or her sorrow.

"You have lost the old person," she told them, "and you may not get him back. You have a loss that is hard to grieve for."

Although in many ways the loss may seem difficult to quantify, there are ways to define it.

"You have a new son, sure," she said. "But you have to grieve your old son, too."

"But that," one mother replied, "means I admit he won't get better, and you know what? I'm not there yet. So I don't want to do that one."

Bauserman assured the mother that the manner in which you grieve for a loved one or choose to accept that they may not recover is an individual process.

"So you know what?" Bauserman told her. "Then treat it as just an idea in your head. That's all it is. You get there when you want to get there—if you want to get there."

She told the caregivers that if they are struggling to deal with the sense of normalcy they've lost in their lives, one way they can process it is to find a place—a shoebox, perhaps—to store their losses. Whether they write down specific items on a piece of paper or use an old photograph that chronicles an earlier episode in their loved one's life, the caregivers can put those items in a storage place and then go to it periodically and examine its contents to remind themselves that their loss was, indeed, calculable.

"There are things that are gone," she said.

Bauserman, a member of the board of directors of the Brain Injury Association of Virginia, heard a similar theme at the group's conference in suburban Richmond, also in March 2013, when she led a session titled, "If I Knew Then What I Know Now...." Some of the several hundred attendees at the conference had been injured in the military, whereas others had been hurt on the job as civilians or in household accidents or vehicle crashes. All had experienced loss and were continuing to work to overcome it, in some cases many years later. The caregivers who spoke at the session touched on the areas of loss, grief, and struggling with the new normal, just as was the case in the support group meetings at McGuire.

Remarks from the caregivers at the conference included:
- "It was almost like raising him from a baby again."
- "It's very difficult to ask for or accept help."
- "The hardest part of being a caregiver was trying to grow with him. I had to learn to grow with him."
- "Patience as a caregiver is the most important thing."
- "There's always someone out there who's got it a little bit worse. You have to remember that."

Remarks from TBI survivors showed that as frustrating as the journey can be for caregivers, the patients have a unique kind of pain—and a unique perspective. The survivors' comments included:

- "My teenager looked me square in the eye and said, 'You're not the boss any more. You can't take care of yourself.'"
- "I didn't like it when therapists tried to make it easy. Don't tell me not to sweat the small stuff. I'm coming to you because I'm desperate and I need help. I need practical solutions. I don't need comfort. I need results."
- "If you plateau, keep working. It will get better. It's a roller-coaster. Enjoy the ride."
- "People talked slower. They looked at you different. You don't want to be the outsider. You want to get back your life."
- "I have to accept the fact that I can't do everything."
- "Divorce was good. Too much negativity. Let me fail. At least let me try."
- "Before, I had a lot of friends. Right now, I speak to two people. The rest are just acquaintances. You find out who your real friends are."
- "Man's best friend truly is a dog."

Finally, one comment drew loud applause from those in the session:

"Don't stop believing in yourself. Keep going. As long as there's breath in your body, keep fighting."

CHAPTER NINE

LUIS AVILA

Early on the afternoon of December 27, 2011, some four hours after the blast of an IED in southeastern Afghanistan's Paktia province killed three US Army soldiers based at Fort Hood, Texas, Claudia Avila was taking part in a ritual every military spouse dreads.

It was 1 P.M. local time at Fort Hood, and Claudia was among a group of army spouses who were accompanying a casualty notification team to the house of Kristi Korte. The spouses were along to offer support to Kristi when the notification officers would tell her that Sgt. Noah M. Korte—her husband, the father of their two young sons and a survivor of three tours in Iraq—was among the three men who had been killed in the IED blast.

The group of seven found no one at the Korte home, so Claudia and the rest of the spouses went back to their battalion headquarters on base to spend the afternoon trying to learn more details about what had happened half a world away when the armored troop transport vehicle went over the IED—and who else was among the dead and injured.

While Claudia tried to focus her energies on helping others who had been affected by the IED blast, a lingering, nagging, persistent question for her was whether her husband, Capt. Luis Avila, was among the casualties. After the identities of the three dead men were established—a list that did not include her husband—her attention turned to whether he was among the wounded. Reports making their way back to Fort Hood indicated that there had been injuries, but it was difficult to get accurate information in the early hours about the number and severity.

"We were making phone calls, trying to find people, trying to figure out what was going on," Claudia said. "I had a feeling. I was asking the battalion commander if my husband was okay, and he said my husband was fine.

"But I had a feeling—because my husband would have called."

She based her assessment on an incident in Iraq in 2007, when Luis had been in the area of an IED explosion that left him with bruises and a diagnosis of a mild TBI.

"It was really far away from him, but it was still big. But he was just bruised," she recalled. "And he was the one who called that time. So this time, I knew that by that time, I should have heard something."

Finally, the battalion commander and his wife came to give Claudia the news that her husband had been among the three men who were hurt. In all three cases, the injuries were extensive and potentially life-threatening. Luis, who was in a seat just behind and to the immediate right of the driver, Spc. Jon McHenry—close enough for the two to touch each other—had sustained massive injuries that would result in the amputation of his left leg at the top of the thigh. His right leg was badly injured as well, including structural damage to the knee and several fractured toes. He also had fractures of the C-5 and C-6 vertebrae.

Worst of all, however, was that the brutal force of the blast had left Luis with an anoxic brain injury—one in which the brain loses oxygen for a prolonged period. Unlike with TBI, in which the tissue is often damaged by being bruised—typically through a violent, concussion-like force—but can possibly heal over time, anoxic injuries lead to the permanent loss of brain cells, which rely on oxygen to survive.

Luis was flown first to a base in Kandahar, Afghanistan, then to the US military hospital in Landstuhl, Germany. The brain damage left him comatose, and infections began to develop in his lungs and his spine. The cumulative effect of the injuries and infections made it possible that Luis, after surviving three tours in Iraq earlier in his army career, might lose his life as a result of his first tour in Afghanistan—a deployment that had lasted less than three weeks.

———

It was no surprise that Luis Avila, a native of Tegucigalpa, Honduras, wound up seeking a career in the military. His father served as a general in the Honduran army, and his last assignment before retiring was a post at the US Department of State in Washington.

Luis was drawn to the United States as well, moving in 1991 to California to attend the University of San Diego, where he earned an undergraduate degree in 1994. He later earned a master's degree in homeland security/business management from Webster University, and he joined the army in 1999 to become a military policeman. His future wife, Claudia, a native of San Pedro Sula, Honduras, came to the United States in 1989 to visit two aunts who were working for the International Monetary Fund. She earned a master's degree in international business from George Washington University and was working as a conference specialist for the Organization of American States, a job in which she occasionally would see Luis's father. He would tell her about his son, always ending the conversation by saying he would one day introduce them.

That day was March 22, 1995. She was walking down a hallway at work, and coming in the opposite direction was the general, smiling broadly and accompanied by a handsome young member of the US Army Reserves.

"We talked for about thirty minutes," she recalled of her first meeting with the man who would become her husband. "We connected pretty well."

It wasn't long before they ran into each other again, this time at a US Embassy party, and she gave him her phone number. He called three days later, and from that point, the relationship quickly gained momentum.

"It was meant to be," she said.

Luis, already a US citizen, and Claudia, who was in the country on a diplomatic work visa, were married by a justice of the peace in Washington on August 4, 1995. Two more ceremonies followed in San Pedro—a civil ceremony on August 31 and a formal Catholic church wedding on September 6, with some eight hundred people in attendance.

"It was almost a whole week of parties," Claudia said.

The couple had three sons—Luis, born on February 18, 1997; Miguel, on June 24, 1998; and Jose, on January 21, 2001—while the elder Luis became a full-time soldier. His orders took him to posts in Georgia, Louisiana, Maryland, Missouri, Texas, Virginia, and Washington, DC.

"We call home the place that they send our soldier," Claudia said. "We really do not have a home until our soldier gets orders."

Because they both had already had multicultural experiences, Claudia said, she and Luis found it easier to raise their children in an environment where move, change, and exposure to new experiences are seemingly constant. Not only did they embrace a lifestyle of being flexible to the adventures and challenges of new states, new schools, and new friends, but the family also traveled as much as possible, no matter where they were stationed. The more the boys saw, the better it would help turn them into well-rounded young men.

"My kids have been in thirty-eight states," Claudia said. "The boys don't know any other way."

It was that kind of open-minded, adventurous attitude that made it easy to take whatever the military lifestyle threw their way, including having to adjust holidays to accommodate their father's duties. For example, when the Avilas found out that Luis's unit was leaving Texas in late November 2011 for deployment in Afghanistan, the family shifted into full holiday mode. Not only did they celebrate Thanksgiving before he left, but they also took care of Christmas. They purchased gifts, put up a tree, decorated their home, and celebrated December 25 on November 15—complete with a family photograph of everyone perched in front of the tree with their dog, Buddy.

Thirteen days later, Luis's unit left for Afghanistan. Barely a month after that, the family had to make another life-altering adjustment, with Claudia hurriedly making arrangements to fly to Landstuhl, Germany, to be by the side of her gravely wounded husband.

She flew eighteen hours to Landstuhl, and when she arrived, she wasn't there long before doctors decided the best course of action was to send the Avilas straight back to Texas. The typical protocol is for those injured in Afghanistan to be stabilized at Landstuhl and then flown to Walter Reed National Military Medical Center for whatever additional surgery and acute care is deemed needed. In this case, however, doctors said Luis would be better served by being close to his family in an environment that would allow him to focus on trying to simply survive. So Luis, with his wife by his side, was put on a military transport plane for an eighteen-hour flight back to Texas, where he was taken to Brooke Army Medical Center, a level-I trauma care facility in San Antonio, to begin the long process of watching and waiting to see if he could overcome his injuries.

As it turned out, the immediate injuries caused by the blast were bad enough, but they were complicated by the infections that developed—infections that proved difficult to purge from an already severely weakened body and became a cause of great concern from those trying to heal him. The days turned into weeks, and the weeks drifted into months. The infections kept lingering, robbing his body of weight, muscle mass, and the ability to fight back, to get up, to start rehabilitation and start regaining strength.

"There were multiple times when they thought he was going to die," one doctor later said.

Throughout the ordeal, Claudia remained a rock—an unrelenting advocate for her husband's care, and a nonstop, multitasking family leader for her children.

"You don't know how strong you can be until you're faced with these things," she said later, adding that she drew strength from her unwavering belief that better days were ahead.

"There is always a calm after the storm. Always."

It was a belief she imparted constantly on her sons.

"We're a very, very unified family, and we believe that the most important thing is to be together. As sad as our situation is, as bad as it is, we haven't stopped smiling. This is God's power. We know that God has a plan."

The three boys seemed to follow her lead.

"They are so resilient. They are so proud of their dad," she said. "They walk with pride and honor."

Claudia wanted her husband back, wanted him healed, wanted him walking and talking again, wanted her boys to be able to take part in father-son activities with him again. So she began lobbying for the army to move her husband from the acute-care hospital in Texas to a facility to begin his rehabilitation, even though he was still struggling with significant infections, was hooked up to a breathing tube, and needed around-the-clock care to have mucus suctioned out of his constantly clogging throat.

Three months after the IED blast, Jon McHenry and Luis Avila appeared headed in opposite directions. Jon was discharged from McGuire on March 28 and sent back to Walter Reed. There he would have follow-up surgery to have a stent removed from his chest and would continue his physical therapy on an outpatient basis while living in what amounted to a small apartment on the campus of the massive suburban Maryland facility just outside the nation's capital. Back in Richmond, meantime, the staff at McGuire emptied and cleaned room 110, Jon's old room on the polytrauma unit, in preparation for the next patient.

That wait didn't last long.

On April 5, Luis was flown to Richmond and taken to McGuire, where the gurney carrying him was wheeled to a bank of elevators in the center of the hospital. He was taken up to the second floor, over to the polytrauma unit—and into room 110.

———

On April 23, surgeons at Walter Reed National Military Medical Center removed the stent from Jon McHenry's chest—a procedure that Jon referred to wishfully as "my last surgery."

It wasn't long before he began attacking his physical therapy sessions. His fractured bones were healing, he didn't face any more surgeries (he hoped), he had graduated from a hospital bed and was now sleeping in a small apartment, and his first child was due any day. Motivation, it seemed, was everywhere Jon looked. He appeared to be gaining muscle mass, strength, and confidence with each passing day. His physical therapy sessions were, in essence, weight-room workouts that resembled what any civilian might encounter at their neighborhood gym under the guidance of a private trainer. Jon was going to a physical therapy studio at Walter Reed every morning and afternoon and getting personal guidance twice a day from therapist Chris Brown, who he described as a six-foot, four-inch, 290-pound bodybuilder who pushed Jon to excel.

The birth of Leo McHenry on May 12 only seemed to boost his father's state of mind.

Jon's left leg was out of a cast, and his surgically repaired right leg was allowing him to get on a treadmill, where he began the gradual process of trying to first walk, then walk briskly, then transition into brief runs. It wasn't long before he reported that he was not only running, but recording ten-minute miles on the treadmill. With his arms, core, and legs getting stronger, Jon no longer was thinking about leaving the military for a new, quiet life as a civilian, possibly in Florida or Arizona. Instead, he had a different goal in mind, one that several months earlier would have seemed unthinkable.

On May 3, Jon went on to his Facebook page and posted the following message: "I'm going to make history."

Several people understood his veiled reference.

"You already have, Bro," one person wrote.

To those who didn't grasp what he was alluding to, Jon offered a simple timetable: His unit's deployment in Afghanistan was not scheduled to end until the end of November. Accordingly, Jon now felt it was realistic that he should be able to rejoin his comrades overseas before they returned home.

Officials within the PSC said it's a refrain often heard from the overwhelming majority of service members.

"Almost every guy says the same thing: 'I want to go back. Get me back to my unit,' " said Sherry Ceperich, a counseling psychologist on Richmond's polytrauma unit. "No matter how severe their injuries, they all believe they can do it. They believe they have to do it. It's a fraternity, and they feel they won't be whole again until they rejoin their comrades."

The reality, however, is that although expressing a desire to return to their units overseas is a common sentiment among wounded service members, accomplishing that feat during the deployment in which the injuries occurred is, for all practical purposes, unheard of. Polytrauma officials were able to cite numerous examples of service members with significant injuries who have been able to return to active duty during the deployment, but those same officials came up blank when asked how many of those service members were able to rejoin their units during the deployment.

Jon said he was the ideal candidate to be the exception. His rehabilitation was going well, and he was committed to setting an example of what hard work could accomplish.

"People have been doubting me all my life," he said. "I know what I'm capable of doing. I'll do whatever it takes. I can do this."

He also dismissed the theory that, with significant line-of-duty injuries, a bride, and an infant son, he was entitled to put Afghanistan behind him and move on with his life. Jon said there were roughly eighty people in his unit, and probably about three-fourths of them had spouses and children.

"So why should I think I'm any different?" he said. "They signed up to do a job, to defend their country, even though they had families back home to worry about. That's all I want to do. Sure, I got hurt, but I'm fine now. So let me go back and finish my job. That's all I'm asking—for them not to treat me any different."

———

On Saturday, June 9, 2012, Jon McHenry, his wife, and his young son made a road trip down Interstate 95 to a place with which he was intimately familiar.

They pulled into the parking lot of McGuire VA Medical Center about 2 P.M. and went to the center of the hospital, took the elevators to the second floor, walked to the PRC, took their first left, and then quickly turned left again, this time into room 110.

It was, not surprisingly, an emotional reunion.

"He saw my child and my wife..." Jon recalled, his voice trailing off.

"There were," Claudia Avila said, "some tears."

Luis Avila, still struggling to put on weight and regain strength as he battled stubborn infections and fought to regain his ability to speak clearly, seemed to get a boost from the visit. He clearly enjoyed seeing one of his men, especially one who had survived the IED blast and appeared to be well on the road to recovery.

"Time just flew by," Jon said. "Next thing I knew, it was eleven o'clock at night. Capt. Avila convinced us it was too late to go back. He kept saying, 'Stay, stay, stay.'"

The McHenrys got a hotel room in South Richmond for the night and then returned to room 110 on Sunday from 10 A.M. until 2 P.M. before going back to Bethesda.

Jon said he and Luis, neither of whom remembered the IED blast, spent very little time discussing the events of that fateful day.

"But we talked about everything else. It was just a great visit," he said. "I had my doubts that he would even remember me. But I was truly amazed. I was really shocked. Man, he's just such a fighter."

CHAPTER TEN

BURNESS BRITT

Saturday, June 4, 2011, found Marine Cpl. Burness Britt on a daily patrol assignment in Helmand province, home to some of the deadliest fighting that US troops had encountered in Afghanistan.

The patrol was nearing an end, with Britt leading ten members of the 2nd Battalion, 12th Marines, 3rd Marine Division through a wheat field, when an IED detonated near the front of the group. The blast injured five marines, none more seriously than Burness.

He was launched airborne, and when he landed, he felt a white-hot pain in his neck. A piece of shrapnel from the IED had torn into the left side of his neck and slashed open a major artery, putting him in grave danger of bleeding to death. His comrades carried the wounded marine to a fast-arriving medevac helicopter that whisked him away to get emergency care. Burness lost consciousness before he could be stabilized for a flight to the US military hospital in Landstuhl, Germany.

Several thousand miles away, his wife of ten months, Jessica Britt, was spending her Saturday morning in the couple's hometown of Georgetown, South Carolina, helping clean and paint her grandmother's garage. Jessica then went to have lunch with a friend before joining a group for a planned softball game in the afternoon. They went to the Seafood Shack and ordered lunch, and they were waiting for their food to arrive when the ring tone on Jessica's cell phone sprang to life.

"I had a bad feeling the minute the phone rang," she said. "Something just wasn't right. I didn't know what it was, but I could tell it wasn't good."

The man on the other end identified himself as a US Marine officer, and he asked if he was speaking with Jessica Britt, wife of Cpl. Burness Britt. With the identity question settled, the officer began speaking in a monotone as if reading from a prepared script.

"As of 0900 on Saturday, June 4, 2011, Cpl. Burness Britt was on foot patrol... "

Jessica slumped, and her thoughts began racing uncontrollably.

"I was losing my mind. I was shaking," she said. "It just felt like an awful nightmare that wouldn't go away."

Burness Britt, the handsome marine who had professed his love for her and convinced her to marry him in August 2010, who wanted to take her from their small town just outside Myrtle Beach, South Carolina, and show her the world, was fighting for his life less than six weeks after arriving in Afghanistan to begin his first foreign deployment.

Details of the extent of his injuries were slow to emerge, and the news seemed to get worse with each communication from the military, making her stress level rise with each conversation. Jessica found some of the information confusing and much of it difficult to digest, but she knew one thing: She needed to get to Germany.

Fast.

———

As she arranged to travel to Landstuhl, Jessica began piecing together more and more details about her husband's condition.

The blood loss led to what doctors called a left hemispheric stroke, which occurred in the left side of his brain and controlled the right side of his body.

It wasn't long before it became apparent that Burness was partially paralyzed, with little use of his right arm and right leg and seemingly no ability to speak.

How long those conditions would persist remained an unanswered question.

In addition, pressure began building in Burness' brain, and surgeons removed a portion of his skull to help relieve it. While the other four marines injured with Britt in the wheat field made it back to their unit within days, Britt faced an uncertain future, beginning with the question of whether the swelling on his brain would prove fatal.

His wife made it to Germany within four days of the IED blast, giving Landstuhl's medical staff and her husband's superiors time to try to prepare her for what she would find upon her arrival.

"It's going to be a bit of a shock when you see him," she recalled being told.

They explained about the intravenous lines, about the myriad other cords he was hooked up to for monitoring various vital signs, and about the swelling. They kept telling her about the swelling, about how his skull would be larger than normal, about how they hoped they had the swelling under control, about how they hoped his head would return to normal size.

No matter how much they tried, nothing could have sufficiently prepared her for what she saw when her long, taxing journey to Landstuhl ended and she walked into her husband's hospital room and saw him, comatose and linked up to a tangle of tubes and wires, for the first time.

"His head," she said in an almost hushed tone, "was close to the size of a basketball."

She paused, took a long, deep breath and slowly exhaled.

"I completely bawled like a baby," she said. "Hysterical. Just hysterical."

Jessica Britt had barely made it to her husband's bedside before Landstuhl's doctors decided it would be best to send him back to the United States and Walter Reed National Military Medical Center. So before she even had a chance to get settled, they were put on a C-17, an aging air force transport plane that had been given new life as a military evacuation aircraft.

As she sat in the cold, loud, steel belly of the massive plane, the long flight to Washington gave her plenty of time to reflect—on her husband's injuries, on their brief life together, on the plans they had talked about, and on their desires to see the world as he worked his way into a career as a marine officer. She flashed back to their courtship, which began after high school and was assisted in large part by technologies that included Skype video chats, Facebook posts, and daily cell-phone calls that routinely reached two or three hours, helping them eliminate the distance between South Carolina and Japan, where he had been stationed.

He had been the first to say "I love you," although it was clouded somewhat by the fact that the two had been drinking that night.

"He was drunk," she said. "But he wrote himself a note to remind himself to call me the next morning and tell me again. And he did. He was so sweet."

That memory, and all the others they had accumulated so far in their brief time together, now had been shoved from prominence, replaced instead by uncertainty about whether he would even live, and if he did, what kind of life he would have—and what kind of life this young couple, still short of their first wedding anniversary, could have together.

They had dreams. They had hopes. And this IED blast had put everything on hold.

"He was the last person," she said, "I ever thought would get hurt."

———

Burness Britt was in Bethesda for less than three weeks before his medical team reached the conclusion that he was no longer in need of live-saving care and was instead ready for the next step. The swelling in his brain had been brought under control and had slowly dissipated. However, he had developed pneumonia, and even though he had regained consciousness, his motor skills were severely lacking, and he was unable to speak.

The doctors at Bethesda had hopes that Burness, with rehabilitation, could regain at least some function, and that made their next move an easy one. The PRC at Richmond's McGuire VA Medical Center, up and running only about five years at that point, had already established a reputation as a leader in the field of TBI rehabilitation. The staff at Richmond's polytrauma rehabilitation unit would work Burness hard to squeeze every ounce of improvement out of him. In addition, not only would moving him to Richmond make sense from a rehabilitation standpoint, but it also would get the Britts closer to their hometown in South Carolina.

So on Friday, July 1, 2011, Burness and Jessica Britt made the trip from Bethesda, Maryland, to Richmond, Virginia, via Interstate 95. The route should have gotten them there in roughly two hours, but with the typical I-95 traffic that has made the road so notorious, it took four.

When they arrived, Dr. Pai made sure that Burness got comfortably established in his new room while the staff got Jessica set up at a nearby Hampton Inn—one of the hotels the hospital uses for family accommodations when there are no rooms at Fisher House.

Then Pai told Jessica to get ready.

"That was a Friday afternoon," she said. "On Monday morning, Burness had his first full day of therapy."

While Burness underwent the polytrauma unit's typical entrance and screening procedures and was assigned therapists accordingly, the reality was that there was nothing typical about him—or any other TBI patient. The common refrain at the unit is that no two brain injuries are alike, and what may appear to be potential doesn't always translate into positive results. Conversely, the staff members have seen plenty of patients who didn't show much potential when they arrived but ended up surprising them by making significant strides.

Burness, as Pai noted, had several factors in his favor: He was young, strong, and energetic.

"I am not one to tell you you're not going to do this or that," Pai said. "We've seen so many crazy things over the years. It's hard to predict with brain injuries."

―――――

By virtue of their therapy field and the time they spend with patients, some of the key staff members in the polytrauma rehabilitation program are the speech-language pathologists—speech therapists, in layman's terms. They are the ones who are charged with trying different types of stimuli on comatose patients before they emerge from that state, and then helping those patients relearn such basic functions as swallowing, speaking, and reading once they do emerge.

Monique Jones, the speech therapist assigned to Burness, was typical of so many staff members on the polytrauma unit—young, energetic, knowledgeable, upbeat, and dedicated to working and communicating well with not only the other members of the team but also the patients and their families.

"People don't just come here for a few days," Jones said. "What happens to them before they get here can play a large part in defining the rest of their lives, and when they get here, a lot of times they're here for months and months on end. They live here. This becomes their home. So we try to treat them like it's their home, like they're our family. Because you know what? They are."

The staff members used Burness' initial evaluation to sharpen their focus on the hurdles facing him now that he had regained consciousness. What kind of future did he face? What would his quality of life be? How many cognitive functions would he regain? Could he feed himself? Could he walk again, talk again, take care of himself? Would he be able to go back to running? Could he go back to active duty with the marines?

It would take time, patience, and hard work before the answers to those and other questions would become clear. As Pai had said, Burness was young, strong, and energetic, and he would need every bit of his marine training to get him through the dark months and years ahead.

The staff's first task was to see if Burness could regain basic cognitive functions. He was classified as "maximum assist," meaning he was so dependent that someone had to do at least 75 percent of his basic tasks for him. The IED and subsequent stroke had sapped a considerable amount of his physical strength, and that wasn't being helped by the fact that when he arrived in Richmond, he was still having difficulty swallowing and remained unable to eat solid foods. So Jones focused her early efforts on giving Burness exercises to help him relearn how to swallow, and with that accomplished, she had him start drinking honey-thickened liquids as a first step to returning to a diet of solid foods.

The next step—working with him to restore his cognitive functions and his speech—was considerably more difficult and frustrating.

He was brought to Jones' office for his therapy sessions, and there the two of them would sit, he in a wheelchair and she in her office chair, facing each other across a small table.

"I would read to him," she said. "I would go through these exercises, one after another, trying anything—everything—to get him to talk. And he would just sit there."

Days passed. Weeks passed. Still Burness would sit there, unable to respond with any degree of success when Jones would go through so-called mirroring or modeling exercises in which she would demonstrate a physical command and ask him to mirror it or model it back to her. She realized that some of his inability to speak could be tied to the fact that he had right-side facial weakness as a result of the stroke. Yet she also knew he was oriented enough that if she gave him choices, he could tell her what day it was, what month it was, and things of that nature, and if she gave him simple questions, he could point to "yes" or "no" for his answers.

However, there was also evidence of cognitive deficits, as evidenced by the fact that when Jones got away from "yes" and "no" questions and asked him, for example, to look at several items she had on the table and show her a pencil or show her a cup, he couldn't do it.

Burness was stuck in what speech therapists call a mode of groping behavior—he wanted to respond appropriately to her, but his body wasn't allowing him to do so.

"He was groping. He was trying," Jones said. "He just didn't know what to do to turn it on."

Jones felt Burness' groping behavior might have been weighing on him to the point where he was giving in to his frustrations and perhaps was not trying as hard as he could.

"No matter what I tried, he just couldn't follow the commands, so he would just look at me and just go like this," she said as she rolled her eyes, threw her arms up in the air, and dejectedly put her forehead on the table.

Those types of physical indicators told Jones that this once-proud marine warrior seemed to have lost his will to fight on a different front—the battle to regain his voice, his physical abilities, and his independence. So one day, while the two of them sat on opposite sides of the small table in her office, once again getting nowhere and once again sending his frustration level skyward, Jones decided enough was enough. She remembered a conversation she had had with one of the military liaisons at the polytrauma unit about appealing to the sense of pride of marines, about sometimes having to keep things on very basic terms.

Jones decided it was time to put her typically effusive demeanor aside for a few seconds, throw all the textbook methods of positive patient advocacy out the window, and take a break from being an unfailingly upbeat cheerleader. It was time to try something completely different.

She reached over to her desk, grabbed a plastic drink straw, slapped it down on the table between her and Burness and glared, first at him, then at the straw, and finally at him again.

"Suck it up, Marine," she told him in a low, stern, almost hissing tone.

It was, Jones recalled months later, a watershed moment.

As Jones had suspected, Burness did indeed have more fight in him—plenty more, as a matter of fact. He began to turn the corner immediately, and Jones sensed a new dedication on his part to work harder, to try and try even when his efforts weren't immediately rewarded with positive results.

Sure, the frustrations still welled up, but by then, Jones had her secret weapon.

"The straw," she said with a smile, "stayed on the table. I'd just look at it every now and then and tell him, 'You've got to keep trying.'"

The straw wasn't the only thing to give Burness a substantial boost on the road to regaining his ability to speak. Jones said he exhibited signs of vocal cord damage, so an ear, nose, and throat specialist was brought in to examine him, and the doctor found that one of Britt's vocal cords was paralyzed. There was a relatively easy remedy for that: Radiesse, an injectable drug that bulked up the paralyzed vocal cord and allowed it to connect with the other one.

Now, Jones had a patient with a new sense of drive as well as newly repaired vocal cords that were ready to give him his voice again. So she and her battling marine set off on a mission to put together his first words since the IED blast, and they settled on three simple ones, three you might not expect from a country boy from South Carolina who grew into a scrapping warrior. The quest became a singular mission for Burness, and he and Jones practiced them over and over again, day after day, until he was finally ready to speak them to his wife, to show her just how strong the power of perseverance could be.

Months later, Burness shook his head repeatedly when asked to describe the struggle that went into uttering his first words.

"Hard," he said simply. "Hard."

When asked to elaborate, Britt looked down at the floor and shook his head again.

"Hardest thing ever."

All the struggles, all the frustrations, all the hours he spent trying so doggedly to follow the coaching of Jones, all the times he was forced to look at that plastic drink straw to be reminded that he needed to put out just a little more effort—all of it was worth it the day Jessica Britt walked into the polytrauma unit and was met by her smiling husband, who gathered himself, steeled his nerves, and then fought to deliver those three words.

They came out in slow, halting, deliberate fashion, but considering where he had been and what had happened—the massive blood loss and stroke, surgeons cutting a hole in his skull to relieve a dangerous pressure buildup, and doctors focusing not on whether he would ever talk again but instead on whether he would even survive—considering all that, no one was going to issue any technical grades about the delivery of his words that day. Instead, Burness Britt made everything right in the world again when he was able to look at his wife and say simply:

"I. Love. You."

CHAPTER ELEVEN

THE LONG HAUL

With his first words providing an emotional lift to his wife and his caregivers, Burness Britt used the occasion as a springboard to commit himself even harder to his rehabilitation.

However, the euphoria of having finally been able to again tell his wife he loved her was tempered by the fact that Burness had a long, arduous road ahead of him. He faced months of grueling therapy, and even then there was no guarantee what the results would be. With brain injuries, there never is.

As the staff at McGuire's PRC frequently points out, patients who wind up in the unit are generally there because they have just experienced the single worst catastrophe that will occur in their lives. Burness was certainly no exception. Mere weeks before he was delivered by ambulance to McGuire, he had been the epitome of a proud warrior, a young marine in the best physical shape of his life. He had a promising job that he loved, and it carried with it a promising future. He had a beautiful young wife from his hometown. He was comfortable, he was happy, and the future seemed limitless.

Then, in the blink of an eye, the world as he knew it was gone. All that had seemed so bright and certain had been thrown into a cauldron of uncertainty.

"IED sucks ass," he would say later. "Sucks, man. Changed my life. Destroyed my life."

Those changes, and the effects they can have, are witnessed constantly by the polytrauma staff. They have a front-row seat for the stark, unforgiving consequences of TBI, which can be devastating not only to the patient, but also to their loved ones. The strains that TBI injuries can put on relationships—be it between husbands and wives, children and parents, brothers and sisters, or families and their in-laws—can multiply like an unstoppable, catastrophic mushroom cloud and tear apart the strongest of bonds. The doctors, nurses, and therapists on the polytrauma unit all have stories about being stunned at seeing the collapse of relationships they were certain were strong enough to survive the devastation of TBI. Ask the staff members, and they can all recite names of patients who came to the polytrauma unit with what appeared to be rock-solid personal relationships only to wind up getting divorced from their spouses or estranged from family members.

As hard as TBI can be on relationships that seem to be on solid ground, it is especially brutal on those who are young and in new, relatively untested relationships. Burness and Jessica Britt fell squarely into that category, as do myriad other young couples who pass through the doors of Richmond's polytrauma unit.

Jessica Flegel had fallen in love with a handsome, young, strong marine. Now, mere months into their marriage, that man had quickly turned into a stroke survivor with limited speech ability, limited motor skills, a hole cut into his skull, and no assurances that he would ever return to his old self. He was easily frustrated by his physical limitations. He longed to rejoin his comrades, and he was understandably scared that he might not be able to.

"He feels like he lost a little bit of himself," his wife said.

Dr. Pai said certain patients are, by virtue of their backgrounds, less vulnerable to strife in their personal relationships in the wake of a TBI. Those would typically include military officers who tend to be in their forties and fifties, have college educations, and have been in long-term personal relationships. Simply put, their emotional capacities have been tested and tested often over the years, be it through the rigors of college and possibly graduate school, the ups and downs of a decades-long career in the military—including possibly repeated exposure to battlefield conditions—the commitment and strength necessary to be in a long-term relationship such as a marriage, as well as the highs and lows of raising children.

On the opposite end of the spectrum, the "high-risk" group would include patients who are young, in new relationships, and are marines—the US military branch with a well-developed reputation for portraying an image of being just a little bit stronger, a little bit more bad-ass, a little bit more invincible.

"So many of these guys think they're going to live forever," Pai said. "There's a certain mindset that goes into it, and that comes with the territory. And when you wind up here, that can shake everything you've known to be true to that point in your life. This changes things in a hurry, and not everyone can adjust to everything that comes with that."

"It's not easy for the patients or their families," said Sherry Ceperich, a counseling psychologist who worked with the Richmond staff from 2008 until 2012 before taking a job in another part of the Richmond VA hospital. "People come here thinking they need to work on getting past their physical injuries. But in many cases, the emotional damages that come with that can be just as severe."

————

Equipped again with the ability to speak, Burness Britt began to blossom, and the polytrauma unit staff started to see his personality emerge.

The portrait of a frustrated Burness sitting in speech therapist Monique Jones' office, banging his head on a table because of his inability to relearn how to talk, quickly gave way to a picture of a young man with a quick smile, a giant heart, a keen sense of humor and practical joking, and an easy way with the staff, especially the ladies.

"He flirted with every woman in here. Every single one," Jones said. "But at the same time he would flirt with us, he would always tell us how lucky he was to be married to Jessica. 'My wife is beautiful. She's the most beautiful woman in the world,' he would tell us all the time. He was so proud of her."

That was evident six weeks into his stay at McGuire, when Britt felt helpless and trapped as his first wedding anniversary approached. When August 18 arrived, however, Burness—thanks to an assist from some staff members—was ready.

"He conspired with the nurses," his wife said. "He bought me flowers and all that. You name it. It was very sweet."

Burness also became a media star of sorts because of two events. He wasn't even aware of the first, because it took root on June 4, 2011, in the frantic, harrowing moments when the medevac helicopter arrived in the wheat field in Afghanistan to rush him to medical care after the IED blast.

Anja Niedringhaus, a Pulitzer Prize-winning photographer with The Associated Press (AP) who is based in Geneva, Switzerland, had built an impressive portfolio as a battlefield specialist for the world's largest newsgathering organization. The AP had arranged for her to be embedded with a marine detachment, and she was aboard the US Army "dustoff" medevac unit that got the call to fly to the wheat field after the explosion that injured Burness and his comrades. When the helicopter landed, Niedringhaus jumped from the craft with the responders and followed them to the wounded, taking one sobering photograph after another as the crew hurriedly carried the warriors back to the helicopter and flew them to safety.

The AP in December 2011 published a story and extensive photo package by Niedringhaus about that day. Her story began:

> Inside the medevac helicopter in Afghanistan, U.S. Marine Cpl. Burness Britt bleeds profusely from shrapnel wounds to his neck. The medevac crew chief clutches one of Britt's blood-covered hands. I take hold of the other.

With my free hand, I lift my camera and take some pictures. I squeeze Britt's hand and he returns the gesture, gripping my palm tighter and tighter until he slips into unconsciousness. His shirt is ripped, but I notice a piece of wheat stuck to it. I pluck it off and tuck it away in the pocket of my body armor.

In my 20 years as a photographer, covering conflicts from Bosnia to Gaza to Iraq to Afghanistan, injured civilians and soldiers have passed through my life many times. None has left a greater impression on me than Britt.

I knew him only for a few minutes in that helicopter, but I believed we would meet again one day, and I hoped to give him that small, special piece of wheat.

Niedringhaus, who wrote that she was especially taken by Burness' courage and smile that day, recalled that the dustoff unit reached him within five minutes of getting the call about the IED blast. He was flown first to Camp Edi, where he was stabilized before the next flight, this one to Landstuhl, Germany, where he would be reunited with his wife and then returned to the United States.

Niedringhaus, meantime, went back to Geneva, where she launched a long, arduous effort to track down Burness. The marines and army would tell her little beyond that he had been seriously wounded, and she was unsuccessful in her bid to see if he was at Walter Reed National Military Medical Center, a popular landing spot for many of the US war wounded. She eventually found his Facebook page, but when she tried to contact him via the social networking website, he didn't respond. Niedringhaus had no way of knowing that Burness, at that point, was not active on Facebook for the simple reason that his right-side paralysis made typing practically impossible.

Fortunately for her, Burness' friends and loved ones were continuing to post well wishes on his Facebook page, and Niedringhaus noticed a post that referred to him being in Richmond, Virginia—the clue she needed to find him. She reached out to Steve Helber, the AP's photographer in Richmond, and he helped her get a phone number for the nurses' station at McGuire's polytrauma unit. Niedringhaus called, and one of the nurses summoned Burness to the phone.

Burness invited Niedringhaus to Richmond, and she arrived on December 13, 2011, carrying a batch of photographs from that fateful day as well as a piece of wheat. She wrote an emotional account of that reunion, describing how Burness was brought to tears as he studied the photographs she took in the wheat field and on the helicopter; how he told her that after he was hit, his only thought was of seeing his wife again; and of how surprised and grateful he was when Niedringhaus gave him the wheat shaft she had plucked from his uniform.

In the days leading up to Christmas, the AP released her story and a series of photographs about Burness, the wheat field, and their reunion. Countless newspapers across the world published the package on their front pages. The global reach of the AP—which distributes news, photographs, and illustrations to some 15,000 organizations across the world, including more than 1,400 newspapers in the United States alone—meant that Burness Britt, the young marine from Georgetown, South Carolina, appeared in newspapers from Sacramento, California, and Tulsa, Oklahoma, to London, England, and Karachi, Pakistan.

The second event that put Britt in the spotlight occurred on January 11, 2012. It was a gray, rainy Wednesday in Richmond when a fleet of dark-colored sport utility vehicles rolled from Richmond International Airport in the Virginia capital's eastern suburbs to McGuire VA Medical Center in South Richmond. The caravan was carrying first lady Michelle Obama, who came to Richmond to make stops at VCU and McGuire to help highlight the administration's efforts to boost treatment of TBI as well as PTSD and related mental-health issues affecting the US military. As part of her visit to Richmond, Obama wanted to visit troops at McGuire.

By that point, Burness was in his seventh month at McGuire. He had spent nearly two months in the main hospital at the PRC then was moved August 29 to the Richmond Polytrauma Transitional Rehabilitation Program, a freestanding facility a few hundred feet south of the main hospital. As opposed to the main rehabilitation unit, which is operated in a more traditional hospital inpatient environment, Richmond's transitional unit allows participants to live in a setting that more closely resembles that of a college dormitory, including private sleeping and bathing quarters as well as common areas.

The transitional unit staff focuses on preparing patients for a progressive return to independent living, with an emphasis on tailoring therapy programs to each person's individual needs and goals. That includes everything from physical therapy to cooking meals in the facility's large kitchen, where patients are expected to fend for themselves under the guidance of occupational therapists. The unit amounts to a finishing school of sorts, and Burness, both with his progress and his outgoing personality, thrived in the environment. That made him a natural choice by the staff to be one of the patients with whom Michelle Obama visited on her stop at McGuire.

The hole that surgeons had cut in Burness' skull after the IED blast to help relieve cranial pressure and swelling had recently been closed, but he still had prominent red scars where the area had been surgically repaired, and they were made all the more visible by the fact that his brown hair was slow to grow back. Burness, who by then had returned to his old joking ways, had developed a comedic shtick in which he used his surgically scarred skull as a prop of sorts. When he would receive visitors and they would chat, the conversation would inevitably work its way to his head, his buzz cut, and his cranial scarring, and he would inevitably convince his guests to reach out and touch the meandering red line. Go ahead, he would tell them with a smile. It's okay, the Southern charmer would reassure them.

Each time, the visitor would reach out and gingerly touch his skull, barely making contact with the tip of an index finger, at which point Burness would let out a howl of "OWWWWWW!" in a booming voice strong enough to make any marine proud. The visitor, of course, would recoil in horror, and Burness would erupt in laughter at having succeeded in pulling his signature prank on yet another unsuspecting guest. He had gotten so good at it, working it to perfection time after time, that the staff was worried he might try it on the first lady. Not to worry, he assured them. He would remain on his best behavior for such an important visitor.

He lied.

Obama made her way through the tour, escorted by various McGuire officials in white lab coats and expensive suits and spending time chatting with several patients. She and Burness seemed to make a quick connection, and it was not long before he began talking about the large, red, winding scar on his head. He pointed to it and motioned for the first lady to touch it.

By then, it was too late. Like everyone else, she reached slowly, tentatively, and barely made contact. Staff members who had been sucked into the prank before now stood by helplessly, wondering whether he would be gentle with the first lady.

"OWWWWWW!"

Burness had snared his highest-profile victim yet, and as the first lady pulled back her hand and shot a stern look at him, he let out a burst of laughter. Photographers captured the event, including Obama waving an accusatory finger at her guilty prankster. He posted the picture on his Facebook page, and the photo quickly became the stuff of lore on the polytrauma unit, prompting one staff member to use the frame as a screensaver on her computer.

———

Tuesday, February 7, 2012, was a sunny, crisp late winter day in Richmond when Burness and Jessica Britt loaded eight months' worth of belongings into their car, pulled out of the parking lot at the transitional center, and drove home to Georgetown, South Carolina, to begin the next chapter of their lives.

They took with them plenty of positive memories from Richmond, where the staff helped point them on the road to being whole again after the most traumatic event in Burness' life.

Days earlier, the manager of the Hampton Inn where Jessica had stayed for eight months held a going-away party for the couple. Now they were off to relax on a thirty-day convalescent leave—"con leave," in military parlance—before Burness reported to his new unit, a Wounded Warrior regiment at Camp Lejeune, North Carolina. The plan was for the couple to spend a month relaxing in their hometown with family and friends and then move into base housing at Camp Lejeune.

The marines launched the Wounded Warrior program to give injured members of the service branch an avenue to work their way back to fitness and active duty, if they so preferred, or to transition to civilian life. Burness was adamant in his desire to remain a marine—and hopefully rejoin his unit—but he needed more rehabilitation to continue improving his speech as well as the movement, flexibility, and strength in his right-side extremities. The Wounded Warrior program seemed like a good way to accomplish that.

However, as the staff at Richmond cautions all patients, the Britts were entering a potentially tricky period, one in which they would no longer be in either a hospital inpatient setting such as the rehabilitation unit or a closely supervised dormitory-style setting such as the transitional unit. They were giving up those tightly controlled environments and replacing them with one in which they would be charged with overseeing themselves. Perhaps most important, the freedom that came with that change in environments also came with a significant change in dynamics, and not all couples make a successful transition to the change in dynamics.

Up to that point, Burness and Jessica Britt had been friends, lovers—equals. When he was injured, she added being a cheerleader to that role, serving as his primary source of positive support during his hospitalization and inpatient rehabilitation. Now that they were leaving the inpatient setting, Jessica would be charged with switching from cheerleader to caregiver, overseeing everything from him taking his medications and doing his therapy work to getting to his appointments on time and eating properly. It remained to be seen how she would adjust to her new role as primary caregiver—and how Burness would adjust to his partner, his equal, adding the duties of supervising his care.

It didn't take long to start getting answers to those questions.

"When he came home, there was nothing for him to do," Jessica said, adding that her husband began drinking more. "He started gaining more weight and he felt worse about himself."

She said Burness had joined the marines to gain confidence in himself, because he had not been comfortable with his body when he was growing up. The IED blast had sapped that confidence. His new normal was a drug regimen that included sleeping pills as well as antidepressive and antiseizure medications that left him feeling lethargic, uncertain, and unworthy of being a marine.

"He felt like his buddies may have lost him," she said, "but they didn't lose themselves."

When Burness' con leave ended and he and Jessica made the less-than-four-hour drive north to Camp Lejeune, things only got worse. Their base housing—a new, spacious, well-appointed garden-style apartment—was fine, but the Wounded Warrior battalion fell far short of Burness' expectations.

After eight months of intensive one-on-one therapy sessions in Richmond, he had hoped more speech and physical therapy at Camp Lejeune would get him in condition to resume an active-duty role with the marines. Instead, he said, speech therapy at Lejeune was nonexistent, and the base's physical therapy consisted of sessions in a swimming pool.

"That's it. Nothing else. A pool!" he said with a tone of disgust, throwing up his arms for emphasis.

He thought that as long as he remained with the Wounded Warrior battalion, he would never get back to the physical condition needed to resume his marine lifestyle.

"Huge disappointment. Big time," he said, shaking his head. "They let me down."

He also was frustrated with his wife, saying she was being negative about his physical condition and badgering him about his sleep patterns and about taking his medications. Trust issues between the two began to bubble to the surface. So did money issues. By the time they went back to South Carolina for the Memorial Day weekend holiday, which coincided with Jessica's birthday, matters reached a head.

On May 27—less than four months after leaving Richmond—Burness Britt told Jessica Britt he wanted a divorce.

By that point, their respective Facebook pages, which for nearly a year had been dominated by news of his recovery, well wishes from relatives and friends, and pictures from their courtship and the early, joyous, carefree days of their marriage, had evolved into a forum for the struggling couple to express their displeasure and frustration with each other—often in not-so-subtle fashion.

The digs, accusations, and admonishments reached a head when, on June 3, 2012—one day short of a year since the fateful blast in the wheat field in Afghanistan—Burness went on his Facebook page at 3:05 P.M. and changed his status from married to single. Within weeks, Jessica Britt was back in Georgetown, South Carolina, living with her mother. She began using her maiden name, Jessica Flegel, on Facebook and began looking for work as a massage therapist.

Meanwhile, Burness Britt was plotting his departure from the marines.

CHAPTER TWELVE

SUPPORT SYSTEM

When a new patient enters the emerging consciousness program at the McGuire VA Medical Center's PRC, it means a fast education in scales for their loved ones.

The list of scales that measure someone's cognitive function includes the Glasgow Coma Scale, the JFK Coma Recovery Scale, the Rappaport Coma/Near-Coma Scale, and the Rancho Levels. Developed at the Rancho Los Amigos National Rehabilitation Center, the Rancho Levels scale assigns rankings to a patient's awareness as well as thinking and memory skills. Depending on the patient's responses to a variety of stimuli and problem-solving exercises, he or she is ranked between Level 1, which is no response, and Level VIII, which is purposeful and appropriate.

Richmond's polytrauma unit used the Rancho Levels as a way to determine the status of new patients and track their progress over the ninety-day program, toward determining whether they are good candidates to remain on the unit. Michael Dardozzi, the speech-language pathologist assigned to work with Bryce Powers, did a baseline assessment upon his arrival at the polytrauma unit. With another speech therapist working alongside Dardozzi to confirm his observations, the pair gave Bryce a Level II ranking. Patients at Level II are starting to respond to sounds, sights, touch, or movement, although those responses can be inconsistent or delayed. Level II patients also can respond in the same way to what they hear, see, or feel, including moaning, moving, sweating, chewing, and breathing faster.

The staff wanted Bryce to reach Level IV by the end of the ninety days. Level IV patients may recognize family and friends some of the time and, with help, accomplish such basic tasks as feeding themselves, dressing, and talking. Although able to speak, Level IV patients may nonetheless be confused and frightened, often acting inappropriately and being unaware that people are trying to help them.

The one thing that all Level IV patients have that those in lower levels do not—the key action that Pai and his staff want to see as a sign of improvement in EC patients—is that they are demonstrating purposeful behavior. Although Dardozzi was just one of the many therapists to work with Bryce on a regular basis, he was in effect in a leading role, largely because his job entailed daily sessions trying to stimulate Bryce to find a way to get him on a road to improvement. It was an especially daunting task, given that Bryce had four different types of significant brain injuries and rated so low on the Rancho Levels.

Dardozzi, with a master's degree from James Madison University and not yet thirty years old, embraced the challenge.

"I just love the complexity of the patients here," he said.

Because there is no way to be certain what patients in a vegetative or near-vegetative state can comprehend, Dardozzi would try to begin each session with an EC patient the same way: He would introduce himself and tell the patients who they were, where they were, and the date and time. Then he would try to reassure them.

"I'm here," he would say, "to help you clear your mind and make sense of your situation."

With that, he would launch into a routine of first trying to determine the level of the patient's cognition that day, and then adjust his therapy goals accordingly. For example, sometimes it could be as simple as ringing a small bell for five seconds on either side of the patient's head with a ten-second gap in between rings to see if that elicited a response from the patient and, if so, whether the response was delayed. Another example would be to take the shaft of a pencil and press it against one of the patient's fingernails. Did the patient withdraw his hand? Moan? Was there a delay? Vision tests might include shining a penlight in the patient's eyes and waiting for a response, or flicking his fingers up close to the patient's face.

These baseline tests would give Dardozzi an idea of how responsive the patient might be that day, and the session could proceed from there. One of his primary goals always was trying to establish and cultivate a line of communication, be it through head nods, verbal responses, or a thumbs-up, thumbs-down mode of responding.

"I'll take anything. Anything at all. Just give me something I can work with," he said. "Establish any mode of communication possible. It doesn't really matter. I need something, and I need it to be consistent."

Naturally, some days would be better than others.

"A lot of times, the patients don't have a high tolerance. You may be scheduled for an hour, but it becomes apparent that that's not going to happen. You may just get twenty minutes."

With Bryce, a lack of consistency was an issue.

"I'd say, 'Close your eyes,'" Dardozzi said. "And some days he was able to do it, but following commands was generally inconsistent. And pretty much everything was delayed. The delay was almost always greater than five seconds."

When there are significant delays in responding to stimuli, it may raise questions about whether the stimuli and response are linked.

Dardozzi was far from alone in trying to coax improvement out of Bryce. The interdisciplinary, collaborative nature of the staff was evident when Bryce began moaning while undergoing stretching exercises in a physical therapy session. The physical therapists told Dardozzi about the moaning, so he sat in on a physical therapy session to watch for anything that might help him or the physical therapists.

"A lot of times you may just be an observer," Dardozzi said. "But what you do may be of help to somebody else on the team. It's a practical universe we operate in here. It truly is a patient-centered approach."

While Dardozzi and the rest of the therapists settled into a daily routine of stimulating Bryce, trying to see if they could get him to advance to a Level III and, ultimately, a Level IV, Cathy Powers settled into her new life as a caregiver.

"I'm just trying to have hope and faith," she said.

Cathy was alone in Richmond while her husband, Jim, a foreman for an electrical contracting company, stayed back in North Carolina with Madi, Bryce's sixteen-year-old sister. Jim and Madi would try to come up to Richmond every other weekend.

"I'm not complaining. I talk to them every day on the phone. We're making it work," Cathy said. "We talk about it like I'm on a deployment."

———

Once it became apparent she might not make it home for an extended period, Cathy wanted to find a way to keep everyone in North Carolina and Japan up to date on her son's condition without having to spend all day on the telephone placing and returning individual calls.

So she turned to social media.

She went on to Facebook at set up a page titled, "Prayer and Support Group for Airman Bryce Powers," and she used it as a tool to get out the word to what she thought might be a few dozen concerned people—a total she figured would be made up of relatives, friends, and members of her church community.

That total almost immediately grew into the hundreds. From there, it wasn't long before the ranks of Bryce Powers' "prayer warriors"—as Cathy called them—swelled past one thousand, and then two thousand, and three thousand, and on and on. Air force comrades passed along the name of the page. Friends told friends. Church groups shared as well. With the total continuing to mushroom, Cathy settled into a routine of posting daily updates to the page. She would generally begin with an update on that day's activities and end the message with requests for specific prayers for her son. Almost immediately after she posted, the reactions would start coming back from all corners of the world, either in the form of comments or "likes" on the page.

She generally would write the daily updates and post them about 11 P.M. Eastern time, using the activity as a way to wind down after a long day at the hospital and to gather her thoughts and put them in writing after she got back to her room at the Fisher House. Cathy said she came to regard the process of sitting down and writing the Facebook entries as "my safe space," a sort of cocoon where she could gain at least some small measure of measure of control in a painful process that often left her feeling helpless.

She also derived comfort from the fact that the number of followers continued to steadily grow and that many of them made a routine of praying for her son and the entire Powers family. Religion had long been a part of her life, and now it was helping her create a powerful community of support.

"For me, it feels like we're not in this alone," she said. "It feels like somebody cares."

Not only did Cathy make specific prayer requests of the followers, but some of them also were not shy about asking things of her. She told the story of two elderly women who wrote and said they had incorporated her posts into their daily routine.

"We don't go to bed until you write," they told Cathy, before gently urging her to "write a little earlier."

Not all the correspondence was as friendly and supportive.

Just as Cathy would typically end each day with her late-night posts, she would rise the next morning and, before going across the parking lot from the Fisher House to spend the day with her son, she would go on to Facebook and review the comments on the page. Although the number of postings was overwhelmingly and unfailingly positive, there were a few negative ones as well.

Some people wrote that she was living in a world of false hope, or that she needed to institutionalize her son and get on with her life. Others wrote that she had no business staying away from her husband and sixteen-year-old daughter for so long and staying with a son who obviously would never recover, or that her son had clearly done something wrong to anger God and deserved to be punished, or that she should just allow her son to die.

Cathy's response to those people was consistent: Not only would she remove the posting from her page, but she would cut off that person's access. She was trying to remain positive about her son's plight, to hold out hope, to keep control during a trying time, and she had no room in her life for negativity.

"I like being able to have some control over the process," she said. "I like having a bit of a wall."

That's not to say Cathy would write nothing but positive news on her page. She frequently wrote in detail about the ups and downs of daily life in the EC program, and she didn't hesitate to chronicle her son's struggles, especially the so-called storms that seemed to occur with greater frequency earlier in his stay at McGuire.

The "storms" were her shortened term for *dysautonomic storms,* which describe periods of autonomic instability—when the body's central nervous system is struggling to regulate his neurotransmitters, the chemicals that transmit signals from a neuron to a cell. Simply put, the instability in the central nervous system manifests itself in ways that include a patient tensing up and breaking out in perspiration. The patient can appear to be in the midst of a personal, physical kind of storm.

Early in his stay in the EC program, Bryce's damaged central nervous system would sometimes spawn repeated storms in a single day. Toward the end of his stay, he would occasionally go weeks between them.

The storms could be unnerving to a loved one who would have to sit by, helpless, and watch as the nurses would come in and try to cool Bryce with wet towels and administer drugs to calm his tensed-up body. Cathy wrote about one such episode that occurred when she walked into his room on the morning of December 17, 2012:

> I waited with him until they gave him his shot of opiates and his body relaxed and returned to normal, then I left his room in uncontrollable sobs. I found a safe, private little space and called my husband Jim at work, hysterical and desperate for his calming and

supportive words. He delivered…and I got my head twisted back on in the right direction. (Thank you, Honey!)

Her posting also described a visit that occurred later that day, and she accompanied her written entry with a picture. The visit and accompanying photograph both involved David Rogers, another air force airman who had been through the EC program and was now living at home. Rogers had come back that day to visit the polytrauma unit, and he spent some time with Bryce and Cathy Powers. Cathy described the moment (and the photograph that accompanied it) thus:

He is so sweet, loving, kind, and has the most beautiful and contagious smile you've ever seen! He told me about Jesus coming to him when he was in a coma, and he asked me if he could pray for Bryce. I said, "YES PLEASE!" This photo above is David bowing his head in his wheelchair, laying his hands on Bryce, and praying for his fellow Air Force brother to be fully healed and restored!

Bryce Powers turned twenty-one on January 9, 2013. The polytrauma unit staff crammed into his room during morning rounds and serenaded him by singing "Happy Birthday," and one of the nurses baked a cheesecake—Bryce's favorite—to mark the occasion.

Cathy's Facebook entry on January 13, posted at 11 P.M., noted that the day marked the halfway point of the ninety-day EC program. Her son's condition was not improving significantly, and he was still being bothered by storms, not to mention bouts of nausea, vomiting, and intestinal problems, prompting his mother to close her message by asking for help from the "prayer warriors":

Specific Prayer Requests:

1. For the "storms" to STOP.
2. For the nausea and vomiting to STOP.

3. For his intestines and digestion process to return to normal and function properly.
4. For God to touch Bryce and miraculously heal him!

Thank you so much! Love, Cathy

On January 31, Cathy went on to Facebook and told the prayer warriors that at the weekly meeting of her son's medical team earlier that day—day sixty-three of the ninety-day program—the staff told her that because Bryce remained at a Level II, they would start making plans to discharge him at the end of the program.

"They do not believe he will be waking up here at the facility...at least not now," she wrote. "Our family is not going to give up our hope for a miracle. We will press on, love, take care of, and work diligently with Bryce, and do everything we can think of to wake him up someday.

"In the meantime, we just follow the orders, and map out a plan to get him safely home."

Cathy ended her posting with prayer requests and the following thought: "The poorer the report...the BIGGER THE MIRACLE!"

"Never give up!" one prayer warrior responded.

"Prayers for peace and rest in decisions that lie ahead," another wrote.

The mushrooming crowd of Facebook followers, by then numbering nearly ten thousand, did not include Jim Powers, who said he didn't see the need to keep up with his wife's daily posts.

"I get all that and more every day," he said with a shrug, noting that he spoke with Cathy constantly, either on the phone or in person.

———

On February 15, Kamee Mayfield, the air force airman who had been injured in the car crash with Bryce and subsequently returned to her family's home in Phoenix, Arizona, to continue her recovery, went on her Facebook page and posted a picture of herself with her father and one of her uncles. The picture had been taken earlier that day while the trio was on a hike at Squaw Peak, which at more than 2,600 feet is the second-highest point in the Phoenix Mountains.

"Asked my dad how long it'd be, he said about an hour. Yeah we were hiking for almost three hours," she wrote. "I should have figured, whenever my dad does an outing with either of his brothers it never works out the way it's planned."

The group was smiling broadly in the picture. Kamee wrote that she enjoyed the outing.

"It was fun for the first hour or so, but then I was kinda ready to be done," she posted. "It did help me sleep well that night though."

Kamee, who was in a coma for five days after the crash, was released from physical therapy at the end of January. She continued to see a speech and oc-cupational therapist.

February 15 was a far different experience in Richmond, where Bryce remained in a state that Dr. Pai characterized as fluctuating between vegeta-tive and minimally responsive. Bryce's mother, Cathy, wrote that she was "up all night trying to deal with hate mail, disgusting and inappropriate posts that only rip at my heart and speak death into Bryce's precious life, and critics that are bullying me and my family."

———

February 26 marked ninety days since Bryce had entered the EC program in Richmond, and even though he remained at a Level II on the Rancho scale, well short of the threshold the polytrauma unit's staff wanted him to reach to remain in the program, there was no urgency to discharge him.

For one thing, casualty levels typically dipped in the harsh winter con-ditions in Afghanistan, so the polytrauma unit did not need the bed space. In addition, there was some indecision about whether the best option was transferring him to a long-term rehabilitation facility in North Carolina or to the family's home. Cathy and Jim Powers opted to take him to their house in Monroe, North Carolina, but that meant special equipment would first have to be ordered and Cathy would have to be tutored on some caregiving functions that were being handled by the polytrauma unit's nursing staff.

There was also the matter of the storms, which continued to come and go on an inconsistent basis, and the significant muscle spasticity issues that were leaving Bryce in pain. Pai wanted to address those two matters before Bryce went home. Cathy continued to hold out hope, telling the prayer warriors that night that she was seeing signs that could indicate he was about to emerge, and she asked them to pray for him "to be miraculously healed, fully restored, and given a second chance to be a walking, talking, faith-filled soldier for God."

On Friday, March 8, Bryce underwent surgery to have a programmable pump implanted in his abdomen to release Baclofen, which is used as a muscle relaxant to counter the spasticity. Doctors were hopeful that instead of having to administer Baclofen orally, a pump releasing it directly into his bloodstream would be more effective. One of the side effects of the drug, however, is that it causes excessive drowsiness, which interferes with efforts to regain consciousness.

"I am hopeful we will see great and wonderful changes in Bryce's body and mind over the next couple of weeks," his mother wrote on the night of the surgery. In the days and weeks that followed, the number of storms dissipated, and Bryce continued to get regular visits from some of his new comrades at Langley Air Base in Hampton, about an hour's drive southeast of Richmond. After Bryce was sent from Japan to Richmond, the air force promoted him to a senior airman and changed his official "duty station" from Misawa to Langley. Even though he had never worked at the Virginia base, the facility embraced him and his family. Every few days, it seemed, a group of air force personnel from Langley would show up in Richmond on their day off to check on Bryce and offer their assistance and support to the family.

———

On March 17, St. Patrick's Day, Kamee Mayfield logged a 4.25-mile run in slightly less than fifty minutes. She had returned to work part time a week earlier and was continuing to see a speech therapist and an occupational therapist.

In Richmond, Cathy Powers celebrated the fact that her son no longer moaned as much now that he had a Baclofen pump to regulate anti-spasticity drugs. She put her son's favorite "lucky" green T-shirt on him and then, with assistance from the staff, got him loaded in a tilted wheelchair so she could roll him outside to enjoy the cool, fresh air of a late winter afternoon.

"I'm not sure he noticed," she later wrote to the prayer warriors, "but it was good for him just the same."

―――――

On Sunday afternoon, March 31, with Jim and Madi in town for the weekend to celebrate Easter, Cathy and her daughter were joking and laughing in Bryce's room when they noticed that the more they laughed, the more Bryce seemed to smile. He remained that way for several minutes, so they asked a nurse to come to the room and take a picture of Cathy, Madi, and Jim leaning over the side of the bed—and all four of them smiling. Cathy later called it the family's Easter 2013 picture.

"OUR GOD IS GREAT!!!" she wrote that night to the prayer warriors, whose ranks had swelled to more than twelve thousand. "With HIS healing touch, I believe these precious WINDOWS of AWARENESS will keep coming, and eventually get longer and longer!

"Thank you for praying and believing with me!!! Love, Cathy"

Madi (who was on spring break from school) and Jim stayed in Richmond for a few days after Easter. On April 2, Madi and Cathy left the hospital for several hours and went to a vintage clothing store in Richmond to buy a dress and accessories for Madi's upcoming prom, the theme of which was "Old Hollywood."

"It was really nice to see her so happy, and I'm glad she has something to look forward to," her mother wrote that night.

On Saturday night, April 6, Madi and Jim took Cathy to dinner at The Jefferson, an upscale Richmond hotel, to celebrate her birthday. It wasn't until April 11, but Jim and Madi were about to go back home to North Carolina.

On April 8, Cathy and a visitor spoke about how Bryce seemed to be more alert and was becoming adept at "tracking," or following the source of movement with his eyes when he was awake. That afternoon, he spent some time in a wheelchair out in front of the nurses' station, and he did quite a bit of tracking, especially when people would walk past and speak to him. Cathy noted that it seemed to be part of an overall improvement that included fewer storms and less spasticity pain, and she expressed optimism that it would continue. Physical therapists were regularly strapping Bryce into a device called an Erigo walking machine, which mechanically creates a walking motion in an effort to keep his leg muscles and joints from tightening.

"He is looking better and better," his mother wrote that night to the prayer warriors, "and I am convinced that someday he will wake up and say 'Hi' to me."

As it turned out, significant change was indeed on the horizon.

CHAPTER THIRTEEN

THE EPIPHANY

Any hopes Cathy Powers had about the significance of her son's seemingly improved tracking were dashed—completely, and with a take-your-breath-away finality—on Wednesday, April 10.

An ophthalmologist and an optometrist both examined Bryce Powers and determined he had cortical nerve damage in his brain, a condition called cortical visual impairment. Even though it was a problem with his brain and not his eyes, it nonetheless affected both eyes, and the nerve damage was such, the two doctors agreed, that Bryce was permanently blind.

His mother, understandably, was devastated.

"I'm not sure what to do about this," she said. "Not sure how exactly to handle it."

Dr. Pai consulted with the ophthalmologist and the optometrist.

"His prospects for normal vision," Pai said afterward, "are zero."

As for what appeared to have been indications of improved tracking that Bryce was demonstrating in the days and weeks leading up to the examination, Pai tied it to Bryce relying on sounds. Even though his eyes were open and he seemed to be following people or objects with them, it may have masked the fact that he was actually tracking them more by what he heard than by what he saw.

"I think he's doing a lot with his hearing right now," he said.

Nonetheless, Pai said it was unlikely Bryce was completely blind. A more probable scenario, he said, was that Bryce might be able to pick out some general shapes or distinguish light from dark. However, being able to determine specific objects or distances would not happen, given the extent of the nerve damage.

"It feels," Cathy told the prayer warriors that night, "like a couple of big scoops of NIGHTMARE packed on top of what we already thought was OUR WORST NIGHTMARE."

Then she quickly went back to her usual positive, supportive mode, telling the warriors there was evidence that God can heal the blind and citing as an example Mark 8:22–25, in which Jesus restored a man's sight by spitting on his eyes and putting his hands on him. Her daily prayer request, which often had three or four items, contained just one that night:

"For God to have mercy on Bryce, restoring his life, and blessing his future.

"Thanks. Love, Cathy"

The next day, April 11, Pai and the other polytrauma unit staff members came to room 159 on morning rounds and surprised Cathy with a hearty rendition of "Happy Birthday."

From there, her day was anything but festive.

Spasticity and cramping issues were clearly bothering her son, so the doctors prescribed a different kind of pain reliever in the morning. Yet as the morning wore on and gave way to the afternoon, Bryce continued to show signs of painful cramping that bent his feet and prompted him to lift his legs every ten seconds or so, punctuating his movements with long, plaintive groans. Finally, as the afternoon progressed, Cathy couldn't stand to see her son in such consistent, lingering pain any more. She asked the nurses if they could have Pai come to check on her son. It wasn't long before Pai arrived, and he saw the same thing she did: that Bryce didn't seem to be responding to the new medication and that he was in obvious discomfort.

Pai said it could be related to a shunt that had been surgically implanted in Bryce's brain after the accident. He ordered a computed tomography (CT) scan, saying the imaging should show if there were problems with the shunt. The CT scan, however, would not address the more immediate concerns of pain management and spasticity. He told Cathy that their options included adjusting the Baclofen levels, ramping up the pain medication, or trying something else. What followed was a simple, matter-of-fact, declarative statement from Pai, but it was profound enough to set in motion the most difficult decision of Cathy's life.

"Of course," she recalled Pai saying, "if we give him more pain medicine, the chances of him emerging go down."

She listened to what the doctor who was overseeing her son's care was saying, and she began to absorb everything. Although there were avenues available to them to ease her son's spasticity and pain, those avenues also might adversely affect what had been the primary mission of Cathy and everyone in the EC program: getting Bryce to regain consciousness.

That's when it hit her—and in practically no time, it changed her outlook, her perspective about what had happened to her son to that point, and what the next course of action should be. Like a massive ocean wave breaking into the surf, Cathy's world crashed down on top of her.

It had been almost six months to the day since the accident, and her son still could not respond consistently to commands. When he did respond, there were significant delays. When stimulated, he could not demonstrate intentional, consistent actions. He was nearly five months into a stay at Richmond—a stay that was supposed to have lasted three months—in a program designed to see if he could emerge from a coma that had been caused by not one but four significant types of brain injuries, any of which could have been fatal. Richmond's program was widely acknowledged as the leader in the military healthcare system for emerging consciousness, and Bryce had received tireless care from a staff of talented, compassionate professionals.

He could not walk.

He could not talk.

He continued to have spasticity and pain issues, and surgery and more drugs not only had not alleviated those issues, but they also could be standing in the way of any chance of him emerging.

In addition to not emerging, he had not advanced past Level II on the Rancho scale, the level he was at when he arrived. Level IV—the target goal for Richmond's EC program—is categorized by patients demonstrating purposeful behavior. Bryce was nowhere near that. His baseline, as Pai simply put it, was between vegetative and minimally responsive.

Now Bryce's outlook was further clouded by the discovery that nerve damage in his brain had left him permanently blind. Although it might not be total blindness, it would be significant, and it would be irreversible.

Throughout the journey, Cathy had been unwavering, relying on her strong Christian beliefs to help maintain a positive, keep-pressing-ahead attitude to give her only son, her firstborn child, every possible chance. Her husband was solidly in her corner. Her sixteen-year-old daughter was solidly in her corner. An online community of what was now more than 13,000 followers, many of them posting messages of support on her Facebook page each day, was solidly in her corner.

She tried to digest what Pai had told her about the possibility that more drugs may serve as even more of a deterrent to her son regaining consciousness. She took stock of how little progress he had made toward that goal since the accident. She considered what might lie ahead for her twenty-one-year-old child. As she processed all of these things, she remembered back to an event that occurred when he completed basic training.

Her son, then only eighteen but mature for his age after several years in the JROTC program, knew he would likely be sent overseas soon, and he knew that, with the United States at war in Afghanistan, he could eventually find himself in harm's way. So Bryce Powers crafted a living will at the end of boot camp, a document that gave his mother power of attorney. It had provisions that included such phrases as "if I cannot make decisions for myself" and "she has permission to withdraw care."

Now, as Cathy and Pai tried to figure out what to do next, she put aside the never-give-up-hope persona that the legions of prayer warriors had come to know. Now it was just her and the leader of her son's medical team, trying to figure out what was best for their patient.

She looked at Pai while fighting off tears.

"What are we doing here?" she asked.

Before Pai could answer, she posed another question.

"What is his quality of life?"

If her son did emerge in, say, six months, or even nine months down the road, what would he be like? What would his life be like?

Cathy already knew he would be significantly blind, if not completely so. It was possible that in addition to not being able to see, he might not be able to speak as well. What, his mother wondered, would life be like for someone who was literally trapped inside his body, someone who was conscious but could not see or speak? Add the possible long-term pain associated with spasticity issues to the mix, and Cathy found herself questioning some of the decisions she had made up to that point.

"When they decided to discharge him from the program, we decided to take him home to let me take care of him. I wanted that. I wanted to do that for the rest of my life—for the rest of his life," she said.

Cathy shook her head and paused.

"I am not going to be able to stand seeing him in pain all the time."

Cathy recalled arriving in Japan shortly after her son's accident and having his doctors present her with paperwork that would have given them permission to remove him from a respirator. He could not recover from his multiple brain injuries, the doctors told her, so she could sign the forms and let her son die in peace.

"I should have listened back then," she said. "He said in the living will he wouldn't want to live like this."

Cathy asked Pai what their options were. Pai explained that if they wanted to withdraw care, as Bryce Powers had described in his will, they could put him in McGuire's hospice unit, where they would stop feeding him and make him comfortable with sedatives. They could arrange to do the same process at the family's home in Monroe, North Carolina, if so desired. A third alternative was to send Bryce home and continue care for another six to twelve months, allowing additional time to see if he emerged and, if so, to what level. If he did not emerge in that period, they could reevaluate the matter.

Pai told her to take a few days to think it over and talk with her family. Cathy told him she would, but also that she knew which way she was leaning.

"I know I can't stand to see him suffer like this," she said.

———

Barbara Bauserman, the polytrauma unit's family education coordinator, had grown to become someone on whom Cathy Powers relied for on-site support. It began with Bauserman's role as the unit's point person for teaching family members the ins and outs of life as caregivers for TBI patients—and Cathy's thirst to learn everything she could about looking after her son. It grew because Bauserman and Cathy had a shared interest in spirituality, and it bloomed because Bauserman has a richly deserved reputation among her peers as someone who is intelligent, a good listener, highly logical, and a calming presence.

"You don't meet people like her every day," Cathy said. "I can't tell you how thankful I am for her. She's amazing. But then, so many people on the staff are amazing."

Bauserman, knowing it was Cathy's birthday and Cathy didn't have a car, thereby effectively confining her to the hospital grounds for what would often be weeks on end, decided to take her out for dinner. They chose as their destination the Tobacco Company, an establishment in Richmond's Shockoe Slip, an area of the city where old red brick tobacco warehouses had been carefully restored to create a popular restaurant and entertainment zone on cobblestone streets. Given everything Cathy Powers had been through on the afternoon of April 11, Bauserman knew that a festive birthday dinner at a high-profile restaurant wouldn't be prudent, so she drove Cathy to her house and got her a glass of wine and some food from her refrigerator. Then the two of them sat down and Bauserman did what she does so well: She listened.

Bauserman knew it had taken Cathy months to get to her current state of thinking, and she wanted to let her begin processing some difficult, painful topics. It was no longer about what Pai, Bauserman, or any other staff member felt; instead, it was up to Cathy, as her son's lead caregiver, to work her way through the issues and find a comfort level. Afterward Bauserman took Cathy back to the Fisher House, which Cathy now had called home for nearly five months. Cathy called her husband, Jim, who was at home with Madi. She told Jim it had been an eventful day and that she needed to speak with him about some important matters, and she asked him to step outside so Madi wouldn't hear their conversation.

Once Jim was outside, Cathy told him everything that had happened with Bryce's spasticity and pain problems that day and about her conversation with Pai. Then she told him she thought it was time to honor the terms of Bryce's living will.

She wasn't prepared for her husband's response.

Just as Jim had patiently listened to her describe the emotionally draining events that led her to arrive at her decision, she listened as her husband told her that because of his love for her, because of his decision to support her, he had not told her that he had arrived at the very same conclusion months earlier—and that he was patiently waiting for her to get there on her own time and her own terms.

Jim went on to explain that he could trace his decision to December 23, 2012, the day he and Madi had driven up from North Carolina so the family could be together in Richmond for Christmas. Jim said he was in room 159, looking at Bryce, when he "saw the light go up" from his son.

The reference Jim Powers made stems from his being one of at least fifteen million people in the United States to report having had a near-death experience, according to various studies. Surveys in the United States and abroad have indicated that as much as 20 percent of the world's population may have had near-death experiences and, as a result, subsequent visions—often involving seeing either their body or that of someone they know. Various studies have been conducted involving those who have reported near-death experiences, and they center on oxygen deprivation or electrical stimulation of the brain as possible links.

A University of Michigan study on near-death experiences released in August 2013 detailed a surge in brainwave activity in the thirty-second period after the heart stops, a burst of electrical patterns that exceeds levels during a normal state of consciousness. In Jim's case, he had been in an electrical accident on the job many years earlier that not only knocked him unconscious but also left him with a vision of his body. He later had similar visions that involved two relatives and a coworker, and in each case, they died soon after. As a result of those experiences, Jim was taken aback December 23 by what he saw when he stood against a wall at the foot of his son's hospital bed.

"He sat straight up in bed, drifted up, and went through the ceiling," Jim said. "It was very peaceful. It was like he just vaporized."

The vision, he said, prompted him to reach a painful, inescapable three-word conclusion—one that had not been swayed by anything that occurred or anything he saw in the months after that.

"Bryce," he told his wife on the phone that night, "is gone."

Just as Cathy had not anticipated what her husband told her that night, she was unprepared for what happened the next morning when she got to the polytrauma unit.

Madi called her from school, and she was distraught, wasting little time before telling her mother what was bothering her.

"I heard you talking to Dad last night," she said.

Cathy, mortified at what her daughter must have thought from hearing only Jim's half of the phone conversation, quickly realized that Madi had figured out exactly what was happening. Cathy tried her best to calm her daughter.

"I told her I don't want her to think we're bad people," Cathy said. "I told her we're not going to play God."

Her daughter, without hesitation, came back with a response that caught her mother off guard—and one that Cathy later said erased any possible lingering doubts about her own leanings.

"She said, 'Mama, don't be mad at me. But we're already playing God. We've been playing God for months now.'"

With that, both were now crying, but Madi wasn't finished.

"She said, 'Mama, he's a shell. Can't you tell Bryce is gone? He wouldn't want this.'"

The following Monday, Cathy met with various members of her son's medical team as well as Dr. Shane McNamee, the hospital's chief of PM&R, the department under which the polytrauma unit falls, to talk some more about her thoughts. As a result, she finalized the decision to withdraw care.

McNamee, noting that Bryce's protein levels were high and that his hydration level was good, estimated death would come in two to four weeks. With Pai in Jamaica with his wife and young daughter for a five-day vacation, one of the few extended breaks he had taken since getting the job as the program's medical director more than two years earlier, McNamee called the polytrauma unit staff together for a hastily arranged meeting. He told them of the decision the Powers family had reached, and he told them he knew it would be a difficult one for the close-knit staff. He told them that they had done everything that could be expected for Bryce, and that as painful as the outcome was, the staff had to make peace with the fact that the family had chosen to honor the terms of Bryce's living will. If the staff members had any personal feelings about the family's decision, McNamee said, now was the time to share them—among themselves, behind closed doors—because once the meeting was over, they needed to once again make taking care of Bryce and his family their sole priority. The meeting, several staff members said, was brief and permeated by a tone that as painful as the outcome was for them, it would be more so for the family.

The next day—Tuesday, April 16—the polytrauma unit staff stopped feeding Bryce Powers.

———

At 5 P.M. on April 16, Cathy Powers went on to Facebook and told the prayer warriors that her son's multiple layers of catastrophic injuries had "continued to pull him farther away from us." She continued:

> We recently received additional, difficult information, and unfortunately, we realize we can no longer sustain his precious and young life.
>
> His amazing doctors and Medical Team have shown such kindness, care, and have literally exhausted every possible idea they could think of to help him beat this, and somehow come back to us. I will always be grateful to them.
>
> Our Family has decided to honor Bryce's written wishes, allowing him to pass naturally and peacefully. I can tell you, as his Momma, it is much harder to put his wishes ahead of mine...Which is why I haven't even allowed myself to consider 'these wishes' prior to this point. I had to try EVERYTHING first.
>
> With all this said, my trust remains solid in The Lord. I trust Him to heal Bryce, like I have always confessed. This 'healing' is the ultimate healing. How could I not be grateful that with his last breath here, his next will be in the presence of The Lord.

Cathy said she initially wanted her son's hospice care to be on the polytrauma unit, where she felt comfortable with the staff and grateful for all they had done over the months. After a brief discussion, however, she realized it wouldn't be fair to ask all of the staff members who had worked so hard for so many months to try to get him to emerge to abandon those efforts and switch directions. Rather than take him home and subject his sixteen-year-old sister to potentially painful memories of her lone sibling's final days, Cathy and Jim Powers decided to move Bryce to McGuire's palliative care unit.

Before the polytrauma staff arranged for Bryce to be moved out of their unit, they displayed their care and compassion yet again by starting the paperwork for him to buried at Arlington National Cemetery in a service with military honors. As a senior at Piedmont High School, Bryce had gone on a field trip to Washington, DC, that included tours of the monuments and a number of key government buildings in and around the nation's capital. His favorite part of the trip had been Arlington National, the nation's iconic cemetery. He had been fascinated by the history, significance, and powerful presence of the vast, rolling cemetery across the Potomac River from the Lincoln Memorial.

Established in 1864, Arlington has steadily grown through war after war, and its tree-lined hills are now home to more than four hundred thousand people, some of them dating to the Civil War. The list of those for whom Arlington is their final resting place includes former President John F. Kennedy, a navy war hero; sports figures such as Joe Louis; military standouts such as Navy Adm. Hyman Rickover, Marine Col. "Pappy" Boyington, and Army Gen. Omar N. Bradley; as well as twelve US Supreme Court justices, including Chief Justices William Howard Taft, Earl Warren, Warren Burger, and William Rehnquist.

Cathy Powers had a black-and-white photograph of Bryce that had been taken while he was walking among the tombstones at Arlington during the field trip, and she considered it one of her favorite pictures of him.

"Now the fact that he's going there blows me away and gives me peace," his mother told a visitor one day while sitting in a lounge outside her son's room. "It's hard to put into words how good it feels to know we can go see him any time we want at such a place of honor."

CHAPTER FOURTEEN

SUE CASH

Sue Cash wanted her visitor to know it's all worth it.

Sitting at her desk in a cramped, windowless office in the center of the PRC at McGuire VA Medical Center, surrounded by endless stacks of papers that would seem to suggest she may never extricate herself from all these piles of administrative minutiae, she insisted that—all appearances to the contrary—her job truly is rewarding.

As she told her visitor this, seemingly a minute didn't pass in which her computer didn't beep to signal yet another incoming e-mail, or her office phone didn't ring to interrupt her train of thought once again, or her cell phone didn't ding to signal the latest incoming text, or a doctor didn't knock on her door with another challenge, or one of her nurses didn't knock on her door with just one more of the myriad little crises that make up her daily routine.

Hour after hour, day after day, this seemed to be Cash's life as the head nurse on the polytrauma unit. Everyone, it seemed, wanted a piece of her time, and it left precious little for her to carve out any for herself.

Evidence of that came when, at 3:15 P.M. on a weekday afternoon, she reached into her desk drawer, pulled out a pack of Lance peanut butter and cheese snack crackers, shrugged sheepishly, and apologized.

"Sorry," she said. "Didn't have time for lunch today. This is it."

If you can just put up with the minute-by-minute interruptions that are the norm in her daily working world, Sue Cash—a widow and grandmother with soft eyes and a soft, reassuring voice—will tell you that there are countless examples of how wondrously rewarding it can be to work on the polytrauma unit.

Granted, you are tending to patients who have just suffered what is likely to be the worst thing that will occur in their lives. Within this darkness, however, the staff on the unit always seems to be able to find these bright beams of light, little snapshots of life that remind them that although it's a job with benefits, it's also a job that can provide the kind of satisfaction that no paycheck or insurance package or retirement plan, no matter how generous, could ever deliver. Ask Cash to give you an example, and she doesn't have to think long before producing one from the heart, one that embodies the type of care offered by the polytrauma unit's staff.

"His name was Jason," she began.

Cash went on to describe a young soldier who, six years earlier, had been serving as a gunner in the end vehicle of a US Army convoy that was snaking down a dangerous road in Afghanistan. The blast of an IED left Jason with serious burns that required repeated and painful skin grafts. In addition, he lost part of one leg and suffered a severe TBI. Like so many patients, when Jason arrived at McGuire, he was still in a coma. How long he would remain that way was uncertain.

So the polytrauma unit staff did with Jason what they do with every other comatose patient: They talked to him. Constantly.

The staff encourages families to bring in photographs, drawings, or other mementos and put them on the walls or elsewhere in the patients' rooms as a way to personalize them. They also suggest that families put some headphones on the patients to play their favorite music. Perhaps most important, the staff encourages the families to talk to their comatose patients, and the staff follows suit.

"We talk to them about their artwork on the walls, their favorite music, current events, their families—anything," Cash said. "The idea is that if you do it long enough, if you keep stimulating them, keep exposing them to familiar things, then eventually, something will click."

Cash remembered taking a particular liking to Jason.

"He was a very handsome young man," she said. "And you could tell from talking to his family that they were all just really good people."

Jason had been at McGuire for about a month when Cash, as was her custom, stopped by his room one evening while making her way across the polytrauma unit and began another of her one-way conversations with another comatose soldier.

"Nothing in particular," she recalled. "I think it might have been about music or something like that."

Cash stayed with Jason for a few minutes, once again trying to offer some verbal cues that might help him make a connection, might help something click in his injured brain. Then Cash turned and began walking out of the room, offering a perfunctory, "I'll see you a little later, Jason," as she left.

Before she made it to the door, it happened.

"Get my mom," came the strange voice from behind Cash in the darkening room.

Understandably startled and frightened, Cash let out a small yell. Then she quickly gathered herself, realizing something special was happening. She wheeled around and went back to Jason's bed.

"What did you just say?"

This time, what she heard instantly washed away her fright and replaced it with unconditional joy. This time, there was no mistaking what was happening in the room that wondrously rewarding evening.

"Get my mom," came the voice a second time, this time with more clarity and authority, leaving no doubt that Jason was indeed emerging into a state of full consciousness.

As she told the story, Cash stopped for an instant and swallowed hard.

"His mother was right down the hall in the kitchen," she said. "Needless to say, I got down there pretty fast."

She paused again and smiled.

"Days like that…," she said, her voice trailing off without finishing.

———

Sue Cash was put in charge of a polytrauma unit operation that, depending on patient needs, generally requires six to eight nurses working the day shift, five or six working evenings, and four or five on the overnight shift.

The level of staff allocation not only depends on the number of patients in the polytrauma unit at any given time, but also what kind of patients they are. For example, those who are unable to bathe themselves or feed themselves or take care of themselves in other ways will require more individual assistance from the nursing staff. Then there are what the staff refers to as one-on-one patients: those who require a nurse to be with them at the side of their bed literally twenty-four hours a day, seven days a week, because they may be subject to involuntary movements that could jeopardize the healing of their broken bones or other injuries, or they may have a level of TBI that puts them at risk to unknowingly leave their beds and accidentally injure themselves.

Life as a nurse in the polytrauma unit requires a certain toughness. It is not limited to just the rewarding moments—the Jasons who wake up seemingly right before your eyes or the patients you help rehabilitate to the point where they can walk out the door, who then come back months later to visit you and thank you, this time as healthy, productive members of society once again.

The casualties of war can and do find their way from Afghanistan back to McGuire, where nurses know better than to walk up unannounced behind a patient suffering from PTSD lest they put themselves in physical danger from a soldier who may become easily confused and disoriented and lash out, unable to distinguish friend from foe as he mistakenly thinks he is back on the battlefield. The nurses also know all too well that patients suffering from TBI can become quickly agitated, frustrated, and verbally abusive— once again, not because of any personal issues they have with the nurses, but because those are some of the ways their injuries present themselves. So the nurses don't take it personally if a patient goes from being kind and considerate one minute to cursing them the next, only to quickly return to again being docile.

"We need people who can meet the challenges that this kind of environment brings," Cash said. "It takes a special person to work here as a nurse, and they make this place run. So much of what people bring to the table is as a team."

Brooke Traylor came to the polytrauma unit almost by accident, instantly fell in love with the place, and later left for family reasons—only to come back a year later because she missed the staff camaraderie, the closeness of the patient contact, and the myriad examples of successful healing and rehabilitation that regularly occur. At age thirty-two, with five years of experience in the unit over two stints, Traylor still found it inspiring to come to work each day and help with the recovery process of those who were severely injured while fighting for their country.

"It changes you on a daily basis. It really does," she said. "You may not always be happy when you walk through these doors, but seeing these people changes you. Let it make you grateful for what you have. When you think you're having a bad day, you come in here and you realize, 'Okay. I really don't have it so bad after all.'"

Adding to that perspective of gratitude, Traylor said, is what she called the gift of seeing a patient wheeled through the doors into the polytrauma unit on a gurney—mangled, afraid, and uncertain of the future—only to undergo a significant transformation over the course of weeks or months through his or her own efforts and those of the McGuire staff.

"You get to really see a team working together," Traylor said. "Think about it. They come in here and they've got these tubes and all that hooked up to them, and they can't even talk and some of them are in a coma and all that.

"And then they walk out. Can you imagine that? They get a new chance in life. I mean, where else can you get that in a job?"

A Florida native who spent her formative years in Richmond, where her father, a Baptist minister, was assigned for many years at Grove Avenue

Baptist Church, Traylor originally went to college to pursue her passion for singing before she decided to get a nursing degree. Cash would have you believe Traylor may have made a mistake in her career choice. As good as Traylor is at nursing, Cash said, she may be an even better vocalist.

Cash vividly recalled the day one holiday season when she walked through the nurses' station in the center of the polytrauma unit and a CD player had Christmas music on. The song that was playing literally stopped her in her tracks. She listened, mesmerized by the pure, gripping, soothing voice, and then asked one of the staff nurses about the origin of the CD. That's when she found out it was another one of her nurses—Traylor—performing on a CD composed of church music.

Asked to describe Traylor's singing skills in greater detail, Cash smiled and offered a brief but powerful summation.

"She has," Cash said, "the voice of an angel."

———

Traylor's nursing career started in the women's surgical oncology wing at a suburban Richmond hospital, where she estimated that 60 percent to 70 percent of her patients had end-stage cancer. Although she found comfort in caring for so many terminally ill patients, the job also provided more than its share of emotional drawbacks.

"I went to several funerals, let me tell you," she said, shaking her head.

She eventually moved to McGuire, briefly taking a job in a different area of the massive hospital before her interest was piqued by an opening in the polytrauma unit, which in 2007 was then in its relative infancy.

It was an instant and lasting match.

"When you think you're having a bad day, take a walk around the unit," Traylor said. "Just one trip. Won't take long. You'll change."

In December 2010, however, there was a change Traylor could not foresee. The father of her young son was diagnosed with pancreatic cancer, and within a few months, he died. In addition, Traylor's father was transferred from Grove Avenue Baptist to a church in Greenville, South Carolina. Suddenly, two of the main cogs in Traylor's support system for her son—his father and grandfather—were gone.

So Traylor took a logical step: She quit her job and moved in 2011 to South Carolina so her son, then ten years old, could be closer to his grandparents.

The Department of Veterans Affairs, in an effort to keep her in the family, so to speak, arranged for Traylor to transfer to one of the VA's outpatient health clinics in Greenville, South Carolina. She was able to keep her son close to his grandparents, and she was able to stay involved with medicine within the VA system. The job hours were more stable than on the polytrauma unit, but other that, Traylor knew almost immediately that it wasn't a good fit for her skills, let alone her professional interests.

Instead of working closely with severely injured patients on an individual basis, instead of helping them progress and work their way back to health, she was now in more of an administrative role, one that was decidedly not hands-on. In essence, she was more of a glorified office manager than a nurse. That would not last.

Her parents were aware of it, too.

"They knew that I didn't like my job," she said. "It wasn't where I was supposed to be."

So in September 2012, she and her son moved back to Richmond, and she was welcomed back to the polytrauma unit.

"Once I was away from it, I realized how much I love it," she said.

Ask Traylor about events that confirm to her that the polytrauma unit is a good fit, and she provides several, including an anecdote about a young, rugged-looking soldier who was a patient there. The soldier, badly injured in a vehicle accident after his return from Afghanistan, was telling his mother in a telephone conversation one night that he was struggling so much emotionally, he was thinking about possibly harming himself.

Understandably concerned, the soldier's mother urgently called the nurses' station and relayed this information. Traylor, aware that the young soldier had a tattoo of Jesus on one of his arms, decided to try a soft approach.

She went into his room and used his tattoo as the basis for striking up a conversation. She spent a long time in his room at his bedside, and the two covered a wide range of topics. Mostly, however, they focused on spirituality. It wasn't necessarily tied to organized religion, Traylor recalled, and she deliberately avoided trying to be preachy with him, attempting instead to help him make some discoveries on his own about the spiritual nature of the world and how he fit in.

The conversation went well—so well, in fact, that the soldier later told one of the polytrauma unit's psychologists that Traylor had changed his way of thinking, and that as a direct result of what they had discussed that night, he no longer harbored thoughts of injuring himself.

As gratifying as that made Traylor feel, it was further validated by something the psychologist told her, something the soldier said to describe what the two had talked about that troubled night.

"He said," Traylor recalled, "it was a life-changing conversation."

She paused and then managed a small smile, a smile that told her that she had undoubtedly made the right move by coming back to Richmond from Greenville.

"It was confirmation," she said, "that this is where I was supposed to be. Those opportunities don't come along very often, but you try to make the most of them when they do."

Traylor paused again and then tried to lighten the mood.

"I'm not the real skillsy type," she said with a chuckle. "But I can surely sit down and talk to you. All day long."

She was quick to add that not all nursing matters in the polytrauma unit are as weighty. The role of the nurses can often involve something as simple as trying to make the patients smile and forget about their troubles for a few minutes.

She recalled one weekend night when the patients seemed a bit restless and in need of something a bit different, so the nurses turned down the hall lights, got several flashlights and used them as strobes, and hooked an iPod to the sound system. Presto: Instant nightclub, complete with blaring lights and pounding music, right there in the hub of a VA hospital unit for severely injured people.

"I mean, where else can you do something like that?" Traylor said. "You've got to do what you can for them. If you can lighten their load and make 'em smile, it's all worth it."

She sees it all as part of a vast job description of helping the recovery and rehabilitation of America's service members and veterans—people she said are deserving of celebrity hero status in this nation but are not getting it because of misguided attention paid to others.

"You pick up a newspaper or turn on the television and you hear about Lindsay Lohan and stupid crap that really doesn't matter when you get right down to it. So much of that really doesn't matter at all," she said. "Then you walk through these doors and come to work here. And this, this is inspiring. It really is.

"It's an honor."

CHAPTER FIFTEEN

SIX MONTHS OUT

June 27 marked six months to the day after the explosion that left Luis Avila and Jon McHenry badly wounded and claimed the lives of three of their comrades on that dark road in Afghanistan.

In Richmond, Virginia, Luis had what his wife and doctors called a good day in room 110 of the PRC at McGuire, another small step on the road to trying to purge the devastatingly stubborn infections from his body so he could begin rehabilitation in earnest.

As had been the case for some time now, Luis' prognosis remained largely a case of wait, watch, pray, trust, and hope. He needed to get his weight and strength back, but the task of fighting the infections was monopolizing what little strength his body had at this stage, strength that might otherwise go to physical rehabilitation. So Luis tried to rest his body, work on his cognitive abilities, and keep waiting for the medicine to wage war against the toxins in his body.

Jon McHenry had a far different day at Walter Reed National Military Medical Center in Bethesda, Maryland. It began when he woke up and logged on to his computer while his wife, Jay, and infant son, Leo, were still sleeping. At 8 A.M. Jon posted on his Facebook page the following:

6 months...Never gets easier.

R.I.P. Brothers

N.M.K.

J.M.W.

K.W.K.

Those we love don't go away, they walk beside us every day. Unseen, unheard, but always near; still loved, still missed and always dear.

Later, Jon said it was hard to believe six months had passed since that fateful day.

"As soon as I wrote their initials out," he said, "I could vividly see their faces. I had no trouble coming up with a flood of memories of all three.

"So I had a good little pout right there and got the crying out of my system right there."

Then Jon went about his business on what he anticipated would otherwise be another typical day at Bethesda, including two physical therapy sessions. His pace of recovery had accelerated to the point that his physical therapy sessions had essentially evolved into personal training workouts, with Jon and the staff able to focus on strengthening individual muscle groups, improve on his cardio conditioning with increasingly brisk runs on a treadmill, and help him gain back the dozens of pounds he had lost during his ordeal.

His body, so mangled, fragile, and uncertain just a few months earlier, was making significant strides on the way back, and Jon would speak excitedly of taking a sort of attack mentality to his physical therapy sessions. However hard the staff wanted to push him, he wanted to push himself just a little bit harder. The aches and pains that the therapy sessions brought out? Jon used those as fuel and motivation to keep focusing on his improvement. He wanted to get back to the point where the army would clear him to rejoin his comrades in Afghanistan before their deployment ended, and nothing, it seemed, would stand in his way. The sweat and the pain of the physical therapy sessions were nothing more than a means to an end.

He was on his way back from one of those physical therapy sessions on June 27 when his cell phone rang. It was one of his doctors, and he had some news for Jon. The results from his two-day, eight-hour TBI test were in. Jon hadn't anticipated hearing the results so soon, and getting an early call left him feeling a bit uneasy. The doctor cut right to the chase. It was the best possible news, and the fact that it came exactly six months after Jon had been gravely injured made it all the better.

He had passed what everyone was calling the final major hurdle to rejoining his unit.

"He said I did outstanding on everything," Jon said. "It was overall above average."

The only area where he did not excel was the test on visual memory, where he was shown a picture for a brief period and then instructed to recreate the lines as best he could from what he remembered of the drawing. Jon said the main reason he did not score well on that section of the test had nothing to do with any possible visual impairments or memory issues. Instead, he had a much more simple explanation.

"I'm not artistic at all," he said. "It took me forever to design a picture."

On all key test sections related to TBI and any possible lingering problems associated with brain injury, Jon said, nothing indicated he would have any problems returning to active duty with his unit.

"As far as he's concerned, everything would be fine for that," Jon said of his doctor. "He said I'm where I need to be, and he said it's only going to get better.

"Bottom line: I passed with flying colors."

Jon made no attempt to hide his relief. He knew that a less-than-satis-factory TBI assessment would at least significantly slow—and possibly de-rail—his comeback bid.

"There was a lot riding on that test," he said. "I'm just glad I did well."

Adding to the angst of the TBI examination was the fact that it was not the kind of test for which one can study in the typical sense of the word.

"You can't really prepare yourself for something like that," he said, "and that's kind of frustrating."

The test, in addition to the visual memory exercise, involved a number of tasks spread out over four hours on each of two consecutive days.

"It was ridiculous," said Jon, who was required to recall a one-paragraph story word for word, solve word puzzles, demonstrate hand-eye coordination with exercises involving computer mouse clicks, and perform such tasks as subtracting three from 171, then three from 168, then 165, then 162, and so on in descending sequence.

"It was kind of frustrating as I was taking it," he said. "So much of it seemed really repetitive, almost like they were trying to get you frustrated, see if you could take it."

Yet Jon was able to keep calm and focused throughout the test, in part by drawing strength from the strides he had already made in his recovery. The way he saw it, focus, drive, and motivation have never been an issue with him.

"Growing up, I was always the shortest kid," he said. "And I was never the heaviest, either. It's always been an uphill battle to prove I belong."

Basketball was the perfect outlet for him as a youth, in large part because it provided a platform for him to show he could excel with tools other than height and weight. A point guard can overcome a lack of size with speed, tenacity, skills, and leadership, and Jon filled that bill. He carried those traits over to the army when he decided to become a military policeman, and he continued to embrace them again in his recovery. In fact, Jon felt those traits would keep giving him an edge over his peers in everything he does in the army.

"I don't want to sound cocky," he said, "but quite frankly, I'd like to think I'm at a higher level than them, and they need to keep up with me."

Just as he believed in his drive and his ability to motivate himself, he knew others may wonder if he might have been a bit overzealous in those areas. More than one person questioned whether Jon, a young husband and new father, had fulfilled his obligation to his country and should pursue the separation route that was made available to him by the army after he was wounded. Jon himself had initially planned to take that option and leave the army, and early in his stay at McGuire, he even spoke of possibly moving to Arizona or Florida to start a new life as a civilian once his rehabilitation was complete.

Yet as time passed and his recovery progressed, he had had a change of heart. Those questioning him, however, had not.

After his May 3 Facebook pronouncement that "I'm going to make history" and return to his unit to be with his buddies in Afghanistan before their deployment ended in November, the first two friends to comment on the posting both raised the issue of whether, given what Jon had already been though, he had met his obligation.

"You already have," one friend wrote.

"Task completed, Bro," another one posted.

Mark Korte, the father of Sgt. Noah M. Korte, one of Jon's comrades who died in the vehicle that day in Afghanistan, offered a similar sentiment.

Jon and Mark had been in contact since the fatal blast, and Mark told him there was nothing else for him to prove in the military, that no one could ever blame him for walking away once he recovered.

"You've done enough," he told Jon.

Jon smiled when he recalled Mark's words.

"That's a really tough one," he said. "Yeah, I've done a lot and stuff, but I really do think I have more to give."

What changed?

Jon said that the more he improved physically and the more he thought about it, he came to the conclusion that he wasn't special, that the fact that he was severely injured should not automatically mean he should walk away from the army. He also realized that the army had given him a sense of purpose, a sense of being part of something bigger than himself, and a sense of camaraderie and that he had come to embrace those qualities. His desire to do the best he could for his bride and young son only strengthened his will to return to active duty and make the army a career.

Jon said that of the roughly sixty members of his unit still in Afghanistan, "I guarantee forty-five of them have family back here. I can't be selfish. I want to do my part and be a part of the team."

Therein lay the problem for Jon, however. His team was shrinking, and the dwindling numbers did not favor his bid to return to Afghanistan, at least not before the end of the unit's deployment.

The unit had been composed of seventy-eight people when the deployment began in November 2011, but because of changing priorities and staffing needs, the outfit had been steadily dwindling. The army was sending members of his unit home instead of adding to their ranks. The bottom line was that it appeared unlikely the army would send Jon—or anyone else, for that matter—to boost the manpower of his unit before the end of the deployment.

That didn't stop Jon from wistfully speaking of rejoining his comrades abroad, of getting back in uniform and getting back to work.

"If they won't let me go outside the wire every other day or whatever the missions call for, I can at least pull guard duty or something like that at a minimum," he said.

A more realistic goal would be for Jon to return to a regular schedule at Fort Hood in some type of security capacity and then, if he wanted to continue in the army, pursuing a promotion to sergeant seemed a logical step. Jon had encountered a number of good leaders already in his relatively brief military career, and he had tried to take some leadership qualities from each of them, hopefully to use in his own career as a leader. Becoming a sergeant would be the first step in getting some men under his wings, some young soldiers to mentor just as Jon had been mentored.

"I know I'm going to be good, so I want to stay in and make a difference in some people's lives," he said. "I'll start with a couple more kids, just like I was when I came in, and try to be a positive influence on them."

One of the leaders Jon admired was Capt. Luis Avila, not only for his strong work ethic but also for his insistence on prioritizing family. Jon recalled one September day at Fort Hood when Luis' charges had been faced with a long list of tasks for the day but had tackled them in earnest, worked well together, and finished their duties by 2 P.M.

"I know some guys would make you stick around, but not Capt. Avila," Jon said. "He just came out and said, 'Good job, everybody. I appreciate you working so hard today. Go home and be with your family, and we'll see you tomorrow.'

"People appreciate leaders like that."

On this day, Luis was in a hospital bed in Richmond, Virginia, his family by his side as he continued to fight to regain some control of his body. Jon, who not long before had been in the same hospital, the same wing, the same room, and even the same bed, was now charting the next chapter in his increasingly active life—one that was on a fast track to a return to normalcy, a return to active duty, and a return to Afghanistan to rejoin his comrades.

Or so it seemed.

CHAPTER SIXTEEN

J.T. MAGEE

The question seemed simple and innocent enough. In fact, it was anything but.

"Do you remember what you did yesterday?" J.T. Magee asked as the soldier sat at a chest-press machine in one of the seemingly endless series of small physical therapy studios at McGuire VA Medical Center.

It had been a mere twenty-eight days since Army Sgt. Eric Petersen was seriously wounded in an IED explosion in Afghanistan, a blast that had killed two comrades. Now Eric was spending an hour with Magee on a Tuesday afternoon in the first-floor studio, a small room crammed with treadmills and weight machines and inspirational signs on the walls, including one that said, "Kinesiotherapy: Improvement Through Movement."

Eric's rehabilitation regimen included five-day-a-week sessions with Magee, each of them sixty minutes long. Their standing appointment was at 2 P.M., and one-third of the way through this day's session, Eric moved to the chest-press machine, sat down, and then paused before he gave his kinesiotherapist a puzzled, hesitant look. He wasn't sure how many repetitions he was supposed to do or how much weight resistance he should set on the machine.

Magee, a nearly twenty-year employee at McGuire and a past president of the American Kinesiotherapy Association, saw Eric's hesitance as yet another opportunity to test more than just a patient's physical progress. He could have just glanced at his chart and told Eric what he had done the day before on the chest-press machine, thereby allowing Eric to proceed with his workout without giving the matter another thought. However, one of the reasons Eric was at McGuire's PRC was because he had not scored particularly well on cognitive tests when he had first arrived back in the United States after the IED blast. That had prompted doctors to express concern about his possible level of TBI, and they sent him from Walter Reed National Military Medical Center to McGuire's polytrauma unit.

There was a wealth of physical evidence that led the staff at Richmond to exercise caution about Eric's TBI. He had been the gunner in his vehicle when it had struck the IED, and the fact that his head and upper body were outside the vehicle exposed him that much more to the powerful, devastating impact of the blast. The IED had knocked the vehicle off its wheels and onto its side, and it had left Eric with not only a torn left quadriceps muscle, a ruptured left quadriceps tendon, and a soft-tissue injury in his right elbow, but serious head injuries as well. He had had significant bleeding on his brain, and surgeons had installed a drain to relieve the pressure caused by the build-up of blood.

Eric's jaw also had been fractured in five places, and he had had extensive facial fractures that had prompted the surgeons at Walter Reed to put eight titanium plates into the right side of his face. One thing the surgeons could not repair was Eric's right eye, which had been damaged so severely in the blast that he'd lost it.

On this day, Eric sat at the chest-press machine wearing an army T-shirt, sweatpants, and a black eye patch, and looked to Magee for help about what he should do next. So Magee asked if Eric recalled what he had done on the chest-press machine the day before.

"It's too easy if I just tell him how many reps and how much weight to put on the machine," Magee said later. "This way, he not only takes charge of his own workout routine, but it encourages him to remember from day to day what kind of progress he's making at the various machines.

"Plus," Magee said with a wink, "it gives the therapists a good barometer of where he is with his cognitive and memory skills. And with any TBI patient, that's always on our minds. That's an important part of the equation."

Sure enough, in just a few seconds, Eric recalled the proper number of repetitions and weight, and Magee smiled and nodded.

"That's right," he said. "Good job."

With that, Eric got right to work on the chest presses, rhythmically going through his repetitions while he focused on his breathing and technique, all the while under the watchful eyes of Magee.

"Let it out. Let it out," Magee said in a low, encouraging tone. "There you go. Excellent."

From there, it was on to another machine that focused on Eric's back muscles. Once again, he went through his repetitions with a quiet, focused determination, seemingly oblivious to the sign on a wall behind him that posed the question: "What fits your busy schedule better—exercising one hour a day or being dead twenty-four hours a day?" Eric was the kind of patient who needed little such motivation. In fact, his get-right-to-work attitude was evident even before he walked into the physical therapy studio.

When Magee showed up at Eric's room on the polytrauma unit to walk him to the studio, the two left the unit and walked down a short hallway on the second floor of the hospital, where they encountered what amounted to another of Magee's little tests to gauge where the patient was in his recovery and rehabilitation process.

Just outside the unit, at the end of a short hallway, Magee and Eric came to a lobby. On the right side of the lobby was a bank of elevators that could take them down to the first floor and the physical therapy studio. On the left side of the lobby was a door leading to a set of four short but steep staircases that would also take them down to the first floor. Magee slowed his pace as they walked into the lobby, allowing Eric to edge ahead, take the lead, and make a choice: Take the elevators or take the stairs.

For a patient barely three weeks off quadriceps tendon surgery, it was not an insignificant decision. The time frame alone dictated that no one would blame Eric for turning right, getting on the elevator, and giving his still-recovering tendon a rest. Then again, if Eric were to decide to take the stairs, that would give Magee an indicator about how the patient felt about his recovery.

Eric walked into the lobby, headed straight to the door on the left, pushed it open, and led the way down the stairs.

Magee looked over at a visitor accompanying the two, nodded approvingly, and offered a smile.

———

Later, after the therapy session had ended and Eric was back in his room at the polytrauma unit, he shrugged his shoulders when asked about how much progress he had made in less than one month following the IED blast on August 1, 2012.

In calm, measured tones, Eric provided a glimpse into the mindset of a soldier who had not only survived a blast that killed two of his comrades, but also had recovered rapidly from significant injuries and rehabilitated himself to the point at which he was about to be released to continue his therapy on an outpatient basis. In fact, to hear Eric tell it, he didn't think there was any reason for the medical professionals to be concerned about his TBI.

"I'm at Walter Reed, and I've got all this surgery stuff going on and everything, and they've got me on all these painkillers," he said. "A lot of times, I'd have a hard time just staying awake. So sure, I probably wasn't as sharp as I could be, probably not as responsive as I could be. But you know what? Once I got off all the strong stuff, everything started getting clearer, getting better. Honestly, I feel fine."

Eric said that once he was taken off the powerful narcotics, he experienced no problems with memory or cognitive issues. However, because the staff at Walter Reed was concerned about TBI issues, he didn't want to make a big issue of being sent to McGuire's polytrauma unit. The way he looked at it, a few weeks at McGuire amounted to nothing more than another example of a soldier getting military orders—and following them.

"It's just checking the box," he said. "Check the box and deal with it. Be a good patient."

By the end of August, Eric was taking no painkillers at all—not even aspirin. The only medication he was using was an ointment designed to prevent infections in his right eye socket. His father, Neal Petersen, who had been with his son since his return from Afghanistan, concurred with Eric's assessment of his mental acuity, saying it had been particularly sharp since leaving Walter Reed.

"I have not noticed anything different—anything," the elder Petersen said. "We can talk about things that happen in great detail."

———

Eric Petersen can recall in great detail what prompted his decision to join the military at an age when many of his peers are instead focused on girls, parties, and college—in no particular order.

Like so many young men in the military, Eric recalls vividly being disturbed and angered as a teenager by the images he saw on September 11, 2001. Yet although the terrorist attacks of that day prompted an immediate surge in military enlistments across the United States, Eric's own response had been more subtle.

September 11 planted a seed, he recalled later, and that seed took root late in March 2003. He was home from school at the family's house in the Philadelphia suburb of Fort Washington, Pennsylvania, and he was waiting for his parents to come home—his father from his job as an attorney and his mother from her position as a school teacher.

Eric grabbed a can of Spaghetti-Os, sat down in front of the couch, and turned on the television. All the major networks were providing coverage of US troops crossing over the border between Kuwait and Iraq and marching on to Baghdad. The more news footage young Eric watched, the more he became entranced by one inescapable fact in particular: The closer he looked, the more he noticed that many of the US Marines appeared to be in their late teens—not much older than him.

"That's when it hit me," he said nearly a decade later, sitting cross-legged in his hospital bed after a kinesiotherapy session at McGuire. "There was stuff going on over there that was so much bigger than what I was doing or what I was thinking about doing. So why should I think I'm better than that?"

The more Eric thought about it, the more he realized that instead of doing what his family expected—go to college and try to chart out some sort of white-collar career—he should do what he felt was right. Neal Petersen said he and his wife were blindsided when Eric sat them down for a heart-to-heart talk about what he saw in his future. Both are college graduates, and both had figured that Eric would follow suit; for them, it had not been a question of whether he would go to college, but rather a matter of where and to study what.

"It was not something that I even considered," Neal recalled. "But I have to give him credit. He clearly had spent a great deal of time thinking about it, and he laid out a strong case. A very strong case.

"He said that not everybody can be lawyers and teachers. In fact, he pointed out that without soldiers, we might not have the freedom to become lawyers and teachers. America needs soldiers. It's an honorable profession. And that's what he wanted to do."

Neal shook his head and peered over his reading glasses.

"You try to instill in them values," he said. "And I have to respect him for making that decision."

That didn't mean it was an easy decision for Eric's parents to accept.

"We struggled with it, sure," Neal explained. "But I told my wife, 'This is what his dream is. He can't live our dream. This is what he wants. We have to be supportive.'"

So with the backing of his parents and the support of army veteran John Baker, his principal at Upper Dublin High School, Eric Petersen spent the late stages of high school preparing not for college, but for the military.

On June 30, 2006, mere weeks removed from his high school graduation, Eric joined the marines.

Although he enjoyed his time in the marines, when his enlistment ended in 2009 he decided to switch to the army, drawn in particular to an affinity for the infantry and intrigued by some of the educational and training opportunities available in that branch that were not available in the marines.

Eric was stationed at Fort Riley, Kansas, with the 1st Infantry Division when they were shipped to Afghanistan in the spring of 2012. He was the gunner on a sixty-thousand-pound assault vehicle, perched high in the turret with an MK-19 machine gun, on the fourth day of an operation in an area of an Afghan valley that had not been touched by US forces in more than two years. On all three previous days in the valley, Eric's unit had come under heavy fire, and this time, it got even worse.

The vehicle struck what was later estimated to have been a 300-pound IED. US Department of Defense News Release No. 652-12, dated August 3, 2012 and carrying the headline, "DOD Identifies Army Casualties," offered the following version of the events:

> The Department of Defense announced today the deaths of two soldiers who were supporting Operating Enduring Freedom.
>
> They died Aug. 1 in Paktia province, Afghanistan, of wounds suffered when they encountered an enemy improvised explosive device. These soldiers were assigned to the 1st Battalion, 28th Infantry Regiment, 4th Infantry Brigade Combat Team, 1st Infantry Division, Fort Riley, Kan.
>
> Killed were:
>
> 1st Lt. Todd W. Lambka, 25, of Fraser, Mich., and
>
> Pfc. Jesus J. Lopez, 22, of San Bernardino, Calif.

Because such Department of Defense releases are limited to those who are killed, there was no mention of Eric, who was stabilized in Afghanistan, then flown to the US military hospital in Landstuhl, Germany, and then flown back to the United States to Walter Reed, where he regained consciousness one week after the IED blast. Weeks later, his recovery progressing steadily at McGuire's polytrauma unit, Eric said he had no regrets, either about joining the military or about suffering serious injuries in the name of serving the United States.

"If you had told me at age eighteen that I would go to Afghanistan, get blown up by an IED, and lose an eye at age twenty-six, I would have said, 'Let's go,'" he said. "Everyone should have the chance to raise their right hand for their country. It's an honor."

Eric said he was focused on completing his rehabilitation, rejoining his unit, continuing with his career, and perhaps even going through Ranger school. He had already been assured that having only one eye would not prevent him from such a venture. His injuries had done nothing to curb his appetite for serving his country as a soldier and for doing it in the infantry.

"The day the army doesn't want me in the infantry anymore," he said, "is the day I'll decide to get out of the army."

———

September 4, 2012, brought word of a suicide bomber blowing himself up at a funeral in Afghanistan. The casualty figures were numbing, even by the standards of a nation that was now mired well into its second decade of war: Twenty-five people were dead and another thirty were injured, many of them gravely.

Half a world away, in Richmond, Virginia, Eric was down in the small, cramped kinesiotherapy studio on the first floor at McGuire for another one of his daily workouts with Magee. The studio, in fact, was not actually a kinesiotherapy studio. It was designed for cardiopulmonary rehabilitation patients, but because of the years and years of fighting in Iraq and Afghanistan, McGuire's polytrauma unit was in the midst of a much-needed massive renovation and expansion, leaving Magee's patient work space in the hands of construction workers. So the hospital's cardiopulmonary rehabilitation studio had been temporarily altered to also accommodate kinesiotherapy patients.

The compact, driven, quiet, look-straight-ahead Eric Petersen presented a contrast to J.T. Magee, a rugged, head-shaved, good-natured type from the rural southeastern Virginia peanut country of Suffolk who had come to Richmond straight out of high school to study economics at VCU.

"Typical teenager," Magee recalled with a chuckle. "I was going to make all the money in the world, be rich, all that stuff."

Then he found out he didn't particularly enjoy the courses, so he switched his major to physical education, which seemed a better fit for his more active lifestyle. As is typical of many college students, Magee found himself in need of a supplementary job. Referred by a member of the VCU staff to an opening at the local VA hospital, Magee quickly embraced working with veterans in a physical therapy capacity.

The son of a Vietnam veteran, Magee got his bachelor's degree in physical education with a concentration in kinesiotherapy in 1994 and then became a full-time member of the staff at McGuire in August 1995. His path to working with polytrauma patients began almost immediately, when he landed a spot on a team working with TBI patients, a job that lasted five years.

"I fell right into it," he said. "Fell in love with it. Still am."

These days, Magee's typical schedule includes five or six hours per day in one-on-one sessions with patients, and the rest of the time doing paperwork or sitting in meetings. Many of his patients are active-duty military who are anxious to get healthy and get back to work, so Magee doesn't have to be much of a motivator. In fact, the opposite tends to be true. He occasionally finds himself telling patients to slow down just a bit.

"Regardless of who they are or why they're here or what their basic level of fitness is, the first couple of times they're in here we monitor their heart rate, blood pressure and talk to them about their breathing level," Magee said. "If you're working out so hard that you can't talk to me, then that's not good."

Eric, whose weight had fallen from 160 pounds to 130 after the IED blast, was one of those patients who didn't need any motivation. He wanted to get back—to being healthy and to being a soldier—and that kind of focus by him and others makes Magee's job that much easier.

"It's amazing how the body heals itself," Magee said. "We provide the patients with education and techniques they can use, but the body heals itself."

Eric's father Neal seemed nonplussed by his son's quiet resilience, a trait the elder Petersen said his son had demonstrated since entering the military. His primary focus had been on being the best infantry soldier he could be; everything else prompted him to a stance that might be best described as keeping his emotions in check, not letting them get too high or too low.

In fact, Eric himself did not mention while he was recuperating at Walter Reed, one of the people who stopped by his room one day happened to be then-Defense Secretary Leon Panetta, who had had some free time and had made the rounds at the hospital to visit with some troops. Eric's father, who seemed more excited than his son about the visit, got a smiling Panetta to pose for pictures with Eric, and it was Neal who told the story and described how gracious, caring, and attentive the defense secretary had been.

Neal also told another story about his son's seemingly casual approach to having been severely injured in Afghanistan.

The backpack that Eric had had with him in the assault vehicle at the time of the IED blast was shipped back to the United States and arrived while he was at Walter Reed. Neal recalled that when he and his son set the backpack on Eric's bed and began taking the contents out, they immediately discovered that someone in Afghanistan had also folded up Eric's bloody uniform and sent it along. Neal carefully took the uniform out of the backpack and slowly began unfolding it as he held it over top of Eric's bed. As he did, some brownish-red crusted soil fell onto the white bed sheets.

"Look!" Neal exclaimed. "Real Afghan dirt!"

His son nodded and managed a slight smile.

"This," he told his father with a deadpan tone, "is tragically beautiful."

The deployment of Eric's unit in Afghanistan was scheduled to last until late February 2013, and Eric, continuing a steady rehabilitation, was hopeful he might be able to rejoin his comrades in some capacity.

"He just wants to be back with them," Neal said, relaxing in an armchair near his son's bed at McGuire after another of Eric's kinesiotherapy sessions with Magee. "It's like it's passed him by."

His son listened, nodded, and repeated a refrain popular in his army unit. "Like they say," he offered. "If you ain't infantry, you ain't."

CHAPTER SEVENTEEN

MARC CRAWFORD

Not everyone who ends up in the PRC at McGuire VA Medical Center has been the victim of an IED blast, riddled by shrapnel, torn open by a bullet, or maimed in some other act of war.

Some active-duty service members or veterans wind up there because of a car crash, motorcycle accident, or any other tragedy that can occur in everyday life.

The events that landed Lt. Cmdr. Marc Crawford in the polytrauma unit began to unfold on the night of January 10, 2011. Marc, a promising navy officer who was about to be awarded command of his own ship, had had a late night at the home he shared with his wife and two small children near Fredericksburg, Virginia, staying up later than usual to watch college football's national championship game.

After he went to bed, he wasn't asleep long before Darin, at fifteen months old the couple's youngest child, woke up with nausea and vomiting. Amy Crawford took Darin into the shower to get him cleaned up, and Marc changed the sheets on their son's bed. On his way down the stairs with the soiled laundry, Marc felt his feet slip out from under him three steps from the bottom—a decidedly unathletic act for someone in superior condition who, at age thirty-six, did regular weight-room workouts and ran twenty to thirty miles per week to keep his six-foot frame at a solid 195 pounds.

Marc banged his tailbone during the fall, but he never hit his head or injured himself in any other way, and he recalled getting back on his feet and telling himself, "I think I'll be okay."

He returned to bed and didn't give the hard tailbone landing another thought.

The next morning, Marc made the approximately one-hour drive north to Washington, DC, for a two-day conference. By the end of the first day, he was experiencing severe headaches, exhaustion, and disorientation. He went out to dinner with some colleagues in a restaurant at the hotel where they were staying, ordered a glass of wine, took a few sips, and excused himself to go use the men's room. By the time he wandered into the hotel lobby, he realized he was lost.

Forty minutes later, Marc was finally reunited with his dinner companions, but his headaches, exhaustion, and disorientation were getting markedly worse. He skipped the conference the next day, opting instead to stay in bed before driving himself home. He called in sick the day after that, again electing for bed rest instead of his job with weapons systems at the navy's surface warfare weapons center in Dahlgren, about a twenty-minute drive from his home.

After sleeping late, Marc decided to take a shower in the hopes it might refresh him; instead, it paved the way for his hospitalization. When he got in the shower, he slipped and fell. His wife heard it and rushed to check on him.

"Amy said I had a bit of a glazed look," he recalled.

Concerned about his state of mind, she asked him to name his mother.

"Betty White," he replied.

His mother's name is Judy White.

Amy asked her husband to name the president of the United States.

"George Bush," he shot back emphatically.

Amy called 911.

Within minutes, an ambulance was rushing Marc to Fredericksburg's Mary Washington Hospital, where emergency-room doctors checked him over and ordered a CT scan of his brain that afternoon. When they reviewed the results, their first action was to order a helicopter. Marc needed to be flown to the University of Virginia (UVA) Medical Center for emergency surgery. Doctors at Mary Washington thought he could be in danger of imminent death, and they did not believe they had the necessary technology for the surgery he needed.

The CT scan showed that a number of blood vessels in Marc's brain had formed a dangerous, tightly tangled nest of sorts, and the nest was cutting off the blood supply that his brain—and therefore Marc himself—needed to survive.

Quickly flying him to UVA Medical Center, however, didn't solve the problem.

He was rushed into surgery, where doctors discovered it was even worse than the CT scan had indicated. Not only was the nest of vessels significant and troublesome, but also a large blood clot was blocking the view of the area they needed to reach, and time was of the essence. The surgery wound up being tedious, long, and especially difficult, the kind of procedure for which no matter what kind of technology you had on your side, you never felt like it was enough.

Marc recalled the surgeon telling him later that he "felt like he was doing surgery with a fork and a spoon."

Marc wound up spending nearly two weeks at UVA Medical Center, and he and Amy were given some sobering predictions about patients with his unusual type of TBI. For starters, they were told that less than 1 percent of the patients with his severity of malformed vessels could expect a full recovery.

Marc recalled hearing two other statements from doctors that hit him particularly hard:

"He is likely to have severe deficiencies," and

"Marc won't be able to even butter a slice of bread for a year."

This was not how Marc had planned his life with Amy. Not at all.

———

After earning a bachelor's degree in criminal justice from the University of Central Florida, Marc Crawford originally had had his sights set on an honors internship program with the Federal Bureau of Investigation (FBI). When the FBI told him that a military background would enhance his prospects, Marc saw the navy as offering him the best options.

He used his early years in the navy to obtain two master's degrees, including a master's of business administration from the University of Hawaii, and began to establish himself in the field of advanced weaponry. The navy sent him to the Naval War College in Newport, Rhode Island, for advanced work in national security and strategic studies.

Marc was told in 2009 that he was in line to be given command of his own ship, and as a final preparation to that posting he was assigned to the navy's advanced weaponry facility in Dahlgren, Virginia, where he focused on operational mission plans for ships with ballistic missile defense systems.

He met his future wife, Amy, in 1998, and they had their first child, Olivia, in October 2005. Darin followed in September 2009. The family lived in a nice home in Spotsylvania, Virginia, about a twenty-minute ride from his job at Dahlgren. They enjoyed their community and were active members of Spotswood Baptist Church. In short, life was comfortable, the family was happy, and Marc was about to get his own ship.

"Everything was good," he said.

Then, seemingly in an instant, it wasn't.

Now, his future as a navy officer seemed very much in doubt, as did his ability to be a husband and father. Doctors were telling him his chances of a full recovery were virtually nonexistent, that he should not expect too much progress, and that any progress at all would likely be slow to occur.

"It was very depressing, but I'll be honest," he said. "I was grateful to be alive. It really changed my perspective on life. We get caught up in our worlds, and we lose perspective on what's important."

Marc was released from UVA on January 24—with one notable exception. To guard against severe swelling in his brain after the surgery, doctors removed a piece of his skull. It stayed behind in a freezer at the hospital when he was discharged.

The navy, wanting Marc to have the best chance at recovery, arranged for him to be taken by ambulance some seventy miles east to Richmond, where the polytrauma unit at McGuire could evaluate his status and gauge what, if anything, could be done for him in terms of rehabilitation.

The first order of business was a neuropsychology test.

"I scored miserably," he recalled. "They had a baseline, and it was not good."

Not only was Marc slow to process matters, but he also had what was described clinically as "a diminished ability of self-assessment." As he later put it, "I was very bull-headed. I didn't have an appreciation for just how bad it was."

After the polytrauma staff completed baseline testing on Marc, they arranged for an aggressive daily routine that included speech therapy, physical therapy, kinesiotherapy, and occupational therapy (OT). Much of the therapy was designed to tax his brain and try to extend it to its limits. Tasks included computer-based exercises that focused on short-term memory, deductive reasoning, and problem solving. Some of it was more primitive—but effective nonetheless. He recalled one exercise that sounded silly but was actually extremely helpful.

"It was essentially a game of let's get Marc lost and see if he can find his way back," he said.

A member of the staff would lead Marc out of the polytrauma unit and to a different part of the sprawling hospital, tell him to find his way back, and then leave him there alone. Marc would time himself and try to improve each day on getting back to the unit.

Not only was he walking, but he was talking and regaining brain function. Marc Crawford was healing.

"We saw McGuire as a blessing," he said.

That wasn't limited to the progress he made while there.

Stories about staff members of the polytrauma unit going the extra miles are legendary, and their treatment of Marc was no exception. Because his hospitalization at McGuire lasted through Valentine's Day, he was unable to go shopping for a gift for Amy. So a member of the staff went out and purchased a necklace that Marc was able to give his wife.

"They took time out of their day to help me be a husband," he said.

———

The therapy administered by the polytrauma staff also took a toll on Marc, leaving him with headaches and cognitive fatigue.

On March 10, that all changed. That was the day of the so-called cranioplasty, when surgeons closed up Marc's skull by reattaching the piece of bone that had been in a freezer at UVA.

"It was a game-changer," Marc said. The headaches and cognitive fatigue nearly disappeared in a matter of days, and that wasn't all.

"My speed of comprehension and conversation improved almost immediately," he added.

After just weeks at McGuire, Marc was sent home to Spotsylvania to be with his wife and children again and continue rehabilitation on an outpatient basis at nearby Mary Washington Hospital. He was able to resume activities at Spotswood Baptist and personally thank the legions of members who had worked him into prayer circles.

"It kind of speaks to me about the power of prayer," he said.

He continued his surprising progress as winter turned into spring, leading to a logical next step—but one that less than three months earlier doctors had said was virtually unthinkable. On April 5, Amy and Mark got in their car, and she drove him the twenty minutes to Dahlgren, where she dropped him off and left him there for four hours.

"I was very nervous," he said. "There were a lot of questions in my mind. You want to believe you're ready, but I knew that I probably wasn't being completely realistic and honest with myself."

It wasn't long after that, however, that he was able to work full days, and within a few months, he was transferred to San Diego, where his initial assignment was as a force personnel officer charged with managing the staffing of the navy's ships on the West Coast as well as Hawaii and Japan.

"There's about seventy thousand sailors that come under my purview," he said. "I make sure that they are manned as best as possible to do the missions that they are supposed to be doing."

Marc described the position as "probably about ten times busier than my last job. But it's going to help me in commanding a ship, no doubt about that."

Following his return to duty, both at Dahlgren and San Diego, Marc continued to go for follow-up tests, all of which showed no problems. Those results, plus the fact that he continued to experience no issues with acuity, dizziness, headaches, or his memory, left him hopeful that the matter was behind him and that he could focus on earning the navy's trust to command a ship.

"I haven't had any issues," he said. "I've been maintaining my weight. I've been exercising. No issues with my head. No headaches. All systems normal."

Marc paused.

"In a strange way," he said, "it's almost like nothing's happened."

CHAPTER EIGHTEEN

JOURNEY'S WAY

On Thursday, April 18, 2013, Bryce Powers was moved from the PRC, on the second floor of the main hospital building at McGuire VA Medical Center, where he had been a patient since November 26, 2012.

His destination was only about two hundred yards southwest of the polytrauma unit. Across a spacious courtyard, where Cathy Powers used to take her oldest child in a wheelchair to get some sun and fresh air, was a relatively small, one-story red brick structure. The building houses the Journey's Way Palliative Care Unit, a ten-bed facility that focuses on pain relief for patients with serious—and often life-threatening—conditions.

Bryce was moved into room 108, which had a spacious layout with a long couch, two comfortable armchairs, and a four-foot-high window taking up the entire south wall of the room. Instead of bathing the room in light, however, the family opted to keep the blinds down to within about twelve inches of the bottom of the window, darkening the interior until it was as dark as though nightfall were only minutes away.

The first day Bryce was in Journey's Way, one of the attending physicians came in to check on him—and began sobbing.

"I'm sorry," she told Cathy. "It's just that I have a son, too."

The staff started Bryce on what was described as a typical level of Fentanyl, a powerful narcotic painkiller, but he didn't respond as well as the staff had hoped. The dosage then was incrementally increased until it reached five times the initial level, which finally seemed to bring him some peace.

On Bryce's first night at Journey's Way, his mother, struggling to come to grips with her new surroundings and the pending finality of the process, decided to do something she had not done the entire time her son was up in the polytrauma unit. She crawled into bed with him and held him softly, hoping to provide a measure of comfort in his new surroundings.

It didn't last long.

She had barely gotten settled when he seemed to tense up, letting out a loud, emphatic moan in the process.

"I had never heard that kind of groan from him before," she said. "He never did anything like that."

Within a minute or so, it became evident that her son was uncomfortable, so she got out of bed and eventually walked over to the nearby Fisher House, to the room she had called home for nearly five months, and spent the night there.

The next morning, a Friday, a steady stream of visitors began arriving at room 108. Staff members from the polytrauma unit, relatives, friends—all came to begin saying their goodbyes. The visitors that day included Bryce's best friend from his childhood, who leaned over and told him that he and his wife would name their first child Bryce—regardless of whether it was a boy or a girl.

Cathy Powers, balancing the roles of looking after her son and serving as a hostess to all the visitors, said she was looking forward to Saturday, when her husband, Jim, and daughter, Madi, would make the five-hour drive up from Monroe, North Carolina.

Cathy said she was comforted by the fact that, for now at least, her son seemed at peace. She, on the other hand, had a million thoughts racing through her mind, most of them associated with fear of the unknown and uncertainty over whether she was doing the right thing by honoring her son's wishes.

"I'm so scared," she whispered to a visitor.

The weekend was a rough one on several fronts.

For starters, Jim Powers, a foreman for an electrical contracting company in Jacksonville, North Carolina, had told his supervisor on Friday that while he was at McGuire over the weekend, he would pick up paperwork that would enable him to take an unpaid leave covered by the Family Medical Leave Act (FMLA), a federally mandated program that requires many employers to grant employees up to twelve weeks of unpaid time off for reasons that include taking care of a child with a serious medical condition. The act's terms appeared to apply to Jim's company, but his supervisor was either unfamiliar with the FMLA laws or unwilling to comply with them. Either way, the conversation ended with Jim being told to turn in his company-issued equipment as well as the keys to his company truck.

"So on top of everything that's happening with Bryce," Cathy said, "Jim got fired. I couldn't believe it. I don't understand how this could happen, how they could do that to him at a time like this."

Jim didn't seem as upset as his wife. He took back the finished paperwork from Richmond nonetheless, and his company called the following Monday and said it had all been a misunderstanding. He was not anxious to return to the company anyway, regardless of the circumstances. He had already spoken with local leaders of the International Brotherhood of Electrical Workers, of which he was a member, and the union brass had assured him they would happily place him with another company in the Charlotte, North Carolina, area when he was ready to return to work.

"None of this matters, because I'm where I need to be right here in Richmond now," he said. "All that's not important. I can get a job anywhere. They'll take care of me. Right now, we need to take care of Bryce."

The weekend got off to a rocky start in Richmond as well, when Cathy left her son's room Friday night and walked back to the Fisher House to try to get some sleep. She walked down the hall to her room and got ready to open the door—then stopped cold when she heard an unmistakable sound, one she had heard over and over and over for months now.

It was Bryce, and he was moaning—a painful, long moan that cut straight to his mother's heart. Even though he was in a different building in a different area of the McGuire campus, Cathy's brain was telling her—convincingly—that her son was right there with her at the Fisher House, and he was making his pain loudly known.

Tired, bewildered, exhausted, and frustrated, Cathy kept listening to the moaning until she couldn't take it anymore. She fell softly against the wall and slowly slid down until she was sitting on the floor, the embodiment of an emotionally drained mother who had spent more than six months putting her needs aside to be her comatose son's caregiver. Now the caregiver didn't know what to do or how to respond to what she thought she was so clearly hearing.

So she cried.

"I was a wreck," she said. "It took me a while to compose myself. A good while."

The other trying part of the weekend involved Madi, who was coming to see her big brother, her only sibling, for what would likely be the last time.

Cathy and Jim had a number of reasons for not wanting Madi to join them on an extended vigil at Bryce's bedside in what appeared to be his final days. For starters, there was Madi's schoolwork. She was a gifted student, as evidenced by the fact that she had been cleared to begin taking classes at South Piedmont Community College after her sophomore year of high school, and her first year at South Piedmont was still several weeks from completion. It was an important time for her with finals approaching, and Cathy and Jim wanted her to focus on academics.

There also was concern that, even though she had demonstrated academic prowess beyond what might typically be associated with someone of her age, the simple fact remained that she was still only sixteen years old, and as such, she should be able to engage in age-appropriate activities. For example, she had already made plans to attend a prom with friends on

Saturday, April 27, and her parents thought it important that she be able to experience that.

Then there was the issue of her spending extended periods at her brother's bedside and watching him slowly deteriorate, and what kind of long-term effects such vivid, visual imprints might have on her.

"She's still just a kid," Jim said. "I don't want her last memories of her brother to be bad ones."

So they decided that it was best for Madi to plan on the weekend of April 20 and 21 for her farewell visit with Bryce. The result was, understandably, emotional for everyone.

"There was lots of crying, lots of meltdowns," Cathy said. "It was hard for her to let go when it came time to leave Sunday."

Jim said he and Madi spent a considerable amount of time discussing the dynamics of grief, death, and saying goodbye, not only on the drive up on Saturday but also on their return trip to North Carolina on Sunday.

"We talked a lot—a whole lot," he said. "And you know what? I'm sure we'll continue to talk about it. It's hard. Real hard. She's just a kid. She's a smart kid. But she's still just a kid."

———

On Monday, April 22, after Jim and Madi had returned home, Cathy was alone again with her son, who was nearing the end of his first week without life-sustaining nutrition.

Given the emotional toll of the weekend, as well as the physical changes she was beginning to see in Bryce, Cathy looked exhausted.

"I never realized," she said, "that grief was so physical."

The blinds were still drawn down almost the entire way, keeping her son's room in a darkened, gray state. The grease board just inside the front door to the room, typically reserved for writing down staff telephone contact numbers, information about nurses on duty, or the like, now instead carried a simple, handwritten message:

"One breath here...the next in heaven."

Polytrauma unit staff members kept coming across the courtyard to check on Bryce. Some made the trip several times a day. That group included Dr. Pai, the polytrauma unit's medical director.

Visitors early in the week were greeted by something new in Bryce's room—the sound of peaceful, comforting music coming from a CD player perched on a nightstand beside his bed. Cathy, asked about the music, smiled gently and said a visitor had spent part of his weekend picking out the songs and burning them on the CD. When he had presented the CD to Cathy, the visitor told her—while fighting back tears—that the CD was for her son's journey home.

"Dr. Pai," said Cathy, now on the verge of crying herself, "is an amazing man."

Pai wasn't the only member of the polytrauma staff to demonstrate acts of compassion.

Barbara Bauserman, who oversees the unit's family education program, kept in almost constant contact with Cathy. When Bauserman couldn't make it to the room to visit in person, she would frequently text Cathy just to make sure she was okay. Michael Dardozzi, the speech therapist who had worked so hard and so long with Bryce, trying everything he knew to get him to emerge from the coma, burned a CD for him as well.

Brooke Traylor, one of the nurses on the polytrauma unit, shared a poignant memory with Cathy. Traylor told of how her son's father had died of cancer several years earlier and that in the days before he passed away, she would rub body lotion on his dry skin. After his death, every time Traylor would smell the body lotion—whether she was using it on herself or noticed the scent of it on a passing stranger in a shopping mall or some other public place—it would instantly bring back memories of him. Touched by Traylor's story, Cathy immediately decided to do likewise with her son in his final days—only to discover that the body lotion supplied at Journey's Way was unscented. The finding left Cathy feeling a slight sense of panic because she didn't have a car, so she couldn't drive to a drug store and buy lotion. Several friends with whom she shared the story quickly brought her some scented lotion for her son.

The visitors on Tuesday, April 23—day seven—included another of the many polytrauma nurses who had made it their mission for so many months to create a comfortable environment for Bryce on what they had hoped would be a road to recovery and rehabilitation. On this day, the nurse stood over Bryce's bed in Journey's Way, took the back of her left hand, placed it softly against the left side of his face, and stroked back and forth in the slowest, most gentle possible way for what seemed like an eternity.

"Poor sweet child," she whispered as she turned to walk away.

Cathy and Jim Powers arranged for Madi to stay indefinitely with friends in Monroe, North Carolina, allowing Jim to return to Richmond to join Cathy for the remainder of the bedside vigil.

On Wednesday, April 24—day eight—with the staff at Journey's Way having taken Bryce off Fentanyl and started him on Dilaudid, another powerful narcotic painkiller, Cathy once again decided to try to get in bed with her son. This time, she encountered no resistance at all. So she stayed with him, side by side, for three hours.

"It was so peaceful," she said.

Cathy and Jim went back to the Fisher House that night, sat down in the facility's kitchen, looked at each other—and began crying. Uncontrollably. It wasn't long before everyone else who happened to be in the kitchen and the other common areas on the first floor broke down in tears as well.

"We've all been there for months," Cathy said later, "and it gets to the point where everybody knows everybody. Everybody knew what was happening."

Thursday, April 25—day nine—found Cathy and Jim devoting a portion of the day to funeral arrangements. Several military liaisons came to Journey's Way, and they sat down with the couple in the large family lounge at the facility, just around a corner from Bryce's room, and got on a conference call with more military personnel to map out plans.

There would be a funeral in Monroe, followed by a memorial service at Langley Air Base, the facility roughly a one-hour drive southeast of Richmond that had essentially adopted Bryce after his accident in Japan. Groups of Langley personnel had routinely shown up at Bryce's room in the polytrauma unit every few days to check on Bryce and offer their assistance to his mother. Their presence and support throughout the family's stay in Richmond had meant a great deal to Cathy and Jim, who felt it important to schedule a service at Langley as a way to show their appreciation for all that the people at the base had done for them. Cathy and Jim had a large photograph of Bryce wearing a tuxedo for a high school prom, and they would take the picture with them for the memorial service at Langley.

After the funeral in Monroe, Bryce's body would remain at the local funeral home until it was time to go to his final resting place: Arlington National Cemetery. Because of the volume of burials at Arlington, the nation's most notable military cemetery, military officials told the family it would likely be three to four weeks before a service could be scheduled. Bryce's best friend from the air force had since been reassigned to Aviano Air Base in Italy, but he would be flown to the United States to serve as the escort for Bryce, staying with his comrade's casket on the trip from North Carolina to Arlington, Virginia.

After the long conference call, Cathy went back in to check on her son, who was getting dark rings around his eyes. His face was now showing signs of being more angular and bony than before, and his mother said his skin was becoming dry and tight.

"He's getting the death mask," she said softly. She paused, looked off in the distance and took a deep breath before exhaling slowly. "I'm so scared. I just want this to be over."

The dawn of Friday, April 26—day ten—found Cathy and Jim exactly where they had ended the previous day—in room 108 at Journey's Way. They had planned to go to the Fisher House on Thursday night to sleep, but Bryce appeared to take a turn for the worse, so they stayed with him. He exhibited signs of discomfort overnight, and there were indications in his urine catheter bag that organ failure and severe dehydration were beginning to occur.

Cathy and Jim tried to sleep in shifts, but it was understandably difficult. By the morning, Jim had been able to sleep some, but Cathy had gotten virtually no sleep.

"It was a pretty rough night," Jim said.

By early Friday afternoon, Bryce had become very quiet and seemed to be resting comfortably. His mother curled up on the long couch beside his bed, pulled a blanket over herself, and finally fell asleep. With Cathy resting peacefully by her son's side, her husband went just outside the door to the room and talked with a visitor for more than an hour about a variety of topics, including his last conversation with Bryce.

It was two weeks before the accident, right around the beginning of October, and Bryce had called home for one of his typical check-in conversations with his family. Except this time, he wanted to speak first with Jim about a subject that was anything but typical. He knew that Jim, himself an air force veteran, would understand: Bryce's unit had been told to expect to leave Japan, likely in the first quarter of 2013, for duty in Afghanistan.

"He knew it was always a possibility," Jim said. "Everybody who signs up knows war is always a possibility. But I'll tell you what. He was very frightened about going over there. He even used the word, 'scared.'"

Jim recalled how their conversation ended.

"He said, 'Don't tell Mom.'"

Jim assured him he wouldn't.

Now it appeared Cathy and Jim wouldn't have to worry about Bryce being in harm's way in Afghanistan—or suffering in Richmond. Instead they were about to turn their focus to doing something every parent dreads: burying a child.

First, however, they wanted to do everything they could to make him feel comfortable and loved as he approached the end at Journey's Way.

"We're not going back over to the Fisher House anymore," Jim said. "We're on 24/7 watch here from now on. I don't know how long that will be, but we need to be here."

As it turned out, that watch was not long at all.

———

Dr. Ajit Pai was supposed to pick up his young daughter from her day-care facility by 6:30 that Friday evening, but first he wanted to stop at Journey's

Way and check on the Powers family. So with his duties on the polytrauma unit complete for the week, he left his office about 4:20, walked to one of the distant parking lots at McGuire, got in his car, and drove over to the entrance to the palliative care unit.

Pai walked in the door and headed for room 108, but he was stopped on the way by one of the unit's nurses, who had some questions for him. The two stood and talked for a few minutes near the door to room 108 until Jim came walking out and looked at Pai with tears in his eyes.

"I think he's gone," Jim said. Pai went in and checked, and sure enough, Jim was correct.

Pai stayed with Cathy and Jim for a while, rubbing Cathy's back and trying to offer words of comfort to the two of them until he was sure they would be okay for a few minutes. Then, aware others would want to stop by and pay their respects, he stepped outside and called up to the polytrauma unit.

"Let the team start coming down," he said.

At 6:45 P.M. on Friday, April 26, 2013, Cathy Powers went on to Facebook and posted what was probably the shortest of all the messages she had written to the community of "prayer warriors," a community of what by then had grown to 13,507 people who had rallied around her firstborn child.

Cathy told them that her "sweet, brave, beautiful son" had completed his journey.

When Senior Airman Bryce Powers took his last breath on Earth at 4:40 P.M., his mother was standing to the right side of his bed, closest to the window shades that had now been raised to let in the warm, healing sunshine of a brilliant, calm spring afternoon. Bryce's mother held his right hand and his father stood on the other side of the bed, holding his left hand. Madi, home in Monroe, North Carolina, was on the phone, which had been placed next to her big brother's head.

All three were able to tell him goodbye and tell him they loved him as he passed.

"Bryce knew The Lord, believed He died for his sins, and accepted Him into his heart," Cathy wrote. Her son, she added, was now in a better place.

She thanked the prayer warriors for all their support and then told them she would update them in the future on exact funeral arrangements.

Within twenty-four hours, there were nearly 2,500 comments posted on the page in response to her news.

"Thank you for allowing us all to be on this journey with you," one woman wrote. "Your loss is Heaven's gain."

"Sir," one man wrote, "Airman Powers reporting for duty...."

"Too powerful of an experience to put into words," yet another "warrior" wrote. "I don't even know you but somehow I feel your loss. RIP."

Senior Airman Bryce Powers, born January 9, 1992, died five months to the day after he arrived in Richmond for what was supposed to be a ninety-day program, the end of which had been extended again and again by a compassionate young physician who kept giving his staff more time, giving Bryce more time, giving Powers' family more time.

―――――

Pai called the Rainbow Station day-care facility and asked for their patience, saying he would be a few minutes late picking up his daughter.

Then he walked back up to his office to get a device that would allow him to turn off the Baclofen pump that surgeons had implanted in Bryce a few weeks earlier in an effort to ease his spasticity problems. While in his office, Pai logged on to his computer and went to a program that allowed him to print a certificate that the staff of the polytrauma unit typically gives to patients when they leave.

The certificate read, in part, that an "Honorable Discharge" had been granted to Senior Airman Bryce Powers from the PRC. It read:

You will forever be one of us. Once Polytrauma, Always Polytrauma.

Awarded this 26th day of April, 2013.

Pai went back to Journey's Way, turned off the Baclofen pump, gave Cathy and Jim Powers the certificate, and made sure they were getting answers to their questions about what would happen with their son's body.

Then he drove to Rainbow Station to pick up four-year-old Ayla, whose big brown eyes got even brighter when she saw her father.

"My daughter was so happy," he said, pausing to take a deep breath. "I gave her a big, big hug."

The following Monday morning, Pai wrote an e-mail to the polytrauma staff, again addressing them as "Team" and telling them that their care for Bryce had earned praise from the director of the hospital, praise that Pai wanted to echo.

"The care you provide," Pai wrote, "is exceptional, and your support of families is second to none. The decision about end of life was not an easy one for this family. They reaffirm that this was in accordance with his wishes and they supported him.

"They also wish to express that they will never forget the exemplary care you provided. Please hold your head high with this thought.

"Ajit"

Two days after Bryce Powers died, Cathy and Jim Powers pulled down the half-mile-long driveway at their house in North Carolina.

Cathy was finally home, back at her house for the first time in six and one-half months, a span during which she had missed most of fall, all of winter, and a part of spring. A span during which she had been away from home for Thanksgiving, Christmas, New Year's Day, her son's birthday, and her birthday.

A span during which she and so many others had tried everything they knew to save her firstborn child.

Cathy got out of the car and was met with an emotional embrace by Madi, who needed her mother more than ever. She went inside and got down on the floor in a "dog pile" with the family's five Chihuahuas.

Then she went about the task of finalizing arrangements to hold a funeral for her son—on Mother's Day weekend.

The main hospital building of McGuire Veterans Affairs Medical Center is on a property that covers 112 acres in Virginia's capital of Richmond.

Drs. Shane McNamee (left) and Ajit Pai nurtured the Polytrauma Rehabilitation Center at McGuire into a unit that became an example of teamwork and compassion within the VA's healthcare system.

Spc. Jon McHenry's US Army career began with a stint in South Korea, where he was able to put his considerable basketball skills on display with a university-level team.

Jon and his good friend, Spc. Kurt W. Kern, are shown in 2011 before their unit left Fort Hood, Texas, for a deployment in Afghanistan.

Jon and Kurt mug it up for the camera on Dec. 26, 2011, in Afghanistan. One day later, the blast of an improvised explosive device (IED) on a dark road would leave Kurt dead and Jon gravely injured.

Barbara Bauserman oversees the family education program on Richmond's poly-trauma unit.

Pat Rudd, the polytrauma unit's clinical case manager, helps screen new patients and paves the way for them to make a smooth transition to Richmond.

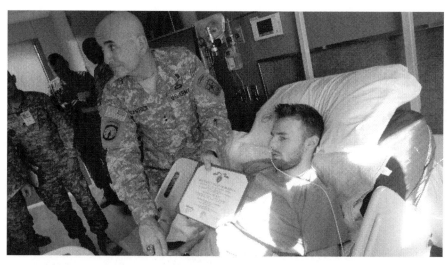

Jon is still heavily sedated when he receives a Purple Heart shortly after his arrival at Walter Reed National Military Medical Center.

Jon's rapid weight loss is evident when his younger brother, Bryan, and his father, David, visit him early in his stay at Richmond.

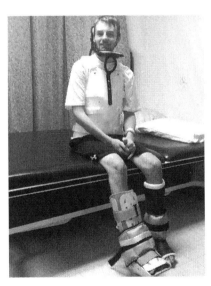

Sitting in a physical therapy studio at Richmond, Jon presents a stark portrait of how far he has to go to get his weight and muscle mass back to the levels that made him a finely tuned athlete and military policeman.

Jon and his wife, Jay, in room 110 at Richmond's polytrauma unit, where they used a spare bed to hold get-well gifts. On the wall behind them is a poster for a benefit basketball game held in his honor at Newport High School.

Bryce Powers walks among the graves at Arlington National Cemetery while on a trip to Washington, DC, and its environs during his senior year of high school.

Michael Dardozzi, one of the speech-language pathologists on the polytrauma unit, spent a considerable amount of time working with Bryce Powers.

Brooke Traylor, a nurse, started her second stint on the polytrauma unit in September 2012.

Luis and Claudia Avila decorated a tree and celebrated Christmas with their three sons at Fort Hood, Texas, in November 2011 because they knew he was about to be deployed to Afghanistan.

On June 9, 2012, Jon returns to room 110 at Richmond's polytrauma unit, this time to visit Luis, his commanding officer.

David and Jon dote on the newest McHenry: Leo, born May 12, 2012, at Walter Reed National Military Medical Center.

J.T. Magee, a kinesiotherapist, and Monique Jones, a speech-language pathologist, pause in the halls of the polytrauma unit.

Jon is nearly back to his old weight and has used an aggressive, sometimes twice-daily workout regimen to regain muscle mass by mid-September 2012, less than nine months after the IED blast, when he visits Kurt's grave at Rio Grande Valley State Veterans Cemetery in Mission, Texas.

Jay, Jon and Leo in the back yard of their home in Copperas Cove, Texas, near Fort Hood.

Alison B. Conley, one of the polytrauma unit's occupational therapists, enjoys a late fall day on the hospital's south courtyard.

Keneshia T. Thornton, a social work case manager on the polytrauma unit, works closely with Bill Haneke, a cofounder and board member of Families of the Wounded Fund Incorporated.

Cathy Powers' visit to her son's grave at Arlington National Cemetery in mid-December 2013 brings a pleasant surprise: Volunteers with Wreaths Across America have placed Christmas wreaths at some 143,000 headstones in the cemetery.

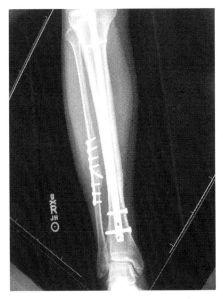

An X-ray shows a long plate and screws that were used to stabilize Jon's right fibula during surgery in Texas on Feb. 1, 2013, as well as the long titanium rod and screws that surgeons at Walter Reed had used more than a year earlier to stabilize his right tibia.

"My little buddy" is how Pai frequently refers to his daughter, Ayla.

CHAPTER NINETEEN

ALISON CONLEY

The smooth plastic device was shaped like a tube, open on both ends and designed to be wide enough to easily slip over someone's foot. It had two sections of soft rope, each about three feet long, attached to one end of the tube.

As her patient sat on the side of his bed and watched intently, Alison B. Conley slipped a red wool sock over one of the ends of the tube, pulling it almost up to where the two sections of rope were attached on the other end. Then she set the device on the floor in front of the patient's bare left foot, handed him the tips of the two ropes, and smiled.

From there, he knew what to do.

Slowly, almost haltingly, he used the ropes to slide the open end of the tube toward the front of his toes. Then he gently and methodically pulled the contraption over his foot, easing it all the way back toward his ankle. When the sock was over his foot, he tugged a bit harder on the ropes and the plastic frame slid away, leaving the sock exactly where it was supposed to be.

He let out a small laugh.

"Hey, that's a pretty neat trick there!" he told Conley.

Just like that, Conley had helped another patient at McGuire's poly-trauma unit move one step closer to independence—a patient who, in this case, was unable to bend down but now had the means to put on his own socks nonetheless.

Conley is one of the staff's occupational therapists, a job for which she spent six years in college on the way to earning a specialized master's degree. However, she prefers to look at her education—and her duties with the poly-trauma unit—in simple terms.

"I got my degree," she said, "in common sense and problem solving."

The device she has used this day, called a Sock Aid, is among a seemingly endless supply of contraptions that Conley and the rest of the staff have at their disposal to help ease the path for patients on the road to recovery and rehabilitation. There are countless closets on the unit filled with various de-vices designed to help patients in myriad circumstances, and what won't fit in the closets is stored in boxes that are piled against the walls. Although many of the assistance devices may look complicated, their purpose is simple—and, most important, vital.

"I wish I had invented it," Conley told her grateful patient as he marveled at how the Sock Aid could make life so easy for someone who was unable to bend over and reach his own foot.

"Although," she added, "if I would have invented it, then I wouldn't be here because I would be rich. And then I wouldn't have gotten to meet you and work with you and help you."

Help.

It is the one common need of every patient who passes through the doors of the unit. Whether it is help regaining consciousness; learning to walk, swallow, or talk again; regaining mobility; or relearning such simple tasks as how to bathe themselves or dress themselves, the patients rely on Conley and her coworkers to provide sensible solutions. Like so many oth-ers on the unit, Conley is young, highly motivated, driven, and dedicated. Those qualities make her a good fit in a place where everyone seems to share a common bond of energy focused on doing everything possible to help their patients succeed.

"There's such a good group here," Conley said. "Nobody really leaves. There's not really a reason to."

Conley grew up in suburban Richmond and then enrolled at Temple University, where she spent a year right out of high school before deciding she maybe wasn't ready to devote her energies to college. A year in Florida followed, and then came another year back in Richmond, where she worked at a Blockbuster video store before going back to school, this time at VCU.

Conley knew her second stint in college would have to be more focused. She would need to get a degree that would land her in a job she could parlay into a satisfying career. The medical field attracted her, and by a process of slow, methodical elimination, she wound up settling on occupational therapy (OT), which not only helps patients develop life skills but also gives the occupational therapists enough variety and challenges to avoid getting stuck in a rut.

"It's never really the same thing every day," Conley said. "Sure, a lot of the things you do are the same, but the patients never are. They all have their own unique challenges."

While in VCU's OT program, which combined three years of undergraduate work with three years of graduate school for a master's degree, Conley was first exposed to McGuire VA Medical Center through a semester-long student internship at the hospital. When she got out of VCU, a job opened up at McGuire's spinal cord unit, and she spent a year there before joining the staff of the polytrauma unit, which was then still in its infancy.

At age twenty-eight, Conley was home, and in 2013, six years later, she was in no hurry to leave.

"I just feel confident in OT," she said, "because so much of it is common sense."

———

Even though McGuire's polytrauma unit quickly established itself as a leader in the field of TBI treatment, making it a popular landing place for wounded warriors returning from Afghanistan, the hospital remained what its name implies—a VA facility. So even when the winter months hit Afghanistan and snow and other rough weather slowed the pace of casualties, McGuire continued to stay busy. That meant the polytrauma unit sometimes became home for retired service men whose problems were unrelated to battlefield injuries.

Such was the case one Tuesday afternoon in late January 2013, when Alison Conley had back-to-back hour-long OT sessions with retired soldiers who were both coming off surgery.

The first was with a sixty-eight-year-old man whose complications with diabetes had necessitated surgery three weeks earlier to have his right leg amputated at midthigh. The patient was undergoing dialysis three times a week and was experiencing problems with his left leg as well. In addition, he had heart problems, poor balance, and his strength, mobility, and flexibility were limited. His mobility was so limited, in fact, that bending down to put a sock and shoe on his left foot was essentially impossible. So Conley showed him how to use the Sock Aid. Then she produced a shoehorn that was identical to one used by able-bodied people, except instead of being perhaps five or six inches long, it was about two feet long. Thus Conley's patient, who was unable to bend over and reach his foot with his hands, could simply take the long shoehorn, wedge the rounded tip under the sock on the back of his ankle, and slide it off his foot.

After that, Conley showed him a shoe that had a Velcro flap on top instead of laces. He could take a so-called reacher—a popular kitchen device featuring a claw-like clamp on one end of a steel rod and a trigger handle grip on the other to help govern the opening and closing of the clamp—and use it to set the shoe on the floor by his left foot. After he slid his foot into the open shoe, he could take the reacher again, close the clamp and use the clamp to push down on the Velcro flap until it securely fastened atop the shoe.

Once again, Conley was able to provide a common-sense solution to a real-life problem.

"If your hands work good," she told the patient, "we can find ways to get to your feet."

The patient's wife was petite and unable to lift him, so Conley devoted time to showing him how to use a tub bench in a shower. She also showed the couple how to set up their shower for maximum efficiency. However, because the patient was married and his wife was able and willing to cook for him, Conley saw no need to devote time to showing him how to fend for himself in the kitchen.

"If it's not important to someone to make their own meals, then we shouldn't address that," Conley said. "We're here to tailor everything we do to each patient's needs. It's important to be helpful, but if we're not giving them what they need, then that's not really helpful."

The one-hour session over, Conley went from that patient's room to the room of another army retiree, this one recovering from a fall and subsequent surgery to repair two fractured vertebrae in his neck. This patient was progressing well in his recovery and, now using a walker to get around, was within a week of being released from the hospital. Unlike the previous patients, this one was not married, so he needed to be able to do his own cooking. Conley had him walk out of the polytrauma unit, down the hall, and into an elevator, which they rode down to the first floor of the hospital and a large OT patient work room.

One wall of the room is adorned with a framed sign that says: "Occupational Therapy. Skills For The Job Of Living." The rest of the walls are lined with floor-to-ceiling closets that store the tools of the occupational therapists' trade. There are splints of various sizes and shapes, electrical stimulation devices to help promote finger movement, and different sizes and types of plastic containers that are designed to test a patient's ability to open and close them, Several closets are dedicated to the Velcro clothing that is so vital to those recovering from fractured limbs and amputations. The clothes provide ease of function and form and, more important, they provide a measure of dignity.

Much storage space is devoted to such items as foam tubing, which can be shaped into widened handles that help those with weak grips or lost fingers gain an easier hold on kitchen utensils or other everyday items. The kitchen supplies include cereal bowls with suction-bottom grips, designed to make it easier for someone with the use of just one arm to eat without having to worry about a bowl sliding all over a table. Among the utensils are rounded wooden handles attached atop half-moon-shaped knife blades. Someone who doesn't have the strength or gripping ability to use a "sawing" motion on a piece of meat, for example, can simply grab one of these knives by the handle, put the device on top of the piece of meat, and rock it back and forth to cut his or her food.

"So much of what we work on in the kitchen," Conley said, "is just to give you that independence of being able to feed yourself and that feeling of not being a baby who needs help all the time. Let's face it: Being able to feed yourself is a pretty basic thing."

One area is devoted to those patients who might be looking to return to work in industrial trades, and it includes such machines as a drill press, a miter saw, and other woodworking devices. The area next to that is where Conley was headed with her latest patient. They were going to give him a test run of sorts in the room's full-fledged kitchen, which includes everything from countertop appliances, storage cabinets, utensils, and cookware to a sink, stove, oven, refrigerator, and microwave.

The patient was scheduled to be sent home in a matter of days, so Conley had him in the kitchen to essentially confirm that he could make his way around the room, prepare a meal, and clean up afterward, even with a walker. She had him describe the layout of his kitchen at home to make sure there wouldn't be any problems that might require some special work before he left McGuire. Satisfied that there weren't any problems, the two went through the process of making sure he could gather cookware, gather food, prepare it, and so on.

With that finished, the two went to a different area of the work room. They spent some time making sure he was developing sufficient strength and dexterity in his hands and fingers to accomplish such everyday tasks as cooking. Conley's exercises for him included taking a glob of putty and rolling it into a ball by using an open palm against the putty while it sat atop a table. With that task accomplished, she had him try to flick off small pieces of the putty ball using one finger at a time. Then she had him roll the ball of putty into the shape of a hot dog. She ended the exercise by having him pinch the hot dog into sections, first using his thumb and index finger and then his thumb and middle finger.

Her next task was to bring out a square wooden rack that had several horizontal wooden wires. On each wire was a group of colored clothespins. The colors on each wire corresponded to varying degrees of tension in the clothespins. Conley had him start with a medium-strength tension set of clothespins and squeeze them hard enough to pull them off one wire and move them to another. He repeated the exercise two more times, concluding it by successfully tackling the highest-tension set of clothespins.

"Look at you, Muscles!" Conley said, prompting him to break into a smile. "Do you remember doing these last week and how much trouble you had? You're doing great."

Although many of the tasks and therapies are individualized based on a patient's needs and level of function, there are ways to gauge and compare the progress of one person against that of another. For instance, the therapists have what amounts to a standardized test that in reality is nothing more than a plastic tray with nine holes and nine pegs that fit into those holes. The loose pegs are placed in a storage area in one corner of the tray, and patients must take the pegs and place them in the holes. The results of the timed test can then be used to chart a patient's progress over the course of weeks and months.

On this day, the way Conley's patient functioned in the kitchen and with the putty and clothespins confirmed that he was making solid progress and was well on his way to once again becoming independent. Conley had him take a seat and offered him a drink of water while he rested for a few minutes. As a reward for his hour of hard work, she pushed him back to his room in a wheelchair while a visitor carried his walker. Once back in his room, he got out of the wheelchair, settled into bed, and warmly thanked her.

"You're very welcome," she said.

It was Conley's final therapy session of the day, and she headed back to take care of some reports and other necessary paperwork. Her office is a cramped, narrow, windowless room that is also home to one other occupational therapist, two kinesiotherapists, and a speech therapist.

No one, however, is complaining.

"It's a real team here," Conley said. "People get along here because we all know why we're here. We want to be here and we know what the goal is."

She shrugged and smiled, satisfied with once again having made a difference for her patients by providing them with common-sense solutions to everyday problems.

"OT, it's life," she said. "It's what you take for granted. But it's also what you do every day."

CHAPTER TWENTY

THE LONG SUMMER

Feeling and looking better by the day and making impressive gains in his sharply focused quest to add weight, muscle mass, and cardiovascular endurance, Jon McHenry seemed to be on an irreversible fast track back to Afghanistan as the summer of 2012 began.

Perhaps too fast, his father wondered, as his son prepared to leave Walter Reed National Military Medical Center in early July and head back to Fort Hood, Texas, for what Jon hoped would be a brief stay before being flown back to rejoin his comrades in the war-torn nation's Paktia province. Although Jon made no attempt to hide his zeal for succeeding in his bid to come back from devastating injuries, David McHenry found it hard to contain his concern for the rapid pace of events.

Could appearances be deceiving? Could what everyone was seeing be too good to be true?

David said he was surprised to hear about the progress Jon said he was making on a treadmill in his physical therapy sessions at Bethesda: from merely stepping gingerly at first, to walking, then to running, and then finally to running at a pace of ten minutes per mile.

When David was around his son, he noticed that Jon would go down staircases by turning to his right and leading with his left leg—the one without the titanium rod in it. It was a stair-descending method Jon had been taught in physical therapy in Richmond when he was first learning to walk again and his right leg was still weak and painful. Months later, however, it was a curious dynamic for someone who had regained his ability to run. Moreover, it was one that left David wondering if his son might be hurting more physically than he was willing to admit.

"He's the type of kid that if he does have pain like that, he's not going to let you know," David said. "He'll just try to suck it up."

That wasn't all. Sometimes it almost appeared as though Jon's recovery and rehabilitation, while surprisingly successful from a physical standpoint in such a short period of time, was not without emotional scars.

David McHenry noted that even though many people had taken the time to send Jon a card, or a letter, or a gift to thank him for his service and wish him a speedy recovery, his son seemed to show little interest in acknowledging those gestures by responding with even brief thank-you notes. David said he had repeatedly encouraged Jon to make time to write thank-you notes, with no success. It seemed Jon was intent on putting the IED blast chapter of his life behind him as fast as possible, no matter the emotional cost to him or those around him. Physically, he was doing everything possible to get his body back to fighting form. Emotionally, the results appeared less conclusive.

David was particularly troubled by an incident that occurred in early July, right before Jon left Maryland to go back to Fort Hood.

Jon had gone home to Newport to see his family one last time. While he was there, he took a supply of large plastic garbage bags into his bedroom on the second floor of the family's red brick Cape Cod-style home and began purging his past.

Football jerseys. Basketball jerseys. Trophies. Commendations. All were placed in trash bags for disposal.

"He loaded up thirteen, fourteen bags of garbage and threw everything away," David said. "Every picture, every poster in his room except a few things that I made him keep."

According to his father, Jon went about the process in a dispassionate manner. The exercise seemed to have the opposite effect on David.

"It brought tears to my eyes," he said. "It was almost like he was breaking off a part of his life."

He tried to talk to Jon and persuade him to hold on to the mementos.

"He really wouldn't go into it," he said. "He said he wanted to just throw everything out. I don't know if it was him changing from his high school room to his manhood or what. I ended up making him keep some things, but not much. It's pretty much all gone."

Jon later said there was no particular significance to that day's events and that it was not indicative of any attempt to put his childhood behind him. Instead it was merely an example of him perhaps not assigning the same sentimental value to objects from his past that his father might.

"It wasn't anything in a negative way or anything," Jon said. "It really wasn't. I was just trying to help out. I made that mess over the years with all that stuff in my room, and I figured it was time to clean it out."

Jon said that in addition to cleaning out some of his pee wee football trophies and other memorabilia from his childhood, he offered some of his old clothes to his younger brother. If his brother didn't want the clothes and they weren't fit for donation, he put them in trash bags for disposal.

"There was other stuff that really needed to go, when you get right down to it. I mean, some of that stuff was nasty. I threw out the tail from the first squirrel that I killed when I was hunting from when I was like nine years old," he said. "My dad got all upset, and I said, 'Dad, it's a freakin' dried up squirrel tail.' I mean, I killed plenty of squirrels over the years.

"So yeah, I pretty much cleaned the room out. But I think he kind of took it the wrong way."

A few days after the bedroom cleanout, Jon was back in Bethesda. He packed his belongings in his Honda sedan and began the twenty-five-hour drive to Texas, which he hoped would be his final stop on his way back to Afghanistan. Back in Newport, Pennsylvania, his father was left to ponder the whirlwind sequence of events that had begun on December 27 in Afghanistan and now, less than seven months later, had his son seemingly on his way back to rejoining his unit, leaving his wife and two-month-old son behind.

When Jon McHenry had announced on his Facebook page that he wanted to make it back to Afghanistan, David had regarded it as a motivational tool, a way for him to stay focused on his rehabilitation.

"That, to me, was just a goal to him," David said. "I figured he just wanted a goal. I figured he just wanted to get out of Bethesda."

Was he really and truly physically capable of returning to a war zone, or were there lingering issues? Was his TBI a thing of the past, or could there be repercussions down the road? Could it manifest itself later in life in some form that no one could predict at this stage? What was his emotional state?

All of these questions had David fighting the issue of whether it was worth it for his son to rejoin his unit in Afghanistan for a relatively short period of time—all in the name of proving that it could be done and that he was worthy of resuming his duties.

"He's my son, and of course, I love him. I respect him. I support him. I always want him to be happy, to be successful in life. But there's another side to it, too," David said. "You gave enough for your country. And now you have a baby to think about. I try to understand his viewpoint, but man, it's tough. He's talking about going back for two months' time."

——————

On the morning of July 19, in the bedroom of his new home in Killeen, Texas, Jon McHenry slipped into his camouflage US Army fatigues, a standard work uniform with the American flag just below his right shoulder and the name "McHENRY" emblazoned in bold black lettering on his right breast pocket.

Jon said goodbye to his wife and son, walked out the door of their home, and did something that would have seemed unthinkable 206 days earlier, when his seventeen-ton vehicle had been airborne in Afghanistan in a horrifying blast that had severely injured him, Capt. Luis Avila, and Spc. Michael Crawford and had killed three of their comrades. After months of surgeries and countless hours of hard, painful work by himself and a small army of physicians, therapists, and other medical professionals, Jon got in his car and drove to work at Fort Hood.

"Total new outlook and respect for this thing," he wrote on his Facebook page that day, under a picture he posted of himself wearing his uniform and staring at the camera with a sharp, no-nonsense look. However, Jon quickly discovered that Fort Hood was a world away from Afghanistan, and the same was true of his job duties.

"They didn't have anything for me to do," he said. "I had no job title. I sat in the operations office with two other people. So I would go in at nine o'clock, hang out, go to lunch at like eleven thirty or so, then at two thirty drink a protein shake, go work out, and then go home."

Although his reintroduction to active-duty army life was anything but fulfilling, life at home was the opposite. Jon was able to settle into a comfort zone with Jay and their new son, enjoying life in their three-bedroom, two-bath, two-car-garage home with a nice backyard in a safe neighborhood. As July stretched into August, however, Jon began to think that the army was stalling his return to Afghanistan. His frustration grew.

"I was getting a little discouraged because they wouldn't give me anything to do," he said. "I couldn't do anything except wear a uniform and play on the computer."

So instead of waiting for the slow-moving medical machine at Fort Hood to get around to him and give him a chance to prove himself physically fit to rejoin his unit, Jon took matters into his own hands. He started calling around to arrange an appointment with a doctor in hopes of getting the final paperwork signed and getting himself on a plane to Afghanistan. On August 14, Jon went in to see the doctor and sat patiently while the physician read through his file.

"He said, 'You're my first patient with something that severe,'" Jon recalled. The doctor checked his reflexes, range of motion, and strength and asked him plenty of questions throughout.

"I told him, 'I'm ready to go back to full duty,'" he said. "I can wear armor, carry a weapon, fire a weapon, stuff like that."

The doctor scheduled a September 7 follow-up appointment and told him that if he continued to exhibit no physical problems, he would be cleared for Afghanistan. Jon, already driven, now had even more motivation.

"I busted my ass for three weeks," he said.

He had been transferred to a different office on the base, but he still found the work unchallenging. He began coming to Fort Hood daily at 6:30 A.M. for a workout before starting his job duties. After his job ended at 4:30 each afternoon, he would work out again before going home for the evening.

It worked. The physical fitness requirements included minimum numbers of pushups and sit-ups as well as a time of sixteen minutes, thirty seconds or better for completing a run on a two-mile course on the base. He ran the course every two or three days, eventually getting his time down to less than sixteen minutes—a pace of less than eight minutes per mile.

The improvements didn't come without some pain. Jon said he experienced some soreness in his knees as well as pain in his right lower leg, where the titanium rod is secured with several screws.

"It was tough. But I just had to kind of break myself in," he said. "I feel a little achy after I run two to three miles, but it's not like I can't get out of bed or anything."

———

On September 7, 2012, Jon McHenry walked into the Thomas Moore Medical Clinic, which houses Fort Hood's Soldier Medical Readiness Center, for the follow-up appointment that he hoped would finally clear him for a return to Afghanistan to join his unit for the remainder of their deployment.

He left carrying a signed memorandum, the subject of which was "Fitness For Duty/Deployment For Active Duty Soldier." The memo confirmed that he had been medically evaluated at the clinic that day, and it offered three check-off boxes underneath to classify his status as a result of the evaluation.

One box, which was unchecked, said the evaluee was unfit to return to duty short term but, with medical treatment, would be fit to return within sixty days.

Another box, also unchecked, said the evaluee was not fit to return to duty long term and would be unlikely to be so for at least four months.

Instead, the doctor had placed a check mark in the box beside the section that said the evaluee was fit for duty, had met the army's retention standards, "and is deployable." Below that, in a box reserved for diagnosis comments, the doctor had written: "Multiple trauma—healed up." In another box reserved for medical treatment comments, the doctor had written: "No further."

The letter was signed and dated, and as far as Jon was concerned, it meant he was home free. After all these months, after all the surgeries, after all the rehabilitation, after all the hard work on the part of so many people, he had validation in the form of a piece of paper that said, quite simply, he was back—all the way back.

"I've done my part," he said. "Now get me a flight back over there."

Even though Jon had hoped for medical clearance, he had not expected it to come in such convincing fashion, in a letter with such no-nonsense wording that seemed to erase any possible doubts about his fitness for duty in Afghanistan. Yet as strong as the doctor's memo seemed to be, an inescapable fact was that the clock was ticking. Jon's unit was less than three months from leaving Afghanistan and returning home, and he knew there was little time to waste. If he was going to rejoin the unit, it needed to happen in relatively short order.

"After today, I'm pretty confident it's going to happen," he said. "If I go back there, it's just like giving a big middle finger to the insurgents. It's like saying, 'Look, you'll never break us.'"

CHAPTER TWENTY-ONE

MONIQUE JONES

Like many of the staff members in the PRC at McGuire VA Medical Center, Monique Jones has a small, windowless office.

Few, however, have one as neat and organized as Jones, a speech-language pathologist—speech therapist, in layman's terms—whose work space doubles as a room where she sees patients for their one-hour appointments.

Whether they arrive in a wheelchair or can walk in on their own, the patients come to an office that is tidy and almost completely lacking in personal effects, save for such items as a few photographs of Jones' teenage son and daughter.

However, the neatness does not extend to a pink plastic tub and a gray plastic toolbox that sit on a bookcase along one of the office walls.

The tub and toolbox are both crammed full with what appears to be a totally random collection of junk. You'll find items such as hand bells, a whistle, marbles, sponges, a flashlight, a package of cigarettes sealed in a plastic bag, a fluorescent green tennis ball, nasal swabs, scissors, ground coffee in a plastic bag, a plastic jar of crushed red pepper, another plastic jar with garlic, and a small mirror. When a curious visitor went through the items in the plastic containers and quizzically focused on the mirror, Jones smiled. As is so often the case with the professionals on the polytrauma unit staff, what appears to be meaningless is anything but.

In this case, all the "junk" amounts to tools that Jones uses in the recovery of so-called EC patients, the polytrauma unit staff's slang for emerging consciousness patients, those who arrive in either a comatose or semicomatose state.

"That's one of the first things we do with EC patients when they first emerge," Jones said, referring to the small mirror. "They like to follow themselves.... They just keep tracking their movements in the mirror."

The other items in Jones' tub and toolbox come into play even before a patient emerges, because even though Jones is technically a speech-language pathologist, her therapy can begin not only before a patient speaks, but also—in the case of a comatose patient——before he or she even regains consciousness.

Many of the items are used to stimulate comatose patients as part of the process to help them emerge. The spices, cigarettes, and ground coffee, for example, might elicit a reaction when placed under the patient's nose. Other examples include the ringing of a bell, the shrill shriek of a whistle, the beam of a flashlight that is scanned across the patient's face, or the placement of a pair of scissors in the patient's hand. Add all that together and still you will have only a small percentage of the tools employed to determine the state of a comatose patient.

Jones, in fact, uses the container items when she is putting patients through a "Coma Recovery Scale" examination, a test that includes twenty-nine specific grades across six topics: auditory function, visual function, motor function, verbal function, communication, and arousal. As patients begin to emerge, other tests are available that can measure their progress. For example, patients' eye movement and cognitive abilities can be graded by whether they can respond to commands to look at certain objects and look in certain directions. Likewise, their limb movement can be graded by their ability to respond to commands to touch or kick certain items, and their vocal ability can be measured by their response to commands to use their tongue and say certain words.

As a patient emerges, the polytrauma unit staff gets a better idea of how to tailor his or her individual therapy program. In the case of Jones and the rest of the speech therapists, much of that work is guided by whether the patient can swallow, speak, and see. Those three areas can be significantly hindered in TBI patients, many of whom suffer strokes as a result of their injuries and are left with significant related physical deficits.

That's a substantial change from the type of patients Jones was working with when she began her speech pathology career. She spent four years in the private sector at a Richmond-area hospital where she focused on elderly patients, most of whom had respiratory issues or stroke-related problems. Many of her patients suffered from myriad health issues and seemed difficult to motivate; they often told her they were resigned to the likelihood that their lives were approaching an end.

She has no such motivational issues at McGuire, where she came in early 2006 after a colleague suggested she would be a perfect fit working with TBI patients in McGuire's polytrauma unit. The unit was then in its infancy, but it was growing by leaps and bounds and was constantly looking to add skilled specialists to its staff.

"I love it. I love working with the young guys. You don't have to put on that cheerleader persona," she said. "They still have all these dreams. They still want to accomplish things. They still have their lives in front of them. So many of them want to still go back to their unit and fight again."

Jones recalled being initially intimidated a bit when she arrived at McGuire, especially considering that her speech pathology colleagues were sent out of the state on business during her first week of work, leaving her to figure out on her own how to test and start working with two newly arrived patients, both of whom were comatose—a new challenge for Jones. As it turned out, the colleagues deliberately didn't offer Jones much guidance, electing instead to see if she could determine the best course of action.

"It was definitely a learning process," Jones said. "But I remember when they got back and saw what I had done with the two patients, they said, 'Wow, that was your test, Monique. You figured it out.'

"Now, I love seeing that process from where they're doing very little to the next week they're doing a little more, and the next week they're doing this and that—and eventually they wake up," she said. "It is very, very rewarding."

With the rewards, however, come some frustrations as well. Not all patients recover completely, and not all show steady progress. In one case, the patient not only didn't seem to be on a fast track to either a full or consistent recovery, but he also presented the staff with a completely unique perspective, one that hit close to home for all of them.

For all the exposure of the staff to soldiers wounded in combat, vehicle collisions, or falls at home or stricken by medical-related strokes or other serious problems, this dedicated team of healers had been able to count on one common bond: the patients coming before them were always either active-duty or retired service members.

Bruce Wallace broke that mold.

When the staff at McGuire first heard in early June 2012 that Bruce would be coming to the polytrauma unit, it hit hard for many of them—for the simple reason that he was one of their own. Bruce Wallace was one of the healers, and now he needed his comrades' help.

"Look, we all put our best foot forward for every one of these patients. That's what makes coming to work here so special. This is as dedicated a group as you'll find anywhere," said one unit staff member. "But we'd all be lying if we said we didn't root just a little harder for him. It's only human nature."

Bruce's name hit hard for the staff at McGuire because he is an internist—a gastroenterologist—at Walter Reed National Military Medical Center, the suburban Washington, DC, hospital with which the Richmond facility works so closely. At least, Bruce *had been* an internist at Walter Reed—until May 17, 2012.

That was the day the extremely active doctor, a former collegiate swimmer, triathlete, and still an avid runner and bicyclist, crashed his road bike while riding home from work on a beautiful spring day when the temperature reached seventy-three degrees in Bethesda, Maryland.

The crash occurred when his bicycle struck a large metal plate that crews had placed on the road surface to cover a hole at a construction site. The impact of the bicycle against the heavy plate snapped the front wheel from the bike's front fork and threw Bruce over the handlebars. The fact that he was wearing a helmet didn't make up for his awkward and violent landing on the concrete road surface.

Thirty percent of his brain stem was severed.

When Bruce arrived at McGuire on June 13, he was still in a coma, and in the months after he regained consciousness, he did little to inspire confidence in his ability to recover and return to his life as a respected physician—a man so academically gifted that he had graduated early from the Massachusetts Institute of Technology before turning his attention to medical school at Temple University.

————

The bicycle accident that caused Bruce's stroke resulted in what was being called *severe left neglect.* Put simply, he had little use of the left side of his body from his head to his toes. The passage of several months, which often proves so vital a component in the healing process, did not seem to be helping in his case, at least not as much as the staff and his family had hoped. They all worked with him tirelessly, but he continued to have a great deal of difficulty generating any kind of significant progress on his left side.

"He just misses everything on that side unless you cue him," Jones said.

It was a sunny afternoon in late October, nearly four months after the accident, and Bruce was getting ready for another of his five-day-a-week, one-hour sessions with Jones. She would spend the first half of the session essentially just asking questions designed to test his cognitive abilities, and the second half would be devoted to trying to strengthen his comprehension. Before the session, Jones told a visitor that Bruce would likely demonstrate periods in which he struggled mightily, balanced against periods in which his intelligence and sharp wit would emerge.

It didn't take long for Jones' words to ring true. Bruce, dressed in a tee shirt from a five-kilometer race, running sweat pants, and running shoes, arrived at her office in a wheelchair pushed by his sister.

"Good afternoon, Doctor, good to see you again," Jones began. "How are you today?"

Bruce didn't hesitate.

"I guess," he said in a flat voice, "that's what we're going to try to find out."

With that, Jones asked him a series of basic questions, ones she asked him at the outset of every session. Some days, he would respond better than others. This day was one of his better ones.

"Doctor, do you know what happened and why you are here?"

"Bicycle accident."

"What is your job?"

"G.I."

"Where do you live?"

"Silver Spring, Maryland."

"When were you born?"

"November. No, March 5, 1950."

"And how old are you?"

"Sixty-two."

After the session, Jones explained that Bruce would often give conflicting answers about his age and would periodically tell her that he was not married and that he had four children when, in fact, he *was* married and had three children, including his son, Teddy, a Gettysburg College student who at the time was spending a semester studying in China. His family members visited him at McGuire often, with the exception of Teddy, who had recently begun conducting Internet video conferences with his father via Skype.

Jones, remembering that Bruce had told her in a recent session about being able to speak with Teddy via the Internet, asked him a question about that subject.

"Tell me one thing Teddy is doing in China," Jones said.

Again, Bruce did not hesitate.

"Figuring out Skype," he said.

"Tell me a joke."

"You're looking at it."

However, the sharp wit and strong memory that Bruce demonstrated in the verbal portion of the session could not be duplicated when it came to the visual tasks that Jones presented to him.

She began by showing him pictures of objects and asking him to tell her what they were. Because of Bruce's severe left neglect, he often had difficulty with this exercise. He could not instinctively or effectively track the objects the entire way over to the left side of the page, even when Jones would tell him specifically that he needed to go two more words or three more letters to his left.

The first picture she showed him was an orange.

"Tell me what this is," she said.

He hesitated for a few seconds.

"Football."

"Frame the picture all the way over, Doctor," Jones said as she flipped to the next picture, this one of a round wall clock.

Bruce studied the image for a few seconds.

"Tachometer," he said.

"Okay," she said, smiling.

The next card had two pictures. At the top was a photograph of a computer monitor, a keyboard, and a hard drive tower. At the bottom was a coffee table. Jones pointed to the top.

"Computer," Bruce said. Then she pointed to the table at the bottom of the card.

"Computer," Bruce said again.

"Frame the picture all the way over," she replied.

He hesitated and cocked his head as if to get a better peripheral view.

"Computer," he said again.

"Try again. Frame it. Trace the outline with your finger if you have to," Jones said. Bruce dragged his crooked right index finger slowly around the perimeter of the table, hesitated, and then spoke.

"Computer."

"Okay," Jones said. "Let's move on to something else."

The next part of the session was devoted to a different set of cards, this one a series of sentences that needed to be finished.

The first card read: "A cup of _____."

Bruce looked at it and blurted out: "Forks."

"Try again," Jones said.

"Spoons."

"Try again."

"Juice. A cup of juice."

"Good," Jones said. "Let's keep going."

The next card read: "Shirt and _____."

"Start and stop," Bruce said.

"Try again."

"Shirt and shoes."

"Excellent," Jones said.

When she held up a card that said, "Make sure you bring your _____.", Bruce struggled with several responses, then answered, "Make sure you bring your shovel."

Jones, smiling, responded: "Make sure you bring your shovel? What are we doing?"

Again, Bruce didn't hesitate.

"Digging up sand."

"At the beach?"

"Yes. I love the beach."

Jones showed him one more card: "Put the dishes in the _____."

"Put the fish in the frying pan," he answered.

"Try again."

Bruce hesitated for what seemed like thirty seconds, his head appearing to droop toward the end of the long pause.

"Put the dishes in the water," he finally said.

"Doctor, are you tired? Do you want to stop for the day?"

"Yes," he said softly, and with that, Jones ended the scheduled sixty-minute session, thirty-nine minutes after it had begun.

"There's always tomorrow," she told him.

"This was actually a good one," she said later. "Some days, when he's struggling, he doesn't even make it that long."

CHAPTER TWENTY-TWO

THE GOOD DOCTOR

The way Helen Wallace saw it, she had every reason to be optimistic.

Granted, her husband's bicycle accident had left him far from being able to walk again, let alone return to work as a gastroenterologist at Walter Reed National Military Medical Center. From her perspective, however, he had been down this road of traumatic injury before and emerged okay, so there was no reason to think he couldn't pull it off again.

Nearly nineteen years before the crash that severed roughly one-third of his brain stem, Bruce Wallace had been in another serious bicycle accident. A car had made a sudden U-turn in front of him, and Bruce had struck the vehicle. That collision had left him with a fractured shoulder and ribs and had required surgery to have a metal plate put in his back.

He had gotten back on his bicycle within six months.

"He worked really hard to come back from that one," his wife recalled. "That's why I have so much confidence now."

Reminded that her husband was no longer in his early forties, that his ability to recover might not be what it once was, and that there was no scientific evidence that his type of brain stem injury either heals or leads to a regeneration of the affected tissue, Helen nodded.

"The doctors at first said he had an 80 percent chance of not waking up from the coma, too," she said.

She noted that Bruce had not only done that, but he also had made good progress up until August 2012, when his recovery seemed to hit a plateau.

Besides, the doctor comes from good stock. His ninety-two-year-old mother was still going in and baking every day at 212 Market, the restaurant she and two daughters had opened almost a quarter-century earlier in Chattanooga, Tennessee.

"It's going to take at least a year," Helen predicted. "I think he will walk again. He will recover as much as he can recover. He's frustrated that he's not walking yet. But he will recover."

———

Being active had been a constant throughout the years for Bruce. It wasn't enough merely to swim in college; he chose the most physically demanding stroke—the butterfly. When he moved to other sports, he also elected the most active route, whether it was with triathlons, to which he was drawn by the grueling triple disciplines of swimming followed by cycling and then running, or with distance running, where he competed in such events as the Marine Corps Marathon, the Honolulu Marathon, the Cherry Blossom Ten-miler and the Army Ten-miler. He was just as serious about his cycling, which was his primary mode of transportation to and from work, weather permitting.

"And, sometimes, weather not permitting," his wife said with a chuckle and a playful smile.

His passion for his bicycle wasn't confined to his Monday-to-Friday work weeks.

"It wasn't unusual for him to go on long rides on the weekends every chance he could," Helen said. "He would go out on a nice afternoon for two, three, four hours. Sometimes he would ride down into downtown Washington and back."

Don't get the misguided impression that Bruce, because he was a well-compensated physician, was some sort of white-collar bicycle snob who spent $10,000 on the latest in titanium-frame machines with carbon-fiber wheels and all the possible upgrades. His mode of transportation had been, for some twenty-seven years, the same maroon Centurion road bike.

"It was so old that no one would steal it. But he said he didn't need anything else," Helen said. "He took very, very good care of it. Maintained it very well. Always stayed on top of maintenance and all that. Anything that needed to be replaced, he did it right away. But he never wanted to get rid of that thing."

On that day in mid-May, however, the combination of an older-model Centurion and a steel plate in the road proved devastating. The crash also left him with fractures to three vertebrae, but it was the partially severed brain stem that did the most lasting damage and had him fighting to regain control of his physical abilities and cognitive functions months later.

Aside from having to use a wheelchair and needing assistance with such everyday tasks as dressing himself, cutting his food, bathing, and going to the bathroom, he also struggled to come to terms with another significant change to his life—one that seemed to be especially painful.

"I think it's frustrating to him not to be the smartest person in the room anymore," Helen explained. Whether he was at the dinner table with his family, in social gatherings with friends, or even with his professional colleagues, Bruce had always enjoyed a reputation for possessing a sharp wit and a superior intellect—and the ability to combine the two in a manner that left others feeling entertained but not threatened.

The accident had robbed him of those abilities.

"He works hard in therapy and all that, but you can see it gets to him some days," his wife said. "And some days he copes with it better than others. I think he's using his sense of humor sometimes as a defense mechanism."

Of paramount importance to Helen was the fact that Bruce's sense of humor was still intact and that he kept employing it, even on the darkest days when it would be easy to give up, to quit fighting, and to say he might not be able to improve any further.

"He still has his personality," she said, "and that gives me a lot of confidence, because he is a fighter. He's got that drive."

That drive had been evident for decades, helping him graduate early at the Massachusetts Institute of Technology before working for a year to help raise money for medical school at Temple. He joined the army in his second semester of medical school and later did his residency in Denver, Colorado, before going to Walter Reed for the first time for a fellowship. From there it was back to Colorado, this time for an army deployment to Fort Carson in Colorado Springs, where he met his future wife.

In 1986, he moved back to the Washington area and Walter Reed, this time permanently, allowing he and his bride to start a family and clearing the way for him to do start conducting research that combined two of his passions—gastroenterology and its relationship to athletes, especially endurance athletes.

As the years passed, opportunities to work elsewhere presented themselves, but each time, Walter Reed—and the family's suburban Washington lifestyle—prevailed.

"He liked what he was doing," his wife said, "and who he was working with. He was happy. We were happy."

———

On November 13, 2012, US Secretary of Defense Leon Panetta confirmed that it was likely that several thousand US troops would remain in Afghanistan beyond the targeted 2014 withdrawal date established for NATO troops. Detailed plans with exact figures were still being finalized, but indications were that the number of US troops staying in Afghanistan would likely be in the range of six thousand to ten thousand.

Given the continuing volatility of tensions in the war-torn nation, such significant numbers of US troops staying behind in Afghanistan pointed to a lasting need for continued strong staffing levels at such specialty centers as McGuire's polytrauma unit and other facilities within the US military medical community designed to cater to the most complicated cases. McGuire's twenty-bed polytrauma unit, in fact, had just one bed available on

November 13, and the staff was understandably busy treating those wounded in Afghanistan and elsewhere, including a certain gastroenterologist injured in a bicycle accident in Bethesda, Maryland.

Monique Jones was in her office that afternoon, once again trying to coax Bruce beyond the plateau that his recovery had seemed to hit nearly three months earlier. Once the two exchanged pleasantries, Jones began by asking him a series of questions designed to determine his cognitive status that day.

"Do you remember what month it is?" she asked.

"December."

"That's next month."

"November."

Next, she asked what city they were in.

"Reno."

"Not Reno. But it starts with an 'R.'"

"Rensselaer."

"No. Try again."

"Rainier?"

In an attempt to help him focus his choices, Jones said they were in one of the following three cities: Roanoke, Richmond, or Riverside.

"Roanoke," he responded.

Jones devoted the rest of the session to addressing such issues as memory, coordination, sensation, and confusion. She began by telling him she wanted him to remember two things—Richmond and Veterans Day—and that she would ask him periodically throughout the session what those two were.

Then she began showing him a series of sentences that he needed to complete.

The first one: "I took an aspirin bottle because _____."

"I can," he replied.

"Give me a better answer than that," she said with a smile.

"I had a headache."

"That's much better," she said.

Jones gave him two more sentences to finish and then asked him what two terms she had asked him to remember.

"Marathon," he said, followed by a long pause.

"Veterans Day and Richmond," Jones finally said. "Veterans Day and Richmond. Let's try again in two minutes."

After he struggled to complete several more unfinished sentences, she again asked him for the two terms.

"Marathon," he responded, again followed by a long pause. When it became clear that he remembered neither Richmond nor Veterans Day, Jones gave him both.

Another two minutes of finishing sentences was followed again by her asking whether he remembered the two terms.

"Running," he said. "And Richmond."

From there, Jones moved on to an exercise in which she would give him two terms and he would tell her how they were similar.

"Grocery store and restaurant," she said.

"They both deal with food," he said.

"And...?" she prodded.

"They both serve hungry people."

"Police officer and firefighter," she said.

"They're both young. And they both work for the government."

"How are they different?"

"They don't serve food."

Jones decided to throw him a curve of sorts.

"Yesterday you spent...," she said.

"Veterans Day," he said.

"Where?" she asked.

"Richmond."

"Yay! Excellent! You did it! Great job!"

Jones resumed the comparison exercise with several more terms, at one point giving him "pipe and cigar."

"Both are tobacco," he said. "Both are served with dinner."

Jones playfully made a face of mock horror.

"I'm not coming to your house for dinner," she said, and he laughed.

After several more comparisons, Jones went back to the Richmond-Veterans Day memory exercise one more time.

"What did you do yesterday?" she asked him.

"Shopping," he said. "Shopping in Richmond."

"You poopin' out on me?" she asked.

"No," he said.

"Good, because we're almost done."

"Hooray," he said.

They worked on memory and confusion issues for several more minutes and then ended the appointment, another session in which he had been sharp at times and struggling at others. Nearly six months after the accident, he could instantly recall such facts as his location in a rehabilitation hospital, the year, and the day. Yet other facts—what city he was in and what he had done the day before, for example—continued to present a challenge.

"There are hard days and there are days that are down," his wife said. "But I have to fight at being positive because that's what works."

She paused, took a deep breath, and exhaled slowly.

"I'm hopeful. I'm very hopeful because basically that's the only choice I have to be able to maintain any kind of mental health."

———

Thanksgiving eve found Helen Wallace in a reflective mood. She talked about the possibility that her husband might be bound for a long-term care facility—or perhaps be moved home, with some alterations to their house to accommodate his limited mobility, and continue to receive therapy on an outpatient basis.

However, she also noted that progress, although not always consistent or in line with their hopes and expectations, was nonetheless evident. For example, her husband had scored a twenty-one on a thirty-point cognitive test the week before after being stuck on fifteen or sixteen for several weeks.

"It'll work out," she said. "It's going to work out. Overall, we're pretty lucky people."

The experience of the accident and her husband's rehabilitation had changed Helen. She used to think she knew patience, especially with the typical trials and tribulations of raising three children and having to drive in notoriously bad traffic in Washington, DC, and its choked suburbs.

"Now I know better," she said. "I've learned a lot more patience."

Patience was a requirement for someone who spent weeks at a time in the hospital by her husband's side, always putting his needs and his care before her own. She didn't hesitate when asked if she had been able to carve out enough time to take care of herself.

"No," she said. "Lately, it's been hard."

She would break away to watch the occasional television crime series, and she tried to make time for knitting and reading and keeping up with friends on the computer. There also were the occasional trips to Williamsburg or Richmond's Carytown shopping district or a visit to a coffee shop—all just to get away from the polytrauma unit for a while to get a change of scenery and escape the strains and stresses of life in a hospital ward.

"I'm doing the best I can," she said. "I don't like to take time away from him. He seems to like me here. He sleeps better when I'm here. Overall, I think he just does better when I'm here.

"It's getting tiring being in a hospital. But this gives us access to the therapists we need."

———

Several weeks later, progress was evident in the memory cue that Monique Jones was using with Bruce. No longer was she asking him to remember just two terms: Richmond and Veterans Day. Their December 17 session instead focused on a worker at a New Hampshire hospital who had been accused of stealing syringes of the powerful painkiller Fentanyl. The suspect had been injecting himself with the Fentanyl, replacing the drug with saline, and returning the syringes—now tainted with his own blood, which was infected with hepatitis C. The worker, who later pleaded guilty and was convicted of numerous federal charges, was said to have infected thirty patients with his tainted blood.

After Jones told Bruce the story and informed him it would be his memory cue for the session, he immediately repeated it back to her almost verbatim.

"Excellent," she said. "We'll try again in three minutes."

With that, Jones took him through a series of exercises designed to address his continuing problems with difficulties tracking and reading with his left eye. Three minutes later, she asked if he remembered the story.

"It was about a guy who was admitted to a VA hospital...," he began.

The incorrect reference to the crimes occurring in a VA hospital turned out to be the only part of the story Bruce got wrong; he nailed the rest of the story.

His recollection was strong again after a five-minute interval, so Jones decided to stretch it, leading Bruce through eleven minutes of exercises before returning to the story to test his memory.

"A man is in a VA hospital...," he began.

"Not the VA hospital," she corrected. "Just a hospital."

"He had a sore foot."

"Not a sore foot."

"Narcan," he said, referring to a drug used to counter effects of certain drug overdoses.

"Not Narcan," she said. "Fentanyl."

At that point, Jones asked him if he kept referring to a VA hospital because the two had repeatedly discussed a VA hospital in one of their exercises the previous week.

"Yeah," he replied.

"Okay," she said. "Then let's take a break from that."

Jones devoted the rest of the session to visual memory exercises, including one in which she showed him a picture of a round dinner table that had five place settings as well as flowers and candlesticks. They briefly discussed the contents of the picture and then she flipped it over, revealing a plain white sheet on the back.

"Okay," she said, "what do you remember?"

"A table," he said. "With turkey."

"No turkey," she responded. "No food on it yet."

Frustrated, Bruce sighed and then reached out and impatiently flipped over the picture to get another look at its contents, a move that surprised Jones.

"Okay," she said with a laugh, "I guess you can turn it over and take another look at it."

She allowed him to absorb the items in the picture before she flipped it over again. This time, he fared much better in recalling the details of each place setting, the floral arrangement, and so on.

Jones decided to try one last time.

"Okay," she said, "what was the article about?"

"This guy who worked in a hospital. New Hampshire," he said.

"Yes," she said, her voice rising in a tone of encouragement.

"He had hepatitis C."

"Yes. Keep going."

Choosing his words carefully, Bruce went on to detail the theft of syringes containing Fentanyl, the worker replacing them with saline solution, and the infection of thirty patients. Jones, leaning forward in her chair, fought to contain her praise and stay silent as he got deeper and deeper into the story, this time nailing detail after detail to perfection.

When he finished, it was time for celebration.

"Excellent!" she shouted. "You rocked that one!"

The two exchanged a high-five, and the session was soon over.

"I think you did enough today," she said. "What do you think?"

"Yeah."

Jones rose from her seat, came around to his side of the table, backed his wheelchair out of her office, and pushed him back to his room.

"Everyone has their good days and their bad ones," she said later. "People get frustrated. That's part of the process. But that also means they're working hard. And that's all you can ask. We all want the same thing. We want them to get better."

CHAPTER TWENTY-THREE

PLAN B

Summer 2012 was down to its final days, and Jon McHenry's unit in Afghanistan was drawing closer and closer to returning home. Jon, meantime, was getting conflicting signals from army brass in his quest to complete his comeback.

Whereas one superior at Fort Hood would tell him his bid to rejoin his unit was in the pipeline and should occur within a span of three to five weeks, another would tell him that reports from above indicated Jon's comrades had all the manpower necessary to complete their deployment and that no one was being shipped back over from Texas to rejoin the unit.

Jon, armed with his doctor-signed memo clearing him for redeployment, was growing weary with the delays and contradictory reports from above.

"It's a little frustrating," he said after work one day, "because all these people at Fort Hood, they listen to me, they hear what my goal is, but they're so quick to turn a shoulder to me and say, 'You're better off here.'

"They don't get it. They don't understand. They're not in my position."

For Jon, it was no longer a matter of how long he would be back in Afghanistan with his comrades before they returned to the United States.

Now it was about the journey he had been on for most of 2012. It was about all of the efforts he had made to rehabilitate his body and all of the people who had helped him along the way. He had made it back, and for the sake of everyone involved in that journey, he wanted to finish it off the only way he saw fit—with a flight back to Afghanistan.

"I told them, 'Look, I don't care if I'm only there a week or whatever,'" he said.

He was able to get his mind off the agonizing wait for a few days in the middle of September by driving six-plus hours to McAllen, Texas. There he picked up the mother of Spc. Kurt W. Kern, one of his three comrades killed in the IED blast nearly nine months earlier, and then drove up to Fort Leonard Wood in Missouri for a service in which bricks honoring Kern and the other two who were killed, Sgt. Noah M. Korte and Pfc. Justin M. Whitmire, were dedicated in a military police memorial.

While at Leonard Wood, Jon got to meet Korte's widow and her two young sons. One had turned three years old by then, and the youngest had just celebrated his first birthday the week before.

The ceremony honoring the fallen MPs left a lasting impression on Jon.

"Overall it was really great of them to do something like that," he said. "But I'll tell you, it was tough and all that stuff, too. I don't know if you've ever been present for a military funeral when they play taps and all that. It was difficult. Very difficult."

Once back at Fort Hood, Jon continued to pass the time working on base at an unsatisfying desk job and working out as much as possible. Although the workouts made him stronger and stronger, he still wasn't at peak physical condition—and he was starting to wonder if, with a titanium rod in his lower right leg, he would ever be able to return to truly top form.

Despite the doctor's memo pronouncing him "fit for duty," Jon said it was a relative term.

"Overall I would probably classify myself as physically I'm not 100 percent," he said. "I'd probably rate myself somewhere in the ballpark of 85 percent to 95 percent. I told them that me at 85 percent is probably better than 99 percent of the people they've got there now."

As September passed into October, it also meant the 720th Military Police Battalion, 89th Military Police Brigade was less than sixty days from the end of its deployment and its scheduled early December arrival back at Fort Hood. Jon was getting more and more frustrated with what appeared to be a growing unwillingness by his superiors to send him back to Afghanistan. Privately, he allowed that if he were going to be cleared to return to Afghanistan to rejoin his comrades, it realistically should have occurred before his unit hit its ninety-day window to return home. Now that the sixty-day window had come and gone, going back overseas was looking less and less likely for him.

Still unwilling to abandon his quest, Jon kept pressing, kept asking, kept badgering his superiors, kept trying to convince them that he was fit to rejoin the fight. When his unit closed in on its forty-five-day window of leaving Afghanistan, however, he realized what little support there had been among his superiors for him to return had evaporated. His telephone calls were no longer being returned, and the meetings with superiors were no longer being scheduled. He finally accepted that his dream was not going to end the way he had envisioned.

It was over.

Jon McHenry, who had been the object of intense work by a massive team of medical professionals from Afghanistan to Germany to Maryland to Virginia to Maryland again and finally to Texas, was now all alone. All the work that he and everyone else had done as one large team to help him reach his goal—getting him back to walking, running, lifting weights, going out on dates with his wife, getting down on the floor to play with his young son, driving again, going back to work—would not get him sent back to Afghanistan. It was a goal he had established months earlier as a key step in healing himself physically and emotionally from the events of December 27, 2011 and in helping him down the path toward closure from what would likely be the most traumatic event of his life.

Not surprisingly, Jon was devastated.

"I believed. I really did," he said. "I'll always believe. I'll always know I could have done it. But they didn't believe in me. Even with the signed letter, they still didn't believe I could do it."

It was an all-too-familiar theme for someone who had spent so much of his youth trying to prove he was good enough, big enough, fast enough, tough enough, strong enough to lead, strong enough to succeed. Time and again, he had proven everyone wrong, but this time, he wasn't given the chance.

That was what hurt the most—the fact that his superiors had so much doubt in him that they would not even give him a chance to prove himself.

"I got it done. I held up my end," he said. "Honestly, I think they did doubt me. But they obviously didn't know me and know how hard I would try."

Jon took a deep breath, slowly exhaled, and paused for a few seconds.

"Maybe," he finally said, "this is all for the best. Maybe this is what was meant to be. I have a family now. Maybe I need to start thinking in a different direction."

————

Perhaps the timing was nothing more than a coincidence. Then again, maybe there was a direct correlation. Regardless of the circumstances, almost immediately after finally accepting that he would not be allowed to rejoin his unit in Afghanistan, Jon McHenry revealed that he had been bothered by two noteworthy physical issues that he had not been sharing with doctors.

The first involved blood in his urine, something he allowed that he had been experiencing as far back as the spring when he was doing outpatient rehabilitation at Walter Reed National Military Medical Center. Jon said he would occasionally see a pink tint in his urine during his time at the Bethesda, Maryland, facility, where he was doing weightlifting sessions and treadmill workouts sometimes as often as twice a day. There wasn't significant pain associated with the discolored urine, and he had spoken about it with his grandmother, a retired registered nurse. She had told him it could simply be a urinary tract infection, and she advised him to drink plenty of cranberry juice. He did, and the problem seemed to disappear, so he figured there was no need to bring it to anyone else's attention.

After he went back to Texas, however, blood reappeared in his urine sporadically throughout the summer and early fall. Each time, the blood didn't seem to be particularly thick, and each time, the condition would quickly abate.

That changed one October morning. Jon went out for a vigorous run at dawn and then showered and went to work. He began experiencing discomfort several hours later, and when he went to the bathroom, his urine was no longer the pink tint that he had so easily dismissed in the past. This time, it was bright, thick red.

"I was like, 'Whoa. This is not good,'" he recalled. "I knew something was wrong. This was not like before."

He went to see a doctor, and it wasn't long before he was diagnosed with a two-centimeter stone in his bladder. Doctors told him that each time he ran or engaged in other high-energy workouts, the stone would bounce off the walls of his bladder, agitating it and leading to the blood flow.

On Friday, October 19, Jon underwent a procedure to break up the stone. He returned to work the following Tuesday.

The second physical problem bothering Jon also was worsening over time, and this one would eventually lead to an extensive surgical repair.

One of the surgeries he had undergone the previous January at Walter Reed was to have a titanium rod inserted into his right leg and anchored with multiple screws to help secure his fractured tibia, the larger of the two long bones in the lower leg. The fibula, the smaller of the two bones, also had been fractured in the IED blast. It had been reset, but surgeons had opted against using rods, plates, or screws to do any additional repairs to it, hoping instead that it would heal itself over time.

As Jon progressed from standing to taking a few steps to walking to jogging on a treadmill and ultimately to running on trails and roads—eventually reaching the point where he could log multiple sub-eight-minute miles and pass his physical fitness test—he would experience what he described as general soreness in the lower right leg.

"It might just be a little achy after, but then it would be okay," he said. "When I'd wake up and I was just walking around, I didn't feel anything."

The low level of pain and the speed with which it abated allowed him to attribute it to typical post-run soreness as he continued to work his way back to fitness. However, like the blood in his urine, which got gradually worse, the pain in his lower leg worsened over the late summer and early fall, and it kept getting more and more intense.

After McHenry had logged a running time fast enough to pass his physical fitness test, the leg pain reached the stage where he knew it was no longer typical post-run muscle soreness. He recalled one day where the pain became so severe that he struggled to keep up with his companions on an early morning run. After sitting at his computer at work several hours later, he encountered even worse pain when he tried to stand up and walk around. Still he kept quiet, and still it kept getting worse. He didn't relent until it reached the point where he could no longer complete his standard two-mile run with his colleagues. Now it wasn't a matter of struggling to keep up with them for two miles; it was a matter of him not even being able to hang with them for half that distance.

"I'd run like a mile or so and I'd just have to stop—not because of a stamina issue but because of the pain in the side of the leg," he said.

So in late October, Jon finally gave in and went to see an orthopedic specialist. The physician compared X-rays over a span of several months and determined that although the titanium rod–supported tibia was doing well, the fibula still had not properly healed.

"He said my leg looked the same from August and the same from June. All the X-rays were just pretty much repeating," Jon said. "Where I was getting all this pain on the outside of my leg matches where the break in the fibula was."

What came next was not what Jon wanted to hear. Still struggling to come to grips with having been denied a return trip to Afghanistan, now he was headed back into the operating room yet again, this time for more work on his right leg.

The plan was for surgeons to use a plate that was three or four inches long and anchor it to the fibula with several screws to stabilize the area of the fracture. Like the titanium rod, the plate would be permanent. The hope was that the plate would relieve the increasingly severe pain that Jon was experiencing on his runs and also that he would be able to return to running, although doctors cautioned that it perhaps might not be at a speed or distance to suit Jon's press-the-envelope style.

"They pretty much told me that the days of going on a five- or seven-mile run might be over," he said. "They said most people who have breaks like that don't go back to that kind of running."

The possibility that he may have to limit his future running to short, easy-paced distances was a tough pill for Jon to swallow. It was made more difficult by the fact that Jon, who when he first got to Richmond had struggled to keep his weight above 120 pounds, had since worked himself back into a strong warrior who was nearly 170 pounds of well-defined muscle. Now he would have to undergo another surgery that would sap his strength and land him back in rehabilitation, once again facing the prospect of rebuilding a body that he and others had already worked hard to reconstruct.

"You kind of get down on yourself a little bit, especially when I see Adrian Peterson and people like that," he said. He was referring to the star running back of the NFL's Minnesota Vikings who overcame a severe knee injury in December 2011 and worked hard in rehabilitation after surgery to get back on the field in time for the next season, during which he rushed for nearly 2,000 yards.

"Hey, it is what it is," Jon said. "I've never had that bad attitude. I'll get back sooner or later."

———

The emotional struggles continued for Jon McHenry on several fronts as he tried to make peace with being denied a return to Afghanistan, and they seemed to increase in difficulty as his comrades drew closer to returning to Fort Hood.

For starters, there was the matter of his future. Jon's enlistment was due to expire in the spring of 2013, and he was of the mind that if the army no longer had any use for him in Afghanistan, then he no longer had any use for the army. A few months after declaring that he wanted to make the army a career, to become a leader and a mentor to young soldiers, Jon now said it was best that he leave the military. Beyond that, however, he was having a hard time identifying his best options for the future.

Then there was his continuing bid to come to grips with the effects of December 27, 2011. Jon had hoped a return to Afghanistan would help his personal healing process. Now that Afghanistan was out of the picture, he continued to look for ways to work his way through the grief and healing process.

One of the ways he coped was by continuing to make the drive of more than six hours to McAllen to visit with Spc. Kurt W. Kern's mother, Martha. Jon had made the trip in September and found it to be beneficial. He missed his friend, and he said that being with Martha seemed to help both of them. He even raised the possibility of moving to McAllen permanently when his enlistment ended.

"It's hard to put into words," he said, "but it just feels right. It's where I need to be."

Jon planned to go back to McAllen to spend Thanksgiving with Kern's family. It would not be his final trip there.

Then there was the not-so-insignificant matter of the fast-approaching return to Texas of the 720th Military Police Battalion, 89th Military Police Brigade.

Jon admitted that as the date drew near—his unit was scheduled to leave its post in Afghanistan on December 1 and return to Fort Hood on December 5—he struggled with numerous feelings, including questions of how he fit in, a perception of having been forgotten by some of his comrades, and nervousness about how he would react to them and they, in turn, to him.

His anxieties continued to swell, and two days before they arrived back on base, "I was getting a little tossy-turny about how I would react seeing all sixty of them," he said.

So the strong-willed, gritty Jon McHenry did something that seemed improbable to many who knew him: He went to the TBI clinic at Fort Hood and asked if he could speak with a counselor.

"I went to the front desk and said, 'Hey, I've got kind of an emergency,'" he said. "They said it would be a three- or four-week wait. I said, 'That's not going to work.'"

Jon walked back to his car, sat down inside, and began looking around for the business card of a psychologist at the base who had introduced herself to him when he had first returned to Fort Hood several months earlier.

"I called her up and she said, 'Come on over right now. I've got some time right now.' So I did."

Jon began telling her about his anxieties associated with the pending return of his unit.

"As soon as the accident happened, all these people come out of the wood-work and they express remorse and all that, and then like a month later, it's all gone," he said. "Months pass and no one calls for an update."

McHenry said a core group of eight to ten of his comrades had remained in touch with him throughout his rehabilitation, but the other fifty or so hadn't had much, if any, contact with him, especially later in the year. He said he had reached out to a number of them in April after he went back to Walter Reed for outpatient rehabilitation, but he had not gotten much of a response.

"I understand," he said. "They've got their own lives. I don't hold it against them."

Still, it left him conflicted, he told the psychologist.

So she had him draw a series of bubbles. The first one had his name in it. Another had his wife's name, Jay, and their son's name, Leo. Then there was one with his father, one with his siblings, another with his grandparents, one with some of his close buddies in the unit, and finally, one with some high school friends. The psychologist then had Jon prioritize the bubbles, first by showing her which one he would put immediately beside his.

"Since I was born, my dad's always been there," he said with a tone of pride. "His bubble has never moved."

After that, it was his wife and son, other family members, and so on down the line until Jon had assigned a priority to all the bubbles.

"Then she told me to show her where on the picture I would put this group of fifty or so people who haven't kept in close contact with me over the last year," Jon said, before letting out a small laugh that demonstrated he clearly got the message that the counselor was delivering.

"Wouldn't you say you were pulling them closer because of what you went through over there, because of what happened to you in Afghanistan?" she asked him. "People will come and go throughout your life. Some will stay, but many will not."

Jon paused.

"She just kind of put everything in perspective," he said. "It was amazing after I walked out of that door. I felt so much better about things. She took a lot of the anger and stuff away. It made it a lot easier about seeing them again."

———

It was 3 A.M. local time on December 5, 2012, when sixty or so members of the 720th Military Police Battalion, 89th Military Police Brigade got off buses in the darkness and strode confidently into Fort Hood's Bronco Youth Center, where they were greeted by a chorus of cheers and hearty applause from family members and friends.

Capt. Luis Avila, still struggling to recover from his injuries, was unable to make the trip down to Texas from Walter Reed, but Jon McHenry was there with Spc. Michael Crawford, the other IED blast survivor, who now was able to stand with assistance as he continued his recovery from surgery for spinal and leg fractures.

Jon said he and Crawford were originally told by one of their superiors that both of them would be a part of the welcome-home ceremony. Right before the unit arrived, another superior instructed them to stand on either side of the gym door as their comrades walked through it. The returning troops were instructed to not shake hands with, salute, or stop and speak with either soldier, Jon said. After the returning troops filed past them and were seated in the gymnasium, Jon and Crawford were seated behind them.

It wasn't until after the brief welcome-home remarks and the soldiers were dismissed to go meet their loved ones that Jon and Crawford were permitted to greet their comrades.

"I guess I understand why they did it that way, but it wasn't what I had planned on happening," Jon said. "After the whole little ceremony type of thing, all of them came over and shook my hand or gave me a hug.

"It was great to see them again. A lot of them I hadn't heard from in eleven months, and I thought they were going to be all fake and all that. But that wasn't the case at all. But a bunch of guys had little parties and stuff like that for a few days, and it was nice to get together again."

Several days after his unit returned, Jon went back to see the psychologist, the second of what would be several visits over the coming months. This time, they not only talked about issues concerning Jon and his recovery, but also about the counselor's background and how she had gotten into her profession.

"She was just super awesome. I can't believe how much she helped me, and now that I'm trying to figure out what to do when I leave the army, I'm thinking it might be good to be able to help other people like that," he said. "A military family counselor would be one way to go. I'll have to research more about that before I jump into it, but it seems like an awesome job, really, so I'm definitely going to have to look into it some more."

Jon was leaving the door open to a number of other career possibilities, although law enforcement didn't appear to be one of them, even with his experience as a military police officer.

"I wasn't really loving the whole law enforcement scheme of things," he said. "As far as regular patrol, I can't really see myself doing that. Maybe an investigator. I don't want to totally close the door on that."

Staying with the army in a different capacity, however, was not an option.

"I think it's time to just pack it up and figure another plan out," he explained. "It sounds pretty bad that I don't really want to do anything for them. But I think I've done enough for them."

Other career possibilities he was considering included moving to McAllen and finding a job; going to professional school to study mortuary science (he had done some part-time work for a mortician in his hometown of Newport, Pennsylvania, when he was in high school); or taking advantage of a generous GI Bill package available to him and going to college full time to get a bachelor's degree. He was undecided on a possible major.

"I need to get some kind of degree. With the GI Bill, it's pretty much all paid for," he said. "I'm just not sold on anything. I've been so busy with everything."

The way Jon saw it, he still had several months to research and consider his possibilities. He'd certainly have plenty of time to think about his options while recovering and rehabilitating from leg surgery, scheduled for February 1.

"Physically, I want to be just as good if not better than what I was before, but realistically I don't know if that's feasible. And you know what? At twenty-three, that's just tragic," he said with a chuckle. "At twenty-two or twenty-three, this is not something everybody should have to go through. But at least I have all my fingers and all my toes. Maybe I should stop bitching and be happy for what I have."

CHAPTER TWENTY-FOUR

SURGERY

Friday, October 27, 2012, marked another deadly day in Afghanistan. A suicide bomber detonated explosives outside a mosque that was packed for a service marking the major Muslim holiday of Eid al-Adha. Even by Afghan standards, it was a particularly bloody attack. Forty-one people died. Another fifty-six were wounded. Most of the casualties were Afghan soldiers and police, representing what appeared to be another example of the Taliban increasingly shifting its focus to the troubled nation's own authorities in light of NATO's move to draw down and withdraw its roughly 100,000 troops by the end of 2014, leaving the 352,000-strong Afghan army and police responsible for security.

Some seven thousand miles away, Burness Britt tried to stay abreast of news from Afghanistan while he was undergoing rehabilitation at McGuire VA Medical Center in Richmond, Virginia, but on this day, his thoughts were elsewhere.

On this day, Burness—newly promoted by the US Marine Corps from corporal to sergeant—would begin a journey he hoped would finally put him firmly on a path to a lifetime of mobility, independence, better health, and happiness. That morning he was wheeled into surgery at McGuire to address what doctors, in layman's terms, called claw toes.

In the nearly seventeen months since an IED blast in an Afghan wheat field had caused Burness' massive blood loss and stroke, doctors and therapists had tried various approaches to help him recover. One of the results of the stroke was damage to Burness' left cerebral hemisphere, damage that led the muscles on the right side of his body to become overactive. His right arm and hand had responded somewhat to rigorous physical therapy and to a special brace designed to limit overactive muscle activity in his hand. Although the arm and hand were still significantly behind those on his left side in terms of strength and flexibility, he at least had some functional use of the limb.

However, the staff wasn't experiencing the same level of success with Burness' right leg and foot. The muscles in his right foot had become so overactive and taut, in fact, that his toes had begun to curl down and back toward his foot. Therapy didn't seem to be helping. Botox injections worked early in the process but later lost their effectiveness. The more time passed, the worse his claw toes seemed to get, and eventually it reached a point where the toes were curled up so tightly that walking became painful. Running was out of the question altogether.

Burness dearly wanted to run again.

It became his one-word, oft-repeated mantra as summer slipped into fall and his second stint at McGuire wore on. Burness would spend five days a week, every week, doing hour after hour of productive but often monotonous and frustrating rehabilitation work.

"Run," he would say, patting his stomach and shaking his head with a look of disappointment.

The disappointment stemmed from the fact that running had helped him early in his stay with the marines. It had helped shape him—literally—into a hardened, fit warrior who blended in with his comrades. He looked like a marine, acted like a marine, *was* a marine. This young man who had struggled to find his niche as a teenager in rural Georgetown, South Carolina, had fit in perfectly with his fellow warriors.

Then came the IED blast and resulting injuries that had robbed him of his physical abilities and fitness. It had cost him in an easily recognizable way.

Strong and trim at less than 200 pounds before the blast, Burness had gradually grown over the months, and when he got on a scale in the days before the surgery, it said this frustrated young marine had reached 263 pounds. When he recounted the reading on the scale, he repeated the numbers slowly, then looked down and shook his head.

"Run," he repeated.

———

The surgery took a little more than an hour and involved lengthening tendons in the toes and fusing bone joints in an effort to reduce the likelihood of the claw effect from returning.

Although Burness made no effort to conceal his hopes that the surgery would open the door to a return to running, the McGuire staff made no such promises. The staff also cautioned that there was no guarantee that the claw effect would not return in the future, requiring more surgery.

Dr. Gary Goldberg, medical director at the hospital's Polytrauma Transitional Rehabilitation Program, said the goal of the surgery was twofold: to undo the claw effect that was causing so much pain for Burness and to make it easier for him to walk again. Returning to a lifestyle of running, Goldberg cautioned, might not be a realistic expectation.

There were two issues clouding the immediate horizon for Burness after his surgery.

First, there was the matter of his weight. The staff made no attempt to hide their collective concern about his steady weight gains, a process they felt was fueled by a variety of factors, starting with the IED blast itself and then fueled by Burness' frustration with the lack of rehabilitation facilities at Camp LeJeune, his marital problems, and his affection for candy and other forms of junk food. He frequently welcomed visitors by offering them candy, and he often dipped into his own stash while entertaining guests. In fact, when a visitor came to see Burness three days after the surgery and asked if he could bring him anything, Britt didn't hesitate.

"Reese's Pieces," he said.

The staff at McGuire had given Burness nutritional counseling, and after the surgery there was talk of revisiting those efforts and intensifying them to get him to embrace a more healthy diet that he could use as the cornerstone of a more active, fit lifestyle.

The second issue facing Burness after the surgery was directly tied to the first: Part of his recovery from the procedure called for him to not put any weight on the foot and to use a wheelchair for as many as eight weeks. As concerned as the staff had become about the weight he'd gained already, they knew the potential existed for the trend to continue for another two months or so. Even Burness expressed reservations being limited in his physical therapy for such a long period and about what effect it might have on his weight.

"Eight weeks," he said, gently rubbing his stomach, "is a long time."

Beyond the immediate postsurgery concerns loomed another matter, one that had gone unresolved in the months since the IED blast.

Before he left McGuire the first time and went to Camp LeJeune, Burness had spoken optimistically of staying with the marines and making it a career. He had been determined to find a way to continue serving in a branch of the military that had helped shape his identity when he first got out of school. The plan was that he would finish up his rehabilitation at Camp LeJeune and then see where he best fit in, whether in recruiting, a hospital setting—wherever. As long as he felt a sense of purpose, he wanted to stay with the marines until he retired.

The experience at Camp LeJeune, however, had soured Burness on the marines, and now he wanted out. He was scheduled to begin the exit process, a so-called Med Board review, in mid-December.

Although Goldberg and his staff had no problems with Burness' change of heart, they were concerned that he didn't seem to have a plan for his future. There were plenty of examples of young service men and service women who were injured on the battlefield, came home, went through the rehabilitation process, and then spent the rest of their lives doing essentially nothing except sitting around, cashing their government assistance checks, living with family members or in substandard housing, playing video games, and drinking too much.

It is an easy existence to fall into, and the staff at McGuire doesn't want to see it happen to anybody, especially considering how many programs are available and how many professionals are working together to make the patients as whole as possible and make them productive members of society again. The staff certainly didn't want to see it happen with Burness, who, even though he had only a high school education, had nonetheless consistently demonstrated a sharp mind, a sharp wit, and plenty of people skills.

"There's some concern," Goldberg said, "because he built a sense of self-worth around his ability to run. Now, you have to find a different pathway."

Many staff members at McGuire had pressed Burness about his post-marines plans only to get the same shrug and same three-word response: "I don't know."

Goldberg noted that because of Burness' outgoing personality and affinity for military history, he might thrive in a military museum setting or something along those lines. Regardless of the setting, the consensus was that even with his stroke-related speech limitations, Burness had the people skills to work in a public setting. He also enjoyed working with animals, although it remained to be seen whether his right leg and foot would improve to the point where he could thrive in a job as, for example, a dog walker or pet sitter or in the veterinary field.

For his part, Burness didn't appear to be particularly interested in spending a great deal of time discussing his career options. He seemed more concerned about getting back to an active lifestyle and seeing where it might lead him. Goldberg said that although Burness' focus on returning to a more physical lifestyle was understandable, he nonetheless cautioned Burness that he was facing some significant decisions about his future.

"The next part of the process," Goldberg said, "will be in large part up to him."

CHAPTER TWENTY-FIVE

SECTION 60

The sticky, warm weather that signals the impending arrival of summer was starting to emerge on the afternoon of Thursday, May 16, 2013, for Senior Airman Bryce Powers' funeral at Arlington National Cemetery.

Intermittent showers that added to the humidity level throughout the day held off long enough for the midafternoon funeral, one of twenty-five on the schedule that day at Arlington, which averages more than twenty-seven services daily and where more than four hundred thousand people are interred.

Bryce's funeral procession of about seventy-five mourners was escorted down Memorial Drive, the main road leading into the facility, then made a left turn on Eisenhower Drive and followed it through a seemingly endless rolling sea of identical, brilliant white headstones to the southeastern quadrant of the cemetery and Section 60, where a left turn onto Bradley Drive, lined on the sides by stands of mature hardwoods, delivered the caravan to plot No. 10379.

One week before Bryce's service at Arlington, his remains had been flown from Virginia to Charlotte, North Carolina. An air force honor guard had met the plane on the tarmac at Charlotte Douglas International Airport and, with Bryce's family standing nearby, had transferred his casket to a hearse in preparation for the ride to a funeral home in his hometown of Monroe. A viewing had been held the next day, followed by a funeral the day after that—one day before Mother's Day. The family had then traveled back to Virginia for a memorial service the day after Mother's Day at Langley Air Base in Hampton. Three days later, it was on to Arlington, his final resting place.

Given the heavy emotional toll that such a protracted series of events must have taken on Bryce's family, it seemed almost merciful that the burial service at Arlington lasted just sixteen minutes.

A large number of staff members from the PRC at McGuire VA Medical Center had made the ride from Richmond to the memorial service at Langley, and nearly a dozen staff members were on hand at Arlington as well to witness what was a typical funeral at the nation's most famous cemetery. After the honor guard delivered the casket with gentle precision to the grave site, an air force chaplain spoke briefly, followed by a twenty-one-gun salute that sent three sharp, crackling sound waves across the cemetery and prompted involuntary flinches from even those who knew the penetrating volleys of rifle fire were coming.

From there, the flag atop Bryce's casket was folded exactingly and then presented—on bent knee, on behalf of a grateful nation—to Cathy Powers. A second flag, also folded tautly into a triangle, was presented to Bryce's lone sibling, sixteen-year-old Madi. After some closing words from the chaplain, the mourners were thanked for coming and excused to walk away from the grave site back toward their cars on Bradley Drive. As they retreated, a kilted man standing some fifty yards southwest of plot No. 10379 played "Amazing Grace" on bagpipes.

Bryce was laid to rest atop a small ridge that affords a view of the Pentagon a few hundred yards to the northeast. Also from that location, when the leaves have fallen in the autumn and the winter, his family visiting him will be able to look just across the cemetery's southern border upon a view of the 270-foot-high US Air Force Memorial and its soaring triple spires.

The memorial, a brightly polished steel formation that reaches powerfully into the sky, stands watch there on a hillside overlooking the Potomac River and the nation's capital.

After the service, Cathy and Jim stayed behind with their lone surviving child to say their final goodbyes to Bryce. Madi, clutching her flag, stood next to her brother's casket and gently touched it. His parents knelt alongside the coffin, slowly leaned over, rested their heads along the gray metal finish, and ran their outstretched arms back and forth, slowly, lovingly, almost rhythmically, for a minute or so.

After the three walked from the grave site and returned to Bradley Drive, cemetery workers approached the plot, lowered the casket into the ground and began taking away the chairs and awning used during the service. As Cathy, Jim, and Madi greeted mourners roughly one hundred yards away, a large yellow plastic cart of dark brown sand was wheeled to the grave site, as were several rolls of fresh sod.

More than seven months after an accident half a world away left him with four different types of significant brain injuries, Bryce was no longer fighting to emerge, fighting the pain, fighting to overcome, fighting to join the 76 percent. Bryce was finally at rest. He was finally home.

———

As the weeks and months passed following Bryce's death, the polytrauma unit staff tried to settle back into a routine. The summer months were coming, and they typically represented the staff's busiest time of the year, a reflection of the increased fighting in Afghanistan as well as injuries to service members in car crashes, swimming pool accidents, and the like.

"I don't think there's any question the staff was affected" by Bryce's case, said Dr. Ajit Pai, the polytrauma unit's medical director. "It made people think about the spiritual side and not just look at things from a rehabilitation perspective. I always want that to be a part of the equation, to be thinking about how what we do here affects what kind of life people can have and what kind of life they want to have. So that's a good thing."

Michael Dardozzi, the speech therapist who had spent endless hours working with Bryce, said the entire experience reinforced his belief that humans are at the mercy of a higher power.

Nonetheless, that belief doesn't hold you back from wanting to do everything possible for the patient.

"You have to make sure that you didn't leave anything on the table, and you try to draw some comfort from that," he said. "You're disappointed because you couldn't do it for the family. But no matter how disappointing it is to us, it's never as disappointing as it is for the family. We have to keep that in perspective."

Just as Bryce's parents and sister had leaned on each other in their moments of grief, the polytrauma unit staff members also relied on each other to help get through what for them was an unusual experience.

"Everyone's door is open to everyone here," Dardozzi said. "This is a pretty special place to work."

Dardozzi thought for a moment.

"It's pretty devastating, because I'm an inpatient rehab therapist," he said. "You're not used to outcomes like that. We're used to seeing people get better, seeing a positive outcome. But you know going in that the outcome might not happen."

With the passage of time after Bryce's death, Dardozzi was able to reflect on the experience of working with him.

"I feel like I've grown," he said. "I feel like it's helped. I feel like it's helped me become a stronger clinician."

———

With the journey that had kept her away from home for six and one-half months now behind her, Cathy Powers returned to the family's residence in Monroe, North Carolina, in search of a new normal.

Madi finished her spring term at South Piedmont Community College and tried to keep busy for the summer with friends. Jim returned to his old job after the International Brotherhood of Electrical Workers intervened on his behalf, telling his employer—which had balked at granting him time off under FMLA—that its actions were putting the company in violation of federal law.

That left Cathy with large periods of time alone at the family's ten-acre home as spring slipped into another hot, humid North Carolina summer. Not surprisingly, she found that not every day was the same, that the emotional peaks and valleys were quite often unpredictable.

"Today I woke up laughing and happy," she said. "Some days, I wake up feeling like I ruined everything."

On those days she is able to draw on the five months she spent by her son's side in Richmond's polytrauma unit and on the lessons she learned there from the staff and how they treated her, her son, and her family.

"The education I received in 2-B was incredible. It really and truly was," she said. "I learned that there's a whole other side of life than just getting up in the morning and worrying about what I was going to get out of it."

So she tries to reach out to others, to show kindness and compassion to them the same way it was demonstrated to her by Dr. Ajit Pai, Michael Dardozzi, and others on the polytrauma unit.

Cathy had expected the range of emotions that she experienced following her son's death. What she had not expected—but what nonetheless sometimes enveloped her and almost incapacitated her—was the gripping physical pain in which her grief could manifest itself.

"It's absolutely horrible. It's so awful," she said. "It's almost disassociated from a feeling. I didn't realize at first it was grief because it was so physical."

The sensation begins in her lower torso, and the first time it happened, she mistook it for a stomach ache.

"After a couple of minutes in the pit of my stomach, I started getting a horrible feeling like I ate some bad food," she said. "But then it just started rising and rising and rising in my chest. And by the time it got to my throat, I was just crying out of control."

Cathy grew quiet for a few seconds.

"There's no way to tell you," she finally said, "how bad it hurts."

With the support of Jim and Madi, however, Cathy was finding ways to have good days as well.

"Since this happened," she said, "I have never stayed in bed all day."

Jim, standing nearby, heard what she said.

"That's because the third day, I brought you coffee and said, 'Get your ass out of bed,'" he said with a laugh.

Cathy also found considerable comfort in the discovery that polytrauma unit nurse Brooke Traylor had shared with her about losing the father of her son to a fast-moving form of cancer. Traylor had told Cathy that as her son's father had approached death, she would often rub a scented body lotion on his dry skin, and that after he died, Traylor found that using that same body lotion on herself—or merely smelling it on someone else—would bring an immediate feeling of serenity and inspire pleasant memories of him.

So Cathy had begun rubbing down Bryce when he was in his final days in Journey's Way. Sure enough, after he died, she found that if she hit a particularly rough patch emotionally, reaching for the bottle of body lotion would have an immediate soothing effect.

"It's hard to put into words," Cathy said, "how wonderful the people on 2-B really are. They gave us so much."

The family worked to find ways together to move on and recover while at the same time honoring Bryce's memory. They erected a large flagpole in their yard and positioned a concrete bench nearby, giving them a place to sit in quiet reflection. Cathy, who had spoken often during her time away from home about her concerns for what effect her absence might have on Madi at such a vulnerable time in her life, planned a two-week trip to California with her daughter for July. Cathy wanted to use the trip as a springboard for Madi to get to know her mother better and to have another successful school year. Madi, who turned seventeen in July, had proven herself to be an outstanding student, and Cathy and Jim didn't want the emotionally draining experience of her brother's death to derail that.

"I'm just going to settle back into that kid," Cathy said. "She needs me. I need her."

They were allowed to choose three lines of simple black type to go at the bottom of Bryce's white headstone at Arlington, under the standard information with his name, rank, service, date of birth, and date of death. They selected

SERVED GOD

SERVED COUNTRY

SERVED FAMILY

The family was slowly healing, slowly finding a new normal following Bryce's death, but their new world would include some changes.

One involved Madi, who since age six had expressed a desire to become a neurologist. Her brother's accident, hospitalization, and death had changed that. About two months after his death, Madi told her parents that she had changed her thinking about a possible career path and now wanted to go to college to study acting and singing. Neurologists, Madi told them, "were responsible for so much stuff," her mother recalled her saying. "I don't ever want to be responsible for so much like that and have to deal with families like us where you can't even help them."

Cathy said she didn't challenge Madi's reasoning.

"I just told her, 'I want you to be happy,'" she said.

Cathy recalled one grief-wracked occasion when she gained some perspective from a nugget of wisdom offered by her sixteen-year-old daughter. Madi was upset, telling her mother that she wished she had been nicer to her big brother, had been more expressive about her love for him, had told him in no uncertain terms how much he meant to her. Cathy responded with words she thought would offer her daughter comfort.

"I told her I would give up everything I had if God could just turn back time and bring Bryce back," Cathy said. "And Madi didn't miss a beat. She said, 'I wouldn't. Bryce is happy now.'"

Times like those, Cathy said, gave her hope for the future, even with all the dark days she knew were surely ahead, days when the pain would be too much, when the grief would become physical and that indescribable sensation would start welling up in her stomach yet again, and she would be powerless to control it. For all the bad moments when grief rules, however, Cathy vowed to allow herself to have joyous ones as well.

"I'm going to make something good out of this," she said. "Bryce would want us to be happy. He would want us to not sit around and cry all the time."

She paused.

"I think I'm going to be a better person because of this. It's going to work out."

CHAPTER TWENTY-SIX

FOR DAVID

Lauri Rogers talked about it like it was the easiest decision ever. When you get right down to it and put it in the context of what might a parent do when one of their children is in trouble—what anyone would do in the name of their love for their child—maybe it really wasn't any decision at all.

David Rogers had been in three different hospitals since suffering massive brain injuries while serving with the air force in Germany, and the doctors' message to his parents, Lauri and Dave, had been essentially the same at all three: Don't get your hopes up. Your son has essentially no chance of regaining cognitive functions. As for such activities as walking again and taking care of himself again, forget it.

Then David was transferred to his fourth hospital, McGuire VA Medical Center and its PRC. A young, energetic physician there named Shane McNamee was willing to be equal parts persistent and patient with David Rogers, and he was surrounded by a staff that seemed just as committed to getting the most from their patients. Something unexpected happened: Rogers' parents started noticing changes in their son. Positive changes.

They knew that medically, David represented the longest of long shots. They knew that his brain damage was not only severe, but also that it might continue to manifest itself in other destructive ways in the months ahead. Yet they also knew what they were seeing—that David, defying the odds, was getting better. Progress was rarely charted in a straight line, but it was progress nonetheless, and there was no mistaking it. Where there once had been darkness, there was now hope.

So Lauri Rogers, who had maintained a constant vigil by her son's bedside for months, had a talk with her husband. Dave had been shuttling back and forth between Richmond and their home in Leroy Township, Ohio, a few minutes from Lake Erie in the northeastern suburbs of Cleveland, where the couple still was raising four school-age children. The family had a beautiful, 3,000-square-foot contemporary home there, complete with a creek and a small waterfall on their property. Lauri was happy, the children were happy, and Dave had a good job as a senior-level programmer for Progressive, the insurance giant that has its headquarters in suburban Cleveland.

Now, however, their oldest son was nearly an eight-hour drive away in Virginia and facing a long and uncertain recovery. They had always been a close family, and his parents were troubled by the fact that, as long as David and Lauri were in Virginia, they were no longer together. All the phone calls, texts, and video chats on Skype couldn't change the fact that they were hundreds of miles and several states apart. As 2009 wound down, the Rogers family decided they needed to be together again. To make that happen, a major change would have to occur.

So the family decided to move to Virginia.

The reasoning, Lauri said, was simple.

"David was getting better," she said with a shrug. "He kept improving."

Even though the family was firmly entrenched in Ohio, the nation was in the grips of a recession that had badly damaged the real estate industry, and there were no guarantees of continued progress with their son, Lauri and Dave Rogers decided to put their house on the market, pull up roots, and move.

Officials had originally suggested David go to Minneapolis, site of what at the time was one of the VA's three other polytrauma units. The units in many cases draw from specific geographic regions, and patients from Ohio were typically sent to Minnesota. Lauri and Dave Rogers had a number of East Coast connections, however, including relatives in Maryland on both sides of the family. So they asked to go to Richmond instead, unaware that McGuire's polytrauma unit was fast developing a reputation for superior work with TBI patients.

"I did not know it was the flagship," Lauri Rogers said.

Once the Rogers family got to Richmond, the work of McNamee and the rest of the polytrauma unit staff and their commitment to keep fighting for improvement—to keep pushing David as far toward independence as he could go—sent a clear message to his parents.

"I hadn't seen enough evidence," Lauri Rogers said, "to tell me to stop. David improved here when no one else at those other places had been saying he would improve. Everyone was just patting us on the back and saying, 'Good luck,' and that sort of stuff."

Lauri and Dave weren't ready to accept that sort of outcome for their son, who was just barely twenty-two years old and already a crew chief for maintaining A-10s, the fighter jets commonly referred to as Warthogs by the air force.

"His whole plan was to become an astronaut," his mother said. "He was inspired by Chuck Yeager's autobiography. He read it, served in the Civil Air Patrol in high school and all that. He wanted to use the air force as a stepping stone to get some experience, then go to college. That was his plan."

———

As Lauri spoke, she was relaxing at a table in an informal dining room that overlooked the backyard of the family's comfortable home about a twenty-minute drive west of McGuire. It is the home they had chosen in 2009 when they made the decision to move to Virginia to be with their son. They had found a contractor willing to work with them to customize a new house that would accommodate David's needs—assuming he would be able to return to a home environment.

Flash forward to late May 2013, four years after the accident and nearly three and one-half years after the Rogers family moved into their new home.

The house, in a subdivision in the Chesterfield County community of Midlothian that was still being developed and was a constant beehive of activity for contractors, did not have a lake or a waterfall, but it did have doors wide enough to accommodate wheelchairs. It had waist-high handrails running along the walls. David had his own suite right inside the front door, complete with a large walk-in shower and a vanity area wide enough to accommodate a wheelchair.

The home back in Ohio remained on the market, and although that represented a financial burden on the family, it paled in comparison to the miracle they got to witness on a daily basis in Midlothian. Because the progress that Lauri and Dave Rogers had seen in their son years earlier—the slow but unmistakable progress that had prompted them to move to Virginia to help foster a better family atmosphere for his recovery—was in full, magnificent bloom four years after the crash, and it had gone further—much further—than even his parents had considered back in the dark days when they were still in Germany.

"I'm surprised," his father said, pausing to gulp and fight back tears, "he's made it back this far. When he was in Germany, he looked so bad.

"There was actually a period right after where I was like, if he passes tonight of if he doesn't make it through the next day, it might be the best thing for him."

That was in the immediate aftermath of May 26, 2009, when David, driving in a light rain and at a speed that authorities later determined was not excessive, hit a patch of oil on a German roadway that sent his BMW sedan across the center line in a curve and into the path of an oncoming Audi.

David had had a shattered pelvis, fractured ribs, organ damage, a punctured lung, and a severe TBI. He had needed a double craniotomy, a procedure where surgeons removed two flaps of his skull so they could reach damaged tissue in his brain.

Whereas doctors at the previous facilities where her son was treated were fond of making blanket statements about the limitations of patients who had

David's types of injuries, Lauri Rogers found that McNamee would take a significantly different tack.

"He wasn't unhopeful," she said. "He wasn't quashing anything. He was just willing to keep trying things."

Lauri admitted she could be aggressive when it came to the subject of how McNamee and his staff could continue to wring more and more improvement out of her son.

"I would badger him with questions about what we could do, what to expect, why we didn't try certain things and all that," she said, and each time, she would get the same response from McNamee.

"I don't have a crystal ball," he would say. "But we should just do what we do and see where it goes."

Rogers shook her head, smiled, and stared off in the distance.

"He's just a great advocate," she said. "His willingness to keep trying, his refusal to quit—I don't even want to think what would have happened if we hadn't made it here."

McNamee smiled later when told about her remarks.

"I have as much respect for her as I have for anybody on this Earth," he said.

A key element in David's recovery was the fact that he was in the VA's healthcare system. Had David been a civilian, insurance companies likely would have been unwilling to be that patient and continue funding therapy that wasn't producing rapid results. A more likely scenario, McNamee said, would have been an insurance company telling the Rogers family after two years that David would have to be moved to a private rehabilitation facility. Instead, Lauri Rogers found her oldest son in a military healthcare system in the hands of a young physician who was willing to be patient, to keep trying, and to keep exploring.

"Up until about five years ago, modern medicine would have told her that was impossible," McNamee said. "They would have told her, 'You get two years. Deal with it. Go on from there.'"

McNamee was far from the only person in the VA community of healing to rally around David.

In addition to tireless work put in by the speech therapists, physical therapists, kinesiotherapists, and occupational therapists, David got a significant boost from Paulette Beasley, the polytrauma unit's recreational therapist.

Beasley has a wide array of community partners lined up in Richmond and the surrounding area to provide services that help the unit's patients reconnect with their lifestyles before their injuries. The services include some activities that might seem unlikely for patients battling back from TBIs, broken bones, amputations, and the like, ranging from a horse stable in nearby Powhatan County, the Lonesome Dove Equestrian Center, which provides riding lessons for physically challenged patients, to Salisbury Country Club in Chesterfield County, which allows Beasley to bring over patients to go fly fishing at one of the golf course ponds on the property.

Lauri Rogers, unaware of the array of services that Beasley can arrange for patients, wasn't sure quite how to answer when Beasley asked her what David, who at that point was confined to a wheelchair, liked to do.

"Well," Lauri said with a tone of hesitation, "he's a rock climber."

"Okay," Beasley responded. "Then we should go to Peak Experiences."

Lauri shook her head later as she recalled the events.

"Her whole approach was amazing, like it was no big deal," Rogers said. "She really went to bat and got the whole ball rolling."

A large climbing center in Midlothian, Peak Experiences told Beasley that David would need a special full-body harness before he could take on the facility's indoor walls. This news was of some comfort to Lauri, given the fact that several months before the car crash in Germany, David had been in a climbing accident in Switzerland that had left him with a fractured clavicle, a fractured scapula, and a punctured lung. The kind of special body harness David would need was offered by Petzl International, a French-based climbing gear and outdoors outfitter. When the people at Petzl found out who would be using it and why he needed it, the company refused to charge for the harness.

Although finding a harness for him proved fairly easy, David was slowed by a case of meningitis, a relatively common occurrence in brain-surgery patients, which in turn slowed his ability to rebuild muscle strength. The prospect of returning to climbing, however, albeit in a restrictive harness that would limit how much work he could do, was enough to motivate him, and when motivated, David could get creative.

His mother recalled one day when he had just begun to demonstrate the ability to once again use his legs to push himself around in a wheelchair, and she was trying to see if he could start building back some strength in his arms as well. Up to that point, he had been using leg drive to propel himself around the polytrauma unit, whose entrance was guarded by a set of heavy wooden double doors that could be opened automatically by pushing a square metal button mounted on the wall just above waist height and about ten feet in front of the doors.

On this day, David had pushed himself through the unit and toward the double doors that separated him from the rest of the sprawling hospital, so his mother decided to issue a challenge.

"I'll take you off the unit," she told him, "if you can push the button."

David pushed his wheelchair over to the wall beside the button, and Lauri waited to see if he could reach out and push it flush against the wall to activate the door-opening mechanism. As he alternated between studying the button and trying to muster the needed strength and movement in his arms, his mother's anxiety grew. This might be just the perfect motivation he needed, she thought to herself, to start relying more on his arms.

In an instant, however, that all changed.

David grew tired of trying to figure out a way to coax into action a pair of arms that were not up to the task that day. So with that, David leaned over, placed his head against the button and pushed. The double doors swung open, and Lauri—holding back laughter—made good on her vow to take her creative, problem-solving son off the unit.

On a day in late April 2010, David went to Peak Experiences and, firmly strapped into a special full-body harness, found a bit of new normal.

"Eleven months to the day after his accident," his mother said. "To. The. Day," she repeated, this time pausing between words to savor the memories of another triumph in a recovery that doctors in Germany had assured her would not occur.

Creative help emerged from other sources as well. Coworkers at Progressive donated leave time to Dave Rogers so he could spend more time with his son immediately after the accident. When the family decided to leave Ohio, Dave didn't have to leave Progressive; instead, the company arranged for him to initially work out of its suburban Richmond office before eventually clearing the way for him to telecommute from the family's new home in Midlothian.

———

Four years after the accident, the Midlothian home had become a haven for David's new normal. He was advancing so well in his quest for progress and independence that it wouldn't be unusual for Lauri to wake up in the morning, go into the family room to let out the dogs—including Jersey the black Labrador retriever, David's service dog—only to find that David had gotten up before her. Not only did he let out the dogs, but when they came back in, he fed them.

David's progress was not confined to the house, either. In the spring of 2013, he got a new walker, this one with four wheels, and it wasn't long before he was logging more than a mile each day, either on a track at a local fitness center or on the streets around the family's home. He was an active participant in family outings and vacations, and when he was at home, he took part in conversations using a small electronic keyboard to tap out words while he continued to work at regaining his ability to speak. He also spent large quantities of time on his computer and posted frequently on his Facebook account.

In early June 2013, he surprised more than one person by using his computer to show just how far he had come.

His mother wasn't sure what to think when she got a telephone call from his primary care physician inquiring about David's right foot, which in recent weeks had begun dragging went he went on walks. Lauri was confused because she hadn't called the doctor recently—about David's foot or anything else. Then the doctor explained to her that he had received an e-mail from David detailing what was happening with his foot and asking the doctor for help. The primary care physician arranged for a consultation with a specialist—which, the more Lauri thought about it, pointed to a significant achievement for her son.

"David," she said, "is beginning to actively and appropriately advocate to get his needs met."

On a recovery scale for TBI patients, benchmarks don't get much higher than that.

McNamee nodded knowingly and smiled when told about what David had done. Years of patience and hard work were continuing to produce rewards, not only in the form of physical gains but also in terms of self-advocacy.

"David's turning another page," McNamee said. "He's putting his hands on the wheel again."

CHAPTER TWENTY-SEVEN

EIGHT PATHS TO FEAR

The final Friday afternoon in March 2013 was one of those typical sunny, early spring days when anyone who drove onto the grounds of McGuire VA Medical Center might quickly form the opinion that there were more people *outside* the hospital than within the walls of the sprawling red brick facility.

With winter finally showing unmistakable signs of releasing its cold, unforgiving grip, the courtyards and outdoor garden areas would become immensely popular hangouts, not only for staff members to eat lunch or take a relaxing break from their work schedules but also for patients and their visiting family members and friends to get away from the structured, enclosed environment of hospital stays.

Some patients would use crutches or canes to help them get outside. Others relied on wheelchairs. A few of the less-ambulatory patients would enlist the aid of loved ones to help them get on a gurney, drape it with a white sheet, and roll them outdoors. This was no time to get caught up in vanity; there were warm, healing rays of sunshine out there, not to mention the peaceful sights of blooming flowers and the soothing sounds of birds— a perfect mix of elements to help staff members, patients, and their loved ones take pause and think about better days ahead, about recovery, about rehabilitation.

On this afternoon, however, while so many others were basking in spring's welcome advances, seven caregivers—spouses, siblings, children, and parents of patients—were joined by two staff members in a windowless conference room on the second floor of the hospital, in the center of the polytrauma unit.

The group had passed over a chance to embrace the sunshine and warmth for an opportunity to learn more about what they could expect in the years ahead as they cared for their loved ones with TBI.

They were drawn to the conference room this day by the latest install-ment in the Polytrauma Family Education series, an ongoing set of talks and seminars designed specifically for the family and friends of patients. Overseen by Barbara Bauserman, the unit's patient and family education coordinator, the one-hour sessions were typically offered Tuesday through Friday each week. Attendance is strictly voluntary; if the topic was something that in-terested you, might help you, and fit your schedule, then the door was open.

Sometimes Bauserman would schedule what she called "Caregiver Support Group" sessions where the topics were whatever happened to be on the minds of the caregivers who came. It was a loosely structured environment designed to give family members and friends a chance to air their concerns and share their stories with each other. Other times, Bauserman would schedule sessions on diverse topics that ranged from amputee care and prevention issues to swallow-ing problems for stroke victims. The sessions were typically led by Bauserman or one of the therapists on the unit. One of the speech-language pathologists working on the unit might lead the discussion of swallowing problems, for example, or one of the unit's occupational therapists would speak with them about a specific aspect of the long-term rehabilitation process.

On this day, the speaker was someone everybody knew: Dr. Ajit Pai, the unit's medical director. The session's title was, "Long-term Management of Brain Injury," and who better to speak to the spouses, siblings, parents, and children than the doctor overseeing the care of their loved ones?

Strong on delegating duties among his entire staff, Pai makes an excep-tion when it comes to regularly delivering the presentation about long-term brain injury management. He has a reputation for relating well to patients and their caregivers, especially when it comes to taking complicated topics and breaking them down into understandable, digestible nuggets, and that approach in turn seems to cultivate trust and put the patients and families at ease. This day would be no different.

"Unfortunately," Pai began by telling his attentive audience, "the brain can get injured quite easily."

With that, he and Bauserman began distributing to the attendees two-page fact sheets that would serve as an outline for his presentation.

"On these two pieces of paper," he said, "are eight things that can really scare people."

For the next hour, Pai led the caregivers on a journey of some of the obstacles they may encounter in the years and decades in looking after their TBI patients. Some of the conditions Pai detailed were more serious than others. Certain ones occur more frequently than others. Yet all of them had one common denominator: From the time the patients left a hospital setting and the structured, closely monitored environment that is a part of it, the burden of being a watchdog for the patient and looking out for someone who may not be able to look out for themselves would rest squarely on the caregivers. The spouses, siblings, children, parents, and friends would have to take on the role of medical detectives, closely monitoring the patients in their home environments to spot signs of change that may signal trouble and taking re-sponsibility for relaying that information to the patient's medical team.

"Make sure," Pai told them, "that you advocate, advocate, advocate. You see them more than anyone else does. You know them better than anyone. You'll know if something is happening, if something has changed. So don't be afraid to speak up. You can make a big difference in the quality of their lives."

The eight points Pai covered were hydrocephalus, posttraumatic seizures, heterotopic ossification, movement disorders, spasticity, mood disorders, sleep disturbances, and posttraumatic headaches. With each of the eight, Pai patiently explained what the condition was, what it could do, what signs the caregivers should watch for, and what the medical remedies are. As he typically does, he stripped away the complex medical jargon and made it easy to digest for his audience, which had not only a number of older adults but also included a fifteen-year-old. As is typical, Pai kept everyone engaged, as evidenced by the smiles, nods, and frequent questions, all of which he deftly fielded.

For example, *hydrocephalus* may sound like a daunting term, but broken down, it is what is commonly referred to as water on the brain. It occurs when extra spinal fluid accumulates in the brain's ventricles, or compartments, and it can lead to dangerous pressure levels in the brain. Pai told the caregivers to pay close attention to their patients for symptoms that include headache, nausea, vomiting, lethargy, difficulty walking, and urinary incontinence. All of these could be a sign that spinal fluid is accumulating in the brain at unsafe levels. If these symptoms occur, the caregivers should call the doctor, who can then order a CT scan to check for a pressure buildup in the brain.

Posttraumatic seizures, caused by irritated membrane nerves, can occur in two forms: the typical convulsive form, which is physically obvious, or nonconvulsive. Pai said that just because there may not be physically apparent convulsions involved does not mean that the caregivers can't detect a nonconvulsive seizure. The patient may report having hallucinations or hearing loud ringing, or there could be another obvious symptom that a nonconvulsive seizure has occurred.

"They could be acting like a jerk," Pai said to laughs. "Once again, watch them. You'll know. Is there an unexplained mood change? It could be that simple. It may be them just acting like a jerk, or it may be a sign of something more serious."

Research indicates seizures are likely to manifest themselves fairly early in the recovery and rehabilitation process. Pai said 40 percent of TBI patients who have seizures are likely to do so within six months of their injury, 50 percent to 60 percent are likely to do so within one year, and 80 percent will do so within two years.

Heterotopic ossification—the formation of extra bone cells on skeletons—typically occurs on the hips of TBI patients, but it can also be found in areas such as the shoulders and elbows. It generally occurs within a few months of the TBI, and patients may complain of swelling, pain in the joints, and a reduced range of motion. Pai said over-the-counter painkillers may help the condition, but if they don't, the next options would likely be prescription drugs or surgery.

Small numbers of patients who have suffered a severe TBI will be more prone to movement disorders, including tremors (involuntary muscle contractions and relaxations that often occur in the hands), dystonia (sustained muscle contractions that produce twisted movements or posture problems), myoclonus (brief, quick muscle contractions), and tics (sudden motor movements that are repetitive but not rhythmic). Pai said the disorders are usually treated with medications, although in some cases the conditions may resolve themselves without drugs.

The fifth item on Pai's list of eight is spasticity, or unusually tight muscles, a condition that can have wide-ranging effects on patients, including their body positioning, personal hygiene, levels of pain, and ability to sleep. Splints, stretching, and ice and heat therapy have been effective at reducing the effects of spasticity, and recently gains have been made in the use of Botox-type drugs and Baclofen to help reduce spasticity.

Number six on the list, mood disorders, is something that affects 50 percent of TBI patients, most in the form of depression but some in the form of anxiety. The key to dealing with mood disorders, Pai said, can be as simple as keeping patients busy and giving them a sense of purpose in their new lives. If they are physically able, it would be ideal for them to have a job, even if it may not be as intellectually stimulating or physically demanding as what they did before their TBI. The mere act of having a daily routine, something they can look forward to on a consistent basis, can produce substantial benefits in the area of self worth.

"Work," Pai said, "is the number one treatment for depression in the country."

The last two items on Pai's outline can both serve as examples of just how far the medical community still has to travel in the field of brain-injury research. Sleep disturbances and posttraumatic headaches both have been studied by various medical researchers, but those efforts have failed to produce consistent findings. For example, Pai noted that depending on the study, sleep disturbances can be expected to occur in as few as 30 percent or as many as 80 percent of people who have had a TBI. For posttraumatic headaches, the range—again, depending on the study—is 30 percent to 90 percent.

"We just don't really know," he said. "There are wide disparities in the numbers."

Patients who have trouble sleeping may see those problems affect cognition, fatigue, irritability, and pain. To ward them off, Pai recommends such tools as reducing caffeine and nicotine use, especially in the afternoons and evenings, and practicing what he called sleep hygiene—in essence, teaching your brain to wind down and prepare to sleep. Examples include not watching television or reading suspense novels within an hour of when you plan to go to bed, using that time instead to gradually ramp down your brain's activity levels.

For posttraumatic headaches, Pai recommends that caregivers keep a headache log that includes as much information as they can document, including when the headaches occur, what happens before they occur, what the patient eats and drinks, how long the headaches last, and what appears to be effective—or ineffective—in getting the headaches to subside. Often the keys to preventing the headaches can be found in the information contained in the logs.

Pai wrapped up the session with some general advice, starting with a plea for compassion and understanding for the new caregivers. He asked them to remember that the patients are not children and that they, like their caregivers, are adjusting to a new way of life.

"Sometimes," he said, "you've got to learn how to back off, because nobody wants to be told what to do. Everybody wants to be treated like an adult."

Patience, while it may be frequently taxed, must be constantly practiced, he said.

"Never get embarrassed by a loved one," Pai said before sharing an anecdote about going to the store with his young daughter, who accidentally knocked several items off a display shelf and didn't seem the least bit bothered by it.

"My first reaction was, 'Oh, my God. I'm so embarrassed,'" he recalled. "But you know what? They're not embarrassed about it at all. So keep that in mind. People do crazy things all the time. Just go with it."

Pai used the anecdote about his daughter to again remind the caregivers that they must be the watchdogs, the chief advocates, for their patients.

"Don't ever hesitate to ask for help," he said. "Your doctors, your therapists should be responsive. Your social workers should be responsive. Communication is the key. Don't be afraid to speak up."

He ended the session with a simple message designed to reassure them as they prepare for their new roles as lifetime caregivers.

"You're going to be fine," he said. "You're going to all be experts."

CHAPTER TWENTY-EIGHT

ALIVE DAY

Filtered sunlight was starting to break through the top of the tree line in McAllen, Texas, on the morning of December 27, 2012, when Jon McHenry logged on to his computer and posted a message to his Facebook friends, telling them that at that approximate time one year earlier, roughly 6:30 P.M. local time in southeastern Afghanistan's Paktia province, his life and those of five others "had forever changed in a matter of a blink of an eye."

> I do not need it to be an anniversary to be reminded of the events that took place that day. I'm constantly reminded of it physically and mentally on a daily basis.
>
> Alive day: the date of an anniversary of a close escape from death, especially one involving permanent injury.
>
> Today is my Alive Day. This is supposed to be a joyous day to be reminded of being reborn and given a second chance at life, but in reality it has tainted the 27th of December

and the holiday season forever in my life because 3 amazing people are not here to celebrate it with me....

I'm where I need to be on this day. It just feels right, not only for myself but also here for an important family, as their angel was always there for me.

Jon's post, filed from McAllen because he had gone there to spend the day with the mother of Spc. Kurt W. Kern, one of his three comrades killed in the IED blast, drew a flood of comments from friends and relatives expressing their support and love.

Those weighing in on his Facebook post included Spc. Michael Crawford, one of the three people who had survived the blast. Crawford was now living in San Antonio, where he was undergoing outpatient therapy as he tried to transition from a wheelchair to crutches in his therapy sessions, slowly regaining his ability to stand and walk following multiple surgeries for spinal and left leg fractures.

"That's real talk right there buddy!" he wrote. "Like you said I'm so thankful to be alive but also every day I have the reminder of the guys that unfortunately didn't and it makes me sick. But I just need to better myself and live for them."

One year removed from the blast, Crawford and Capt. Luis Avila—who remained hospitalized at Walter Reed National Military Medical Center in Maryland—were struggling to get back their physical independence. Jon, meantime, was struggling to figure out what to do with his independence and what role the IED blast would play in shaping it. Disappointed that the army would not return him to his unit before the end of the deployment, even though he had a signed document from a physician saying he was physically fit to do so, Jon no longer wanted to remain in the military. His enlistment was about to expire in the spring of 2013, and now it was just a matter of figuring out his next move.

Determining his initial path in his postmilitary life was proving to be elusive, however. He was having a difficult time deciding between college, professional school, or some other option. Furthermore, deciding where he would go to start the next chapter of his life also was proving elusive.

One thing he knew was that McAllen, a city of 130,000 people in the Rio Grande Valley, at the southern tip of Texas along the Mexico border, remained a strong draw. He continued to want to spend time in the city where his friend and comrade, Kern, had enjoyed his youth, and where Kern's mother, Martha, still lived. Not only did Jon find solace spending time with Martha in McAllen as he tried to chart his future and make peace with his past, but he also spoke of possibly moving to the Rio Grande Valley once he left the service. The latest journey he made to McAllen, a drive of more than six hours from Fort Hood, was his third in slightly more than three months.

After expressing his sentiments on Facebook about the blast that had changed so many lives, he joined Martha and several other members of Kern's family on a picnic—of sorts. Their destination was neighboring Mission, Texas, home of Rio Grande Valley State Veterans Cemetery. Once they drove into the cemetery, they went to Section 34, Row H, Site 222.

They had food and family and friends—and they had Kurt Kern.

"It was pretty nice," Jon said. "We had some lawn chairs and all that, and we just hung out and spent some time around him. We were there for most of the day, really."

There were only a handful of other visitors that Thursday at the cemetery, a seventy-five-acre site that had been opened by the Texas Veterans Land Board in December 2006. The cemetery was designed to eventually accommodate up to twenty-five thousand graves, but because it was still in its relative infancy, the Kern family's December 27 gathering didn't draw much attention at a facility that is adorned with brass signs advising visitors: "BE SILENT AND RESPECTFUL. HERE PATRIOTS REST."

The group at Kern's grave was able to pass the hours sharing remembrances of him, retelling his favorite jokes, and building new memories of each other and that day. In the evening they all attended a mass for Kern at the church where his family worships, and Jon was able to meet a number of Kern's childhood friends.

"It was a good time," Jon said. "Good day. It was definitely a good experience meeting so many people who knew him.

"But yeah, glad I made the trip. Don't want to forget."

At various points throughout the day, Jon found himself drifting back to one year earlier. Even though he didn't have any specific memories of the IED blast or what had happened in the minutes and hours after it, he still drifted, still tried to remember, to go back to the moment and piece together events using information his comrades had told him about what had happened during the blast and its aftermath. Looking back later, Jon said that day in McAllen was at least a step in the direction toward him achieving closure. Just how big of a step it was remained to be seen.

"I really didn't have any expectations," he said. "The whole thing that really took me was just thinking exactly one year ago, reliving it, what really happened at this time and that time. That really took me away a little bit. I remember at one point thinking that my ankle was pretty much behind my neck right about now. That was weird. But the whole day kind of went like that. There were moments. Lots of little moments."

The next day, Jon drove back to Fort Hood.

———

Jon's trip to McAllen for the December 27 remembrance capped a busy week that included the first Christmas he and Jay celebrated with Leo, who was, not surprisingly, showered with gifts.

"That little guy," Jon said, "means everything to me."

The dynamics at his job were considerably less joyous. Several days before Christmas, one of the dorm rooms at the operations center where Jon worked became the temporary home of a colleague who had been arrested a few days earlier for domestic violence. The colleague, with a wife and two young children, had been barred from returning to his house following his arrest, so he was instructed to stay at the dorm room and check in daily at the operations office where Jon worked.

Jon, who had been deployed to Afghanistan with the colleague, felt sympathy for him with the holidays approaching, so he tried to make sure the man was coping as well as possible under the circumstances.

"I don't know what happened with him and his wife, and it's none of my business," Jon explained. "But I was cool with him. We used to talk and work out and stuff like that."

On December 23, the man told Jon that his wife had cleaned out their bank account, leaving him without money to even buy food. So Jon took his colleague to a local Wal-Mart and, using his own money, paid for about fifty dollars' worth of food so the man would have something in his room to eat. The colleague expressed his gratitude to Jon, who told him to stay in touch.

"On Christmas Eve, I talked to him and he said he talked to a lawyer about getting a divorce and all that stuff. He said he was good and didn't need anything," Jon said. "On Christmas, I sent him a message. He said it was tough not being around his two boys. I said if he needed anything, don't be afraid to hit me up."

When Jon went to work on the morning of December 26, he discovered that the man had failed to check in with the operations office that morning as required. Jon was sent to his room to check on him.

Jon knocked on his door and got no response. He left, went back about an hour later, and knocked on the door again. Getting no response a second time, he returned to the operations office, got a master key, and went back to the man's room.

"The key worked fine," he said, "but the door wasn't opening. I don't know if it was barricaded or what, but you could tell it wouldn't move."

Jon then went around back, slid open a window, poked his head inside, and tried to look around, only to realize it was too dark inside to see anything.

"So I yelled, 'Hey, it's McHenry! What's up?' Still nothing."

Jon returned to the operations office and told his supervisor, who told him to wait in the office while he went to the room and crawled in the window to check around inside. The supervisor wasn't gone long.

"Next thing you know," Jon said, "he came running back in and screaming to call the commander."

The man had hanged himself in the bathroom.

"He was a happy-go-lucky kid," Jon said. "He had two sons and everything."

That afternoon, Jon got in his car and drove six-plus hours to McAllen. He had plenty of time during the trip and in the weeks afterward to think about why his colleague's suicide didn't have more of an impact on him. Sure, he felt sad, but it was not an overwhelming, wrenching, sit-down-and-have-a-good cry sorrow. He felt shocked, but not to the point where it left him feeling particularly traumatized.

"Throughout the whole ordeal and stuff, I don't know if it was what I was through before in Afghanistan and everything, but I wasn't really like— I was thinking I should be showing some emotion, but I really couldn't feel anything," he said.

Not long after the man's body was discovered in the bathroom, the counselor Jon had been seeing arrived at the operations center to check on everyone.

"She talked to everybody who was directly involved in it," Jon said. "She talked to each of us, but I said I was good. And you know what? I was. Normally, that kind of emotion is kind easy to gauge your feelings about something. But I wasn't feeling much. Maybe I just had a lot going on."

He saw the counselor several times in January, but as the weeks passed, Jon's thoughts about the suicide did not necessarily center on the man's death or the manner in which the man had taken his life, but rather on his own actions in his comrade's final days. For example, should Jon have invited him to his home on Christmas day?

"But in hindsight, I don't know," he said. "I could play, 'What ifs' all day."

The more Jon thought about it, the more he realized that his perspective on death had been altered by the horrific events on that dark road in Afghanistan a year earlier.

Before the IED explosion, death had been an unmatchable tragedy to Jon. There was no qualifying it. Death was a devastating event no matter who died or what the circumstances were. Now, however, he had been exposed to death as a cost of war. Some die, some live, and those who are left behind have to move on. There was no way anyone could reasonably explain why Jon had been one of three people inside that armored vehicle to survive, and there was no way to answer why three others had died. Why was Jon—blown out the driver's side door and still strapped into the driver's seat—able to resume running within months of his devastating injuries, while Capt. Luis Avila—who was sitting a mere three feet away from Jon in the vehicle, literally close enough for him to reach out and touch—was still struggling to walk and talk a year after the blast?

What Jon could determine was how his feelings about death had changed, not only in the months after the IED blast in Afghanistan but also in the weeks after his colleague's suicide and his trip to McAllen for the one-year remembrance of the death of Kurt Kern. What he now knew was that he no longer viewed death the same way. Now, he was more accepting and less inclined to feel devastated by death unless it involved his son, his wife, his father, or some other family member. His new perspective on death frightened him a bit, especially considering how little of a reaction he had to his colleague's suicide.

"I don't know if that whole experience—I think I'm just kind of numb," he said. "I don't know how to explain it. It's not something that shocks me. And I wonder about that."

Part of that fear was based on the fact that he was still trying to make sense of the IED blast, still seeking closure from those events.

"The more and more I thought about it and stuff, maybe it's just me, but it'd be different if we all made it out alive," he said. "But I really don't want to reflect on myself too much."

Jon was beginning to think that closure was something he might never get.

"A part of me is always going to want to get that. A part of me is always going to want to know how it would have been if they had let me go back," he said. "I hate to say I'm bitter about it, but that's the truth of the matter. That's exactly what it is."

As a result, Jon—who had planned on making a career of the army—decided that once he was denied the chance to return to Afghanistan and complete his remarkable comeback, he could no longer in good conscience stay in the service.

"That's when I made my mind up that I didn't want to be in the military anymore," he said. "I just really felt let down."

Although Jon wasn't particularly fond of playing, "What ifs," he found it difficult to avoid doing so when the subject was about him returning to Afghanistan to rejoin his comrades for the end of their deployment.

"In a perfect world, I would have loved to go exactly where I was laying. That would be in a perfect world. But that specific area would be difficult because it's hostile," he said. "But at least getting on the same base that I was on, that would have helped fill the void a little bit. Something. Anything."

As 2012 rolled over into 2013 and Jon moved closer to leaving the army and beginning a new chapter in his life, however, he found that his quest to make peace with what happened in Afghanistan was slowly giving way to a new quest. Now he was trying to make peace with not being able to rejoin his comrades at the end of their deployment and being denied the chance to finish off his comeback on his terms. He was also trying to make peace with the fact that in war, some people die while others live, and when you get another chance at life, you try to capitalize and make the most of it.

"There's a level of acceptance to the matter, sure," he said. "I don't know. It's just that I kind of wish things would have been a little bit better. But I've definitely accepted it. I know it's real. It happened. I'm okay with it. I just wish the story would have ended a little bit different."

He paused.

"I think I'd feel a lot better about it if I had that closure about it and got to go back and finish.

"I think I'll always have a piece of me missing."

CHAPTER TWENTY-NINE

ART THERAPY

The soldier's wife didn't know.

She didn't understand why her husband, home from his second tour in Afghanistan, had difficulties sleeping.

Sometimes she would go to bed and he wouldn't join her, instead staying up all night. Sometimes they would go to bed together, but he wouldn't make it long before he'd get up and spend the rest of the night awake, alone with his thoughts.

She didn't understand why he seemed so quiet, so distant—always processing his thoughts, but rarely able to express them or to explain to her what was going on inside his mind or to open up with the woman to whom he had committed to sharing his life.

Afghanistan had changed him, and now she worried that she may have lost him forever.

"All she knew was that he wouldn't talk to her anymore," Felix Cruz said, "and all he knew was that he didn't know how to tell her what he was feeling, what he had seen, how he had changed over there."

As Cruz spoke, he was standing in a long, narrow room at the McGuire VA Medical Center's Polytrauma Transitional Rehabilitation Program building. After injured service members complete their stay in the PRC on the second floor of the main hospital, they can be shifted to the transitional unit in a separate building, several hundred yards south of the massive main hospital, as a final stop before their release. The transitional unit can be regarded as a final tune-up of sorts, a place where injured service men and women can get the help they need to learn—or, in some cases, relearn—specific skills that can help them succeed in the workplace and at home.

One example is the unit's fully equipped kitchen, where therapists can work with those who have lost one or more limbs or have limited mobility and motor skills because of a brain injury and teach them how to accomplish such seemingly routine tasks as preparing meals alone and cleaning up after themselves.

Another area in the unit that prepares the war wounded to reenter society is the long, narrow room that Cruz oversees. Bathed in light from the windows that line one of the room's long sides, the space is part art gallery, part classroom, part therapist's office. It is also a place where some patients can make important discoveries about themselves.

The three walls that aren't covered in glass are almost completely covered with works of art by the unit's patients. There are charcoal drawings, oil-on-canvas paintings, wood carvings—all of varying degrees of difficulty and expertise. What's important to Cruz, however, isn't the technical prowess that is or isn't displayed in the works of art. Instead, his goal is for the patients to use art as a tool of healing, communication, and discovery.

Cruz smiled softly and nodded when a visitor inquired about an oil painting, perhaps not even eighteen inches by eighteen inches, that featured a leafless tree done in almost menacing dark gray tones with a black, badly contorted, pained-looking face drawn into the center of the main trunk. Large, blood-red droplets appeared to be raining from the branches of the tree.

This painting, Cruz explained, was what had helped the sleepless soldier, the one back from his second tour in Afghanistan, finally reconnect with his wife. The soldier had been exposed repeatedly to IED blasts that had left him suffering from TBI as well as PTSD.

"In his two tours, I think there were at least five IEDs, maybe six," Cruz recalled.

One was particularly traumatic and left the soldier battling demons long after he returned to the United States. When the soldier found himself unable to talk with his wife about those demons, Cruz gave him another outlet, another way that eventually helped him open up the lines of communication and start down the road to healing.

Cruz told the man to paint.

When the man told Cruz he couldn't even draw a stick figure, Cruz said it didn't matter. Just paint, he told him. Draw something. Draw anything. Start somewhere. Take the first step. See where it leads you.

It wasn't long before the soldier had a number of pieces of art work, including this one in particular, this pained-looking tree with what appeared to be blood raining from its branches.

"Turns out he lost somebody. He lost one of his buddies," Cruz recalled. "See the face there in the tree? His buddy got his face blown off. That's what that is.

"And all the red? When his buddy's face was blown off, he got blood all over himself. It's his buddy's blood."

Cruz shook his head.

"That's how he was finally able to talk to his wife," Cruz said, his voice rising with excitement. "He couldn't tell her all the terrible things. But when he showed her this, then she knew. Then she finally had some idea of what he was dealing with, what kind of pain he was in."

Cruz paused.

"They're talking now," he said. "He's doing better. They're doing better."

––––––

Dr. Gary Goldberg, the medical director at the transitional unit, has a staff that covers a wide gamut of services, including physical therapists, occupational therapists, kinesiotherapists, psychologists, and psychiatrists. Felix Cruz is technically considered a creative arts specialist, but to Goldberg he is much more.

"He's a very unique individual, and he brings so much to the team," Goldberg said. "He's a fascinating person. He really is. He always seems to find a way to connect with people. We're very fortunate to have him."

Cruz, who works within the recreation therapy division, spent nine years in the navy before taking a job with the VA in compensation and pension to help finance his way through Cedar Crest College in his hometown of Allentown, Pennsylvania. After earning a bachelor's degree in fine arts, Cruz decided to move to Richmond, home of VCU, when his son enrolled at the school.

Cruz was still working in the compensation field, this time at McGuire, when he saw a job posting one day for a recreation therapist's assistant at the hospital. He applied for the job and made a pitch to incorporate art into the position.

"It was going to flourish, and I knew that," he said. "But I had to sell everything."

These days, he has a small, cramped, windowless office next door to the long, narrow studio. His cubicle, one of three in the office, is adorned with dozens of pictures ranging in subject from Miles Davis to Muhammad Ali and from Pablo Picasso to a logo of the Philadelphia Flyers. Over in the studio, Cruz has amassed a small library of textbooks and biographies with titles that include *Drawing Animals, Living With Art, Flowers, Leonardo da Vinci, The Power Of Feminist Art,* and *Art Nouveau.*

He began his therapies by offering thirty-minute art sessions for the patients, but that soon proved inadequate.

"When the patients started giving feedback, they said they needed more of this," Cruz said. "Now we have one-hour time slots. But I'll stay as long as they want. There are no time limits."

Not surprisingly, the hardest part is getting the patients to initially believe in the process, especially considering that most of them have no background whatsoever in the arts.

"At first, they're real reluctant," he said. "But then they learn how to express themselves."

Once that happens, regardless of the relative quality of the art, regardless of whether the patients are drawing glorified stick figures or intricate landscapes, they begin to appreciate what their sessions with Cruz can produce.

"I see it as a release of emotions," he said. "They find it a way to release the anger, to release the depression."

The key is to establish a rapport with the patient—something that Cruz seems to do easily, both because he has a military background and can relate to the patients and because of his engaging personality. Once the rapport exists, then Cruz can begin helping the patients help themselves.

Yes, he will acknowledge to them, your stick figure really wasn't all that good. But I'm going to help you make it better, to improve on that, little by little, and here's how we're going to accomplish that. Once that occurs, Cruz will inspire confidence in his patients and give them more and more responsibilities to take charge of their own discoveries and to branch out and explore areas they may not have been willing to previously examine. It isn't solely about helping a patient express himself and explore creative areas he might have been reluctant to visit without prodding, however.

Cruz, who also is certified as a brain injury specialist, is careful to make sure the art sessions address such concerns as mobility, cognitive skills, and other areas that may need attention in the aftermath of a TBI. For example, one of his patients, a twenty-year-old soldier with a TBI, was nearing the end of his rehabilitation at McGuire but still had only limited use of his left arm. So Cruz, rather than give him a canvas and paintbrush and turn him loose in the studio, opted for a more structured approach, one that would incorporate exercises designed to not only work his brain but also his left arm.

He had the young man build a jewelry box. Using a kit that included soft pine wooden panels as well as metal fasteners and nails, the patient had to first read the instructions and then follow them by using both hands to put the box together. The patient came into the studio, exchanged pleasantries with Cruz, popped an Eminem album into the CD player and began working.

Cruz, hearing some of the obscenities on the CD, gently needled the patient.

"What are you doing listening to Eminem? You're too young for that," he said. "You should be listening to Justin Bieber."

The young man laughed, then began putting two pieces together, struggling to incorporate his unsteady and slowly responsive left arm. He stopped as a look of confusion crossed his face, and he asked Cruz if he was doing it the right way. Cruz smiled and put one hand on the patient's shoulder.

"I don't know," he said in a gentle tone. "What do the directions say?"

"I don't know," the young man said.

"Well, take a look," Cruz encouraged him. "You can do it."

With that, Cruz said he would be right back, excused himself, walked out of the studio, and closed the door behind him. Once outside, Cruz reviewed his actions.

"If I put those two pieces together for him, then he's not using his left arm," he said. "And if I tell him what the directions say, then he's not reading them himself. So we leave for a few minutes and let him figure it out himself. And he will. He'll get there. He doesn't need me."

Sure enough, Cruz went back in about ten minutes later and found that the patient had successfully finished that part of the assembly and had moved on to another task. Not only was the patient smiling, but Cruz was as well.

"It's therapeutic for me, too," Cruz said. "I always have a grin on my face when I get home."

———

Cruz generally arrives at his office at 7:30 A.M. and starts his work day with a pot of coffee. In addition to art leisure education and working with patients on an individual basis, he also plans outings such as trips to baseball games, movies, and VFW posts.

It's all designed to get the patients out in the community and learning to function again by using parts of their bodies that have been injured, whether it's an issue related to mobility, cognitive function, stress, or something else. It can add up to some trying, time-consuming times for the staff, whether they have two people or two dozen on any given outing.

"I've been doing this for four or five years," Cruz said, "and I've never seen a complete movie, never seen a complete ball game. It's always something.

There are always challenges. Each day is different. It's never the same around here.

"My day is supposed to be done at four thirty. Some days, I'm lucky to get home by nine."

Not that he's complaining. Like many employees at McGuire, Cruz worked at enough different jobs before his arrival in Richmond to give him an appreciation for the sense of camaraderie and the commitment to serving those who have served their country. In his wallet he carries what appears to be a business card, worn and dog-eared. Instead of containing his name, job title, and contact information, however, the card has a quotation from the late Arthur Ashe, the tennis champion, historian, and humanitarian.

"True heroism is remarkably sober, very undramatic," it says. "It is not the urge to surpass all others at whatever cost, but the urge to serve others at whatever cost."

Affirmation for Cruz that he was in the right job for him came in the form of a patient who was sitting in his studio one day, working away at an art project, when the door swung open and one of the staff psychiatrists came in and walked up to the patient.

"You're late. You know you have a therapy appointment with me, don't you?" the psychiatrist said.

The patient showed no interest in moving.

"No," he told the psychiatrist in a matter-of-fact tone. "This is my therapy right here."

CHAPTER THIRTY

OUTSIDE HELP

Bill Haneke was the picture of quiet confidence as he got off the elevator on the second floor at McGuire VA Medical Center and walked straight for the section known as 2-B, or the PRC.

"Hi Bill," came the greetings as he approached the nurses' station. Haneke cheerfully returned the salutations and kept walking to the back hallway of the unit, where he turned left and headed purposefully for a patient's room.

Haneke had met this patient a day earlier in a brief visit. His second visit was not terribly long either, but unlike the first meeting, this one ended with the patient and his loved ones wiping away tears. His mission complete, Haneke left the room and walked out of the unit, once again exchanging pleasantries with the nurses and other members of the staff on the way.

"See you soon, Bill," they said—for indeed, they would.

It can seem as though Haneke is at the unit on an almost daily basis, and each time he comes, the scenario repeats itself. He goes to see however many patients are on his list that day, spends a few minutes with each one, makes them cry, and leaves—and everyone is satisfied.

The reason he makes them cry is also the same reason everyone is satisfied.

Haneke is a cofounder and board member of Families of the Wounded Fund Incorporated, a charitable nonprofit that has produced remarkable results in a remarkably short time after being founded under remarkable circumstances. Although it is the basic mission of all charitable nonprofits to help those in need, Families of the Wounded has found a singular way to be particularly effective and to strike back at a major chasm that opens and threatens to swallow up so many families whose worlds are turned upside down literally in an instant when a loved one is wounded in battle.

The medical treatment for the war wounded costs the service member nothing, and the military will pay to get certain immediate family members to the side of their wounded loved one and for lodging while he or she is hospitalized. However, myriad other expenses may be associated with being suddenly uprooted and traveling across the country to live somewhere else for what can be months at a time during their loved one's recovery and rehabilitation. For example, a wife who is flown to Richmond with her two young children and then driven to McGuire to be by her wounded husband's side at McGuire during his six months of rehabilitation may quickly be overcome by a sense of impending doom when she thinks about the family's immediate financial future. Sure, her husband's paychecks will continue to come in, but the several hundred dollars a month she was making at her part-time job back home in, say, Texas? That's gone. Their lodging in Richmond may be free, but the mortgage on their ranch house back home? Still due every month. Sure, the army flew her and her children to Richmond, but the payments on their new minivan back in Texas? Still due every month.

Throw in day-care expenses the families may encounter over the course of a long-term stay in Richmond, the cost of diapers and baby food, clothing expenses to make up for the fact that they traveled to Richmond with only what they could cram into a suitcase, various homeowners' and car insurance bills that continue to come due, and other miscellaneous costs associated with day-to-day living, and it can be easy to see why a family already worried about a loved one's long-term recovery can also be overcome by anxieties about their own immediate financial future.

Then Haneke walks into their room and says that, on behalf of a grateful nation and on behalf of the Families of the Wounded, he'd like to give them this check. For $6,000.

"It's amazing the reactions we get," Haneke said. "Ninety-nine percent just burst into tears immediately. I can't tell you how many say we're the answer to a prayer and that they were down to their last three dollars or their last five dollars or that they were even broke and were borrowing from friends and family."

Haneke paused, looked down, and shook his head.

"Reactions like that," he said in a tone only slightly above a whisper, "continue to tell me we're doing the right thing."

As improbable as it seems that a Richmond-based charity would give $6,000 to a family that is merely passing through the city, consider that it is not unusual for Haneke and his group to deliver as many as three checks a day to the patients on the polytrauma unit. In addition, if Families of the Wounded sees that the patients and their loved ones are still in need in the weeks and months after the donation, the group will give them another check. For another $6,000.

Families of the Wounded also will keep tabs on the patients after they leave Richmond, and if need be, a further donation is not out of the question.

———

This well-funded, well-run financial lifesaving operation that lives by the simple motto "Help us help the healing" got its unlikely start from a group of mostly Vietnam-era marine veterans from the Richmond area who like to get together for an informal breakfast every month.

One morning in early 2005, the marines chose as their gathering spot a restaurant on Midlothian Turnpike, a busy commercial stretch in South Richmond, not far from McGuire. After they got seated, they noticed two young women, both with babies, who came in and sat at a table beside them. Both women were visibly upset, and it wasn't long before one broke into tears. One of the marines went over to their table and asked the women if they were okay and if there was anything he could do to help.

The women explained that both had just gotten into Richmond because their husbands had been injured in Operation Iraqi Freedom and had been sent to McGuire for what looked like lengthy rehabilitation stints. One woman had driven drove two and one-half days from Texas and was out of gas and out of money. The other woman had just arrived from Massachusetts and was down to one-fourth of a tank of gas and five dollars.

The man told the women that he and his friends were all marines and would be honored to pick up their breakfast tab. Then he went back and told his comrades the women's story, and after everyone finished eating, the marines took the women shopping for gasoline, diapers, and other essentials. The marines not only paid for everything, but they also gave the women some spending cash. They expressed their gratitude to the women for their service in support of the military, and the women expressed their thanks to the marines for helping them in a time of crisis. With that, the women went back to the hospital, and the men went on with their day.

Instead of ending there, however, the encounter kept percolating with the marines, and it wasn't long before the men, all either retired or approaching retirement, began asking each other if there wasn't something else they could do to address what was an obvious need in their community. Their conversations grew to include other Vietnam-era veterans in the Richmond area, including Haneke, a West Point graduate and retired army captain. Pretty soon, this informal collection of veterans was banding together to buy gift cards and cook meals to be delivered to McGuire to the families of service members who had been injured in Iraq.

Yet the more time the members of this group spent at McGuire trying to help these out-of-town families, the more they realized there was much more that could be done. McGuire had yet to even start its polytrauma unit, but the war in Iraq was producing large numbers of injured US service members needing treatment, and Richmond was being flooded with families in need, many of them young, with children, and with limited financial means.

The group of Richmond-area veterans possessed two key qualities that made it easy for them to grasp the significance of the issue and to respond the way they did. First, the group included a number of men who were career military—men who had so many medals and commendations that it would be difficult to accurately count them—so they knew well the challenges facing service members and their families. Second, the group was well-connected; among them were a bank president, a retired university president, corporate titans, and Pentagon brass. Together they possessed not only a can-do attitude but also the means to get it done. So they did—in relatively short order—and the results were nothing short of astounding.

In April 2006, Families of the Wounded Fund Incorporated was granted status as a so-called 501(c)3, a tax-exempt nonprofit, by the IRS. In its first fiscal year, Families of the Wounded reported contributions of more than $411,000. That total surged to nearly $801,000 the next year, in 2007—as a recession was starting to hover over the nation—and by the time the charity was a mere five years old, it had taken in donations totaling $2,537,594.

Perhaps even more astounding was the amount of expenses that Families of the Wounded reported to the Internal Revenue Service: $0.

Printing costs, use of office equipment, travel expenses—anything you can think of that is associated with running a charity—is completely absorbed by the members of Families of the Wounded. Their volunteer duties include everything from maintaining contact with the polytrauma unit staff and screening prospective recipients to making fundraising appearances on behalf of the charity and keeping track of the group's financial records.

"It's important to us when we go speak to a group of prospective donors that we be able to look them in the eyes and say one hundred percent of their contributions will go toward helping these families," Haneke said. "It's not just that it builds credibility. It's the right thing to do."

Haneke, who has retired from a second career as a hospital administrator, estimated he puts in an average of fifteen hours a week in his role as what amounts to the organization's point man with the polytrauma unit. He is the unit's primary contact for prospective recipients, and he then goes and personally screens them. If they are qualified, Haneke then polls the fifteen board members to see if they approve a check—a simple majority of eight votes is all it takes for approval. After that, Haneke arranges to get a check from Village Bank—whose president, navy retiree Thomas W. Winfree, is a Families of the Wounded board member—and then delivers that check to the recipients. Haneke, as are most other board members, also is active in the group's fundraising efforts.

"I guess," he said with a sheepish grin, "it's become a labor of love for me. My wife thinks I'm in too deep. But I love it. I really do. Truth is, we all do."

Families of the Wounded began by distributing checks of $1,000 to eligible families, and the amount gradually increased, first to $3,000, then to $5,000, and eventually to $6,000, where Haneke said it is likely to remain. In its first seven years of operation, Families of the Wounded helped more than 450 families of patients in Richmond, many of them more than once.

———

The list of officers and directors for Families of the Wounded does not include Keneshia T. Thornton, but anyone associated with the organization will tell you she is, in effect if not in fact, a gatekeeper for the nonprofit. A social work case manager on the polytrauma unit, Thornton is familiar with the patients who pass through the doors. Accordingly, she is aware of who appears to meet the criteria for assistance from Families of the Wounded.

The qualifications are simple and straightforward. There are various assistance programs available to US military veterans and their families, but outside financial help is less structured for active-duty personnel, so Families of the Wounded limits its assistance to those who are still on active duty. In addition, the service member must have been injured in combat operations or as a result of line-of-duty activities in support of combat operations. If Thornton sees someone who fits those qualifications and who has a family appearing to be in need of help, she picks up the phone, calls Haneke, and gives him some brief information about the patient.

"Some weeks, I won't have any patients for him," she said. "Sometimes, I'll give him three names in one day. It doesn't matter. He's always the same: 'No problem, Keneshia. Thanks for calling. I'll get right on it.'"

If his schedule allows, Haneke typically stops by the unit the same day Thornton calls him and visits with the patient and his or her family. He introduces himself, says he's from Families of the Wounded, and identifies it simply as a nonprofit designed to reach out and help families of service members who have been wounded in the line of duty. He gives them a brief overview of his background—his education at West Point, severe wounds in Vietnam and lengthy recovery, much of it at McGuire—and gives them some encouraging words of hope for their recovery and rehabilitation. He asks the patient a few innocent questions about his or her service status and injuries just to confirm the service member's eligibility. He then gives them a business card with his contact information and tells them that they will no doubt have many questions about their stay in Richmond, and they should feel free to contact him if they don't get their questions answered or if they don't feel comfortable asking certain questions of the staff. With that, he leaves without ever mentioning a possibility of financial assistance from Families of the Wounded. Having gone through the routine literally hundreds of times, he keeps it positive, brief, and to the point.

When Haneke gets home, he logs on to his computer and sends out what amounts to a brief synopsis of the patient to the nonprofit's fifteen board members and then waits for the responses to come in. When he reaches the magic number of eight votes needed for approval, he contacts Village Bank and arranges to pick up the check—typically the next day—and with check in hand, he returns to the patient's room. He tells the family that the group appreciates all that they have done for their country and that Families of the Wounded hopes this check will help them with their financial needs.

Then the tears come.

Some charities would use such events as publicity-generating opportunities, making sure television cameras would be on their heels to record the moment and boost their visibility. Families of the Wounded avoids this approach for simple reasons.

First, the group makes its funds available only to active-duty personnel injured in battle or battle support functions, and it does not want to create any animosity with polytrauma unit patients who have suffered brain injuries in off-duty activities, including vehicle crashes, swimming-pool accidents, bar fights, and the like. Second, the nonprofit's fundraising prowess is such that it doesn't need to use individual check presentations to boost its image. The list of people serving as Families of the Wounded's officers and board includes not only corporate titans able to make persuasive pitches to potential donors but also such military heavyweights as Gen. Richard B. Myers, a retired chairman of the Joint Chiefs of Staff. Quite simply, when someone from the Families of the Wounded makes a pitch for donations at a military retirees' dinner, a service organization, or a church group, people listen, as evidenced by the donation totals in the group's IRS returns.

"We'll go anywhere and talk to anybody—anyone who will have us," Haneke said with a chuckle. "It helps that we've had a good track record, and frankly, it really helps that a lot of these groups need a speaker every month. So we can go back to a lot of these groups on a yearly basis, and if they've had a good experience with us in the past, then we've got some credibility built up with them."

"They are a fabulous, fabulous organization," Thornton said. "There are lots of groups out there that can help patients and their families, but we love Families of the Wounded because we have no other organization that can provide that type of support. Others can help, but not like that."

In the winter of 2013, when fighting in Afghanistan was slow because of poor weather conditions, resulting in a relatively low number of war wounded in McGuire's polytrauma unit, Families of the Wounded got in touch with Thornton and asked for contact information for roughly thirty former patients the group had helped. The group wanted to see how each patient was doing and if there was anything more the nonprofit could do to help.

"They really wanted ones who have really needed it in the past," Thornton said. "And that wasn't the first time. They've done it from time to time. They really are incredible."

For many recipients, that starts with Haneke, who after graduating in 1966 from the US Military Academy eventually found himself in Vietnam, where he was severely wounded by what is now called an "improvised explosive device" or IED but was then known simply as a land mine. Thrown eighty feet by the force of the blast, Haneke landed sideways on a barbed-wire fence. He lost his left eye. He lost his right leg above the knee. His jaw was shattered, part of his brain was exposed, and he had a carotid artery that was so badly damaged it was missing a two-inch section.

"I said a prayer that was at the time probably the simplest prayer in the world, and that was, 'Oh, God, help me,'" he recalled.

Haneke was given 178 pints of blood over thirty-six hours after the blast, and he said he was pronounced dead five times in a two-day period. Over the next two-plus years, he underwent more than two hundred major medical procedures.

"Here I am, forty-four years later," he said, gently rubbing his skull, an estimated one-third of which is comprised of a plastic plate-like material.

"Death," he said with a slight smile, "is not an option."

He went on to a lengthy career in hospital administration, including seven years as an assistant director at VCU Medical Center at a time when the university established the facility as a Level I trauma facility. He also has done extensive counseling work with veterans, and he was named the recipient of the 2008 Daughters of the American Revolution Veteran of the Year award.

Haneke, who cowrote his autobiography, *Trust Not,* willingly shares his story of survival and hope in fundraising pitches and with patients and their families on the polytrauma unit. Because of his background in hospital administration and his experiences as a war-wounded service member, he knows the value of having the family at the side of an injured service member—and having them be able to go through the recovery process without fretting about financial emergencies.

"Everyone gets to focus on what they need to focus on, and that's such a key," he said. "Our donations have enabled people to spend more time by the patient's bedside—where they should be."

Haneke admitted that when Families of the Wounded was founded, the group of well-meaning veterans had no inkling the nonprofit's efforts would go on as long as they have. The group figured the United States would wrap up operations in Iraq and that would be the end of it. The board members even discussed what they would do with any leftover funds at the conclusion of the Iraq war, agreeing to transfer the money to the Red Cross or a similar charity.

Iraq morphed into Afghanistan, the years went by, and terrorism continued to keep US troops busy abroad—and getting sent back, severely injured, to Richmond's polytrauma unit.

Fortunately for Families of the Wounded, the group's fundraising efforts and good stewardship left the charity well positioned for the future. In 2012, at the end of its most recent IRS reporting period, Families of the Wounded had assets of nearly $1.2 million—a remarkably far cry from the morning in 2005 when a few marines coming to the aid of some distraught military wives in a South Richmond breakfast joint pitched in to buy them some gasoline, diapers, and other essentials.

"We started out thinking this war on terrorism was only going to last a couple years," Haneke said, pausing to stare off into the distance as he sat in the breakfast nook at his suburban Richmond home. "It appears now that this will not end in our lifetime."

CHAPTER THIRTY-ONE

THE PARACHUTE

The tone and length of the newspaper story that appeared in the *Winston-Salem Journal*'s online edition suggested that what happened on September 27, 2012, was relatively minor.

The first of the story's five paragraphs said a military skydiver had been injured in a publicity event at Victory Junction, a nonprofit camp in Randleman, North Carolina, for children with chronic medical conditions or serious illnesses. The story went on to say the skydiver had been taken to Moses Cone Hospital in nearby Greensboro with an ankle injury and that it was not life threatening.

The story did not identify the skydiver by name.

Several months later, US Army Sgt. 1st Class Marc Owens sat in room 110 of the polytrauma unit at McGuire VA Medical Center and calmly and methodically spoke about what few details he could recall from that day when he and several other military skydivers performed at Victory Junction. Marc remembered that his first jump of the day had been routine. His second had begun in similar fashion, but as he had approached the ground, something happened.

"I was in a slow spin and caught a down draft," he said, "and it pushed me into the ground."

As Marc spoke about having been "pushed" down, he leaned forward in his wheelchair and adjusted the tan-colored sanitary hose that was covering his right leg at a spot just below the knee where surgeons at Moses Cone had amputated. There was another sanitary hose on his left leg. That leg had been amputated above the knee.

However, the true indication of the devastating power of what he matter-of-factly referred to as a "push" was borne out through an accounting of his other injuries higher up in his body.

The accident left Marc with a fractured pelvis.

Surgeons also removed two feet of his small intestine.

He had a ruptured aorta.

His right elbow was fractured.

His left eye socket was fractured.

And he was diagnosed with a TBI.

"I pretty much was out for the whole month of October," he said. "My first surgery took twenty-one pints of blood, and then there were five or six surgeries after that."

By the time he regained consciousness, he had been moved from North Carolina and was at Walter Reed National Military Medical Center. He was moved again on November 19, this time to Richmond, to begin rehabilitation. It became immediately apparent that he was not ready.

"I was a hot mess," he said. "I was a limp noodle. I couldn't do anything for myself."

Not only was Marc weak and ineffective in his physical therapy sessions, but he also was having difficulty eating. Once sturdy at five feet, eight inches tall and 200 pounds, Marc was now down to 123 pounds. It wasn't long before the polytrauma unit staff figured out why.

Marc was diagnosed with ulcerative colitis, an inflammatory bowel disease. The staff tried to treat it with drugs, but still he seemed to keep getting weaker and weaker.

"They were saying, 'Pills, pills, pills, pills,'" he said. "But my body was saying it needed a rest. I'd go down to PT and I couldn't do anything."

So Marc and his girlfriend, a registered nurse, did some research and came up with an alternative to the drugs. They suggested an organic diet, one that eliminated sugar and focused on such items as raw honey and aloe juice. Dr. Ajit Pai, the polytrauma unit's medical director, studied what Owens and his girlfriend had presented him, and he agreed to give it a try.

"One of the nice things about working here," Pai said, "is we've got some flexibility. Marc felt like it might make a difference, and he was pretty down about the way things had been going up to that point. I'm always interested in what the patient thinks, what they want, what they're feeling. That said, I'm not going to do anything that might put them in harm's way. But what Marc was proposing made sense from a nutritional standpoint."

Within five weeks, Marc had engineered a significant turnaround. The stomach troubles abated and he began gaining weight. He was able to parlay that into productivity in his physical therapy sessions, where he started rebuilding muscle mass. Because he showed enough initiative to advocate for himself, and because the physician overseeing his care was interested in input from his patient, Marc was on the road to walking again.

"I never had a doctor do anything like that for me," he said. "He was willing to take a chance. The staff here is just remarkable."

———

A native of Albion, Michigan, Marc Owens joined the army in 1985 straight out of high school. After a few years, he still was unsure about his future and left the military branch for eight years before rejoining in 1997, this time with more focus.

He spent almost eight years with the Golden Knights, the army's Fort Bragg-based aerial demonstration skydiving team, traveling the country to perform at special events, before becoming an instructor for the Black

Knights, the parachute team at the US Military Academy in West Point, New York, for two and one-half years. After an eleven-month tour in Afghanistan, where he served in an aerial delivery unit, he returned to Fort Bragg in March 2012 and at the time of the accident was jumping with the All Veteran Parachute Team, a mix of active-duty and military retirees, most of them from the Fort Bragg area.

Marc refused to harbor any ill feelings about the injuries, including the loss of both legs that left him facing a long course of rehabilitation.

"It's just one of those things that happens if you stay in the sport long enough," he said. "You're bound to get hurt."

Pai and his staff on the polytrauma unit tell patients that the loss of one or more limbs can leave them trying to cope with a wide range of emotions, including anger, embarrassment, depression, and frustration. The staff tells them that those emotions can be expected, because your body can help define your career, especially in the military, and a drastic body change such as amputation can lead to a difficult adjustment period. Patients don't know what will happen to them, how they will be defined, or how to cope. Marc, according to Pai, seemed determined to not let that happen.

"He's got a real willingness to push and push and push. And that's on him," Pai said. "I just admire him. You see him work, you see him smile. The world is open to him."

That drive, determination, and positive spirit came in especially handy in Marc's physical therapy sessions as the staff worked to help him regain his strength and learn to walk again, this time with prosthetics. The staff's number-one concern for amputee patients' emotional needs—the support of family and friends—seemed to get met as well in Marc's case; his girlfriend quit her job at a hospital in Wilmington, North Carolina, and came to Richmond to be with him, and his longtime best friend made frequent trips to visit Marc. A common fear of amputees is that their family and friends will view them differently and treat them differently, but that did not appear as though it were going to be an issue with Marc.

By late January 2013, Owens' stomach troubles appeared to be behind him, and he was regaining strength and starting the process of trying to learn to walk with artificial legs. Prosthetists and physical therapists say patients with below-knee amputations generally have easier adjustment periods than above-knee amputees because they can use their knee joint to help control the prosthetic. Those without a knee have to rely on core muscles above the leg to help control the prosthetic.

Because Marc's right leg had been amputated below the knee and his left one had been amputated above, he faced the challenging task of trying to learn and coordinate two different sets of dynamics into his efforts to walk again. It was further complicated by the fact that his right leg, which should have been easier because of the below-knee amputation, was giving him significant pain because of what the staff determined was a portion of the fibular bone that was rubbing against a nerve.

On the afternoon of January 29, however, Marc wasn't bothered by the right-leg pain as much as he was by his inability to control his new left leg—specifically the prosthetic's knee joint. As he stood on both artificial legs in a physical therapy studio, using waist-high parallel bars to steady himself, he found that the left knee joint would give out easily, making it almost impossible to support himself.

"Your knee is bending. You know how to stop it?" asked Patty Young, the polytrauma unit's amputee rehabilitation coordinator. "Lean forward and squeeze those butt cheeks."

As Young smiled, Marc grimaced while trying to carry out her directions. Beads of sweat began to form on his forehead as he leaned forward on the parallel bars and tried to tighten his buttocks. He clenched his teeth as though that might somehow help the process.

"You're doing fine. Keep it up," Young said. "You should have buns of steel by the end of this. I'm serious. Bounce a quarter off them."

Marc half laughed, half grunted, and then said he needed to take a break. Young helped push a wheelchair up behind him, and he practically plopped into it for a minute or two to rest up for another attempt.

Pulling himself back to his feet, Marc tried to incorporate the forward lean and buttocks tightening that Young had described. Using the parallel bars again to steady himself, he slowly slid one hand forward, then the other, all the while trying to keep his buttocks as tight as possible while lifting one leg, then the other.

"That's it. Keep going. You've got it," Young said calmly as Marc took one step, then two, then three, and finally a fourth, alternating between smiles and grimaces as sweat reappeared on his forehead.

Finally, some eleven feet down the parallel bars, Marc stopped, deciding that that was far enough and that he needed another break. This time, when the wheelchair was rolled up to the back of his legs, he eased slowly down into it, trying to focus on using his stomach muscles to control his descent into the chair.

After another brief break, he got back up again, once more going four steps, but this time demonstrating a good, solid swinging motion with his left leg, which had been stiff on his previous walk. Once he eased back down into the chair, Young praised him and told him that because of his earlier stomach surgery and its effect on his abdominal muscles, he would have a more difficult rehabilitation road than many amputee patients.

"Unfortunately," she said, "you're going to have to work harder than the next guy."

Marc smiled.

"One day at a time," he said. "I'm getting better and better. I'm slowly but surely progressing. I'm not a hot mess any more. Now I'm just a warm mess."

His girlfriend, dressed in a runner's sweat suit and leaning against a wall near the parallel bars, chuckled.

"I want to be able to do everything I could before. Everything," Marc told a visitor. "That's one of my goals—to be able to run beside her and be able to go boating. I want to do all the things we like to do again. I'll get there. I know I will."

As Marc returned to room 110 from physical therapy, a nurse saw him in the main hallway of the polytrauma unit and asked how his session had gone.

"I walked four steps," he proudly told her.

Marc got back in his room and called Mike Elliott, the head of the All Veteran Parachute Team.

"Hey, how are you doing today?" Elliott asked him.

"I walked four steps," Marc shot back, once again making no attempt to contain his pride.

———

Marc Owens was progressing so well that in the first week of February, Dr. Pai gave him what amounted to a weekend pass so that he and his girlfriend could return to Fayetteville, North Carolina, home of Fort Bragg, to visit friends.

The visit was over almost as soon as it began.

Marc's girlfriend, who had been with him for almost two years and had quit her job after his accident to be with him in Richmond, told him she was leaving him.

"For my best friend," Marc said, shaking his head. "My best friend for almost thirty years."

He stared out the window in his hospital room.

"And then she has the audacity to say she thinks she loves him," he said. Marc paused.

"It's a tough pill to swallow," he said. "I just have to try to keep moving forward. No choice."

An hour earlier, he had done just that. In his latest physical therapy session, Marc had exhibited so much strength and resolve that therapists took him off the parallel bars and had him instead use a walker. When a visitor asked Marc how far he was able to go using the walker, he thought for a second.

"Almost out the door," he said.

A long period of silence followed.

"Almost," he repeated, this time in a more melancholy tone, "out the door."

Pai said the polytrauma unit staff was concerned to learn that Marc had lost two key people on whom he had relied for support. Pai had a long talk with Marc when he got back from Fayetteville.

"I gave him my cell number and told him, 'If you get in trouble, or you need anything, give me a call,'" Pai said. "I told him, 'No matter what, we're here for you. You know where my door is. I'm not your psychologist, but if you feel more comfortable talking to me, I am here for you.' "

———

On February 12, Marc Owens, using a walker, covered 135 feet in his physical therapy session.

"I think I stopped one time to turn the walker," he said with a smile. "It felt great. I'm getting a little bit more comfortable with the prosthetic."

Less than a week after that, he surpassed four hundred feet.

The artificial left leg—and its tricky knee joint—were becoming less and less of an issue, thanks in large part to what Marc said was expert guidance from Patty Young, who would literally stay with him every step of the way, offering no-nonsense guidance.

"I have a good rapport with her," Marc said. "She just gets right to the point."

Young, who has a master's degree in physical therapy from Northeastern University and went to Cal State-Dominguez Hills for a certificate program in prosthetics, joined the polytrauma unit in December 2010. She quickly established a reputation as a tireless worker, especially in the field of patient care. To get an idea of just how industrious she is, consider that she worked a fifty-hour week at McGuire while she was thirty-eight weeks pregnant with twins.

"I'm the queen of multitasking," she said. "I need to be doing as many things as possible at one time."

Young almost always seems to be hurrying down one hallway or another at the massive hospital, heading off to an appointment with another patient or to take care of details in her role as a point person for organizing weekly clinics for veterans who have had amputations. The Wednesday afternoon sessions last several hours, providing a chance for a steady stream of veterans—many of them living in threadbare conditions—to have Young and other medical professionals check their prosthetics, see if they need any supplies, and make sure they are taking care of themselves as best they can.

The one time Young appears to slow down is when she's with a patient. She calmly allows them to vent their frustrations, which often involve their struggles to adjust to a new prosthetic device, and she will respond with simple, easy-to-understand advice delivered in even, reassuring tones. She will have the patient try her suggestions, and generally, within a few minutes, the frustrations have evolved into smiles.

If the patients are smiling as they leave, that tells Young she has made a difference in someone's life.

"I could sit here all day," she said, "and watch people walk."

Young said it's difficult to put into words how satisfying it is to help the nation's service members and veterans who have lost limbs.

"I can't imagine doing another job," she said. "They are such wonderful people. And to be a part of this team here? It's a dynamic group."

In the case of Marc Owens, his rehabilitation went so well that the polytrauma unit staff decided to transfer him at the end of February 2013 back to Walter Reed. He would get more surgery on his fractured elbow at the suburban Maryland facility, and there were plans to have surgeons also try to reshape what remained of his right fibula so it would no longer cause him nerve pain that made it difficult to try to walk with a prosthetic device. In addition, because Marc had demonstrated such solid progress with his first set of prosthetic legs in Richmond, he would be fitted at Walter Reed with more advanced devices, ones more suited to the active lifestyle to which he aspired.

"It's kind of like a baton pass," Young said of transferring Marc to Walter Reed. "I look forward to going up there in a few months and seeing him absolutely rock—because that's what he's going to be doing."

With the staffs at McGuire and Walter Reed coordinating the care of Marc's fractures and prosthetics, he took an active role in addressing his TBI. The injury had been originally classified as mild, but Marc freely admitted that it had left him struggling with memory deficits.

"I'd say at this stage my cognition is, I guess it's maybe a little below par," he said. "I have to be honest. I have some memory problems for the short term. But it seems like my long-term memory hasn't been affected as much as I thought it would."

In an attempt to keep his mind sharp and hopefully improve his memory skills, Marc decided to pick up the pace of his online college coursework. He was closing in on a bachelor's degree in hospital administration, and he figured he could take advantage of his free time while being hospitalized to compile the remaining credits he needed to graduate. When he wasn't reading coursework-related material on his laptop, he was watching television—with a purpose. He would seek out shows such as *Jeopardy!* and others that would test his memory, keep his brain engaged, and force him to challenge himself—all in an effort to fight back against the TBI.

"Sure, TBI concerns me," he said. "They don't really know what will happen down the road. But for now, I figure anything I can do to use my brain will do nothing but help. It certainly can't hurt, right? Exercise for the brain, right?"

Whether he was at McGuire or Walter Reed, Marc had another constant in his life: a framed quotation that was given to him by his sister as a birthday gift in 2013. Marc kept the quote on the wall at the foot of his bed, just above waist high, so that every time he woke up it was one of the first things he saw. The quotation is two sentences—the first from Maya Angelou and the second from Eleanor Roosevelt.

"I've learned that no matter what happens, or how bad it seems today, life does go on, and it will be better tomorrow," it reads. "You gain strength, courage and confidence from every experience in which you really stop to look fear in the face."

CHAPTER THIRTY-TWO

STAR

Just as the PSC grew out of the US Department of Veterans Affairs' desires to improve its services, the establishment of STAR became a logical outgrowth of that program.

STAR originally stood for Servicemember Transitional Amputation Rehabilitation, but it quickly morphed into Servicemember Transitional Advanced Rehabilitation. Established as the result of a recommendation of a joint task force involving the VA and the US Department of Defense, STAR was launched in early 2012 as a three-year pilot program.

Brought to life by Dr. Shane McNamee at McGuire, the program—as its original name suggested—was first intended to provide vocational and physical education specifically for active-duty military personnel or veterans who had TBIs and were amputees—and who were trying to return to military, federal, or civilian jobs. It wasn't long, however, before administrators realized that the scope of the program could be broadened to serve amputees and others, and it was expanded to essentially include any service members coming through the PSC.

Because it was, in effect, a finishing school for polytrauma patients, the STAR program found a natural home at the Polytrauma Transitional Rehabilitation Program, already in existence as a finishing school in a building along the southern border of McGuire's sprawling campus. The transitional center has twenty beds, and ten of those were designated for STAR participants.

The overall goal of the transitional center was to take polytrauma patients who no longer needed to be inpatients at the PRC on the second floor of the main hospital, move them into a less-structured setting in the transitional building, and provide them a range of services and therapies that would help them make a successful return to their homes. Those offerings include such services as physical therapy, speech therapy, and adaptive therapy to help them learn how to accomplish such tasks as driving a car again, balancing a checkbook, or preparing meals and cleaning up for themselves in a kitchen.

Whereas those patients in the transitional rehabilitation program used their stay in the building as sort of a final tune-up before returning home to live with their loved ones, the STAR program ramped it up a notch by catering to those patients who were looking to return to specific jobs or explore specific areas of study. The STAR patients had access to the same therapists and services as the other patients in the transitional building, but they also had the benefits of not only staff members who helped them identify employment possibilities but also a network of corporate and military employers throughout the Richmond region who were willing to help them make that transition back into the workforce.

STAR patients spend several hours a day seeing therapists or taking advantage of other services available to them at the transitional center, and then they spend an average of four to six hours daily out in the community, either at local jobs or at schools where they work on skills that help them prepare for a return to the work force.

"The program is providing a different intensity level than has been provided for the patients," said Dr. Joseph A. Webster, the STAR program's medical director.

Early in the program, it became apparent that the decision of the joint VA/Department of Defense task force to create STAR, and the efforts of McNamee and Webster to get it up and running, were filling a need for patients who were trying to work their way back from multiple traumatic injuries.

"It really can be kind of a snowball effect and build their confidence and build their hope that there really is something out there, life out there, beyond this," Webster said.

He was working in the VA's amputee care system in Seattle when he was recruited by McNamee to come to Richmond in 2011 to guide the STAR program from its infancy.

"Like anything within the VA system, it took a little bit longer than we thought to get up and running," Webster said. "But we've really been able to broaden the scope of the program. It's evolving quite a bit, and it's clear that it's serving a very real need."

That need grew out of the success stories that were emerging from the PRCs. The stated goal of the staff at Richmond, for example, is to return the patients to as high a level of function and independence as possible. In some cases, that can mean simply being able to walk out the doors of McGuire's PRC and go home with their families, but a growing number of those being released from the unit not only were finding themselves able to do more, but also wanting to.

"Returning to some kind of meaningful activity can mean employment," Webster said, "but it can also mean volunteering or going to school. There are many avenues available, and we want to help them get there."

When patients first enter the STAR program, they go through an interview process, part of which includes the patients and vocational specialists teaming up to identify anywhere between three and ten possible future endeavors. The reason multiple possibilities are identified is because, depending on the severity of their injuries and their pace of recovery, their top choice may not always be realistic.

Webster recalled one active-duty service member who was recovering from a moderate TBI and thought he might like to go into police work. So the STAR program set him up with not only the police force at McGuire but also the Richmond Police Department and the Chesterfield County Sheriff's Office. The man was able to spend extensive time with each agency, asking questions, observing, and going on ride-alongs to get a feel for daily life in law enforcement.

The result?

"He ended up concluding that the intensity and the stress levels that could be involved in that type of work may not have made him a good fit for it," Webster said.

That change highlights another benefit of the STAR program: Because there are ten private bedrooms available for participants and because the program is set up to allow individuals to stay for three to nine months, they have time to explore their options. In this case, the man switched from pursuing a possible career in law enforcement to looking at other, less-stressful possibilities, including driving a truck.

Another participant used the STAR program to see if he was ready to return to the field in which he had been working at the time of his injury. This man, who had suffered a TBI while stationed in Germany, where he was an army videographer, felt he could resume that role. So the STAR program arranged for him not only to work with videographers within the VA system, but also to spend some time with the staff of a Richmond television station. His work with the VA and the television station confirmed his beliefs that he was, indeed, capable of resuming his career, and he left STAR and returned to active duty with the army as a videographer.

———

Working to help amputees is a natural for Webster, who in addition to overseeing the STAR program is the medical director for the VA's amputation system of care.

"These guys have served and they've sacrificed," Webster said, "and they deserve the best we can do for them."

Unfortunately, the STAR program occasionally encounters the red tape and delays that are so often a part of the federal government's bureaucracy, especially when the military is involved. For instance, although the STAR program can take in and evaluate a new patient and then work with an employer or employers to train that person for a new career, the patient's release from the program—and into the working world—may not always coordinate with the timing of their release from the military.

Most active-duty personnel who come into the STAR program and are attempting to leave the military are doing so via the so-called Med Board process, a method in which a military panel judges the severity of the service member's injuries, determines a level of disability payments due to the person, and then processes the paperwork to release him or her from the service. Webster said there have been occasions where STAR has been able to get an individual trained and then lined up with a job in the outside world, only to learn that he or she is not yet free to leave the military and take that position because the Med Board process, which frequently takes six to nine months and occasionally longer, has yet to run its course. STAR officials are working with the Department of Defense and the VA in an attempt to better coordinate the timing of the release of patients from the program with the completion of the Med Board process, an endeavor that Webster called "a little bit of a moving target."

Another unwanted reality is that motivation—or lack of it—can also be an issue with some polytrauma patients who are considered good candidates to join the STAR program, and it can be a direct result of financial considerations associated with the Med Board process.

As the Med Board works through the process of determining disability payments, it arrives at its conclusions by rating an individual's abilities. If a person has little cognitive and physical function and therefore has limited abilities, his or her ratings will result in larger disability payments. Conversely, if a person has demonstrated that his or her cognitive and physical functions have returned to a higher level, then his/her ratings will result in smaller disability payments.

That, Webster noted, can leave some polytrauma patients in a quandary: Should they elect against participating in the STAR program, go through the Med Board process and hope it results in a rating that will produce the highest possible disability payments, or should they enter STAR and work toward a return to the working world in a meaningful capacity? If they have a successful experience at STAR, they may not be looked upon as favorably in the Med Board process when it comes time to determine the size of their disability payments.

"If they get too good, it's going to affect their rating," Webster explained. "And let's face it: That compensation is going to affect their security."

Those cases are rare, however.

"The majority of people want to work," he said. "They want to be productive and they want to benefit from the program."

Those benefits have been aided significantly by the willingness of community partners to help the STAR program succeed, and that willingness is not limited to the corporate world.

VCU, the thirty-four-thousand-student school based in Richmond, has fostered a close working relationship with the STAR program, offering everything from help to determine a course of college study to employment counseling and job opportunities at VCU Medical Center. Another active participant is the Defense Logistics Agency (DLA), which is the Department of Defense's largest logistics combat support agency and is headquartered at Fort Belvoir in Northern Virginia, about a ninety-minute ride from Richmond. The DLA offers its operation as a place where those whose injuries prevent them from serving in combat roles can continue their military careers in an office environment.

The list of corporate partners has grown steadily since STAR was launched and crosses a broad spectrum that includes such companies as CSX, the railroad giant, and Dominion Resources Inc., Virginia's largest utility.

"The community employers have really been willing to bend over backward to facilitate whatever they could to make opportunities available," Webster said. Knowing that people in the community are willing to step up and help them is a vital aid to the emotional well-being of the STAR participants. That's especially true with relatively young active-duty personnel who were wounded in action shortly after coming out of high school and suddenly find themselves struck with a jolt of new reality as they struggle to overcome a TBI as well as the loss of one or more limbs. They had planned on making the military a career and figured they would have plenty of time throughout that career to take advantage of educational opportunities and work their way up the promotional ladder.

"When they don't have that any more, they really are lost," Webster said. "They've lost all control over everything they had previously."

CHAPTER THIRTY-THREE

MOVING ON

It was a foggy, gray Saturday afternoon in Newport, Pennsylvania, as David McHenry led two visitors up the staircase to the second floor of his red brick Cape Cod-style house and then slowly pushed open the door to Jon McHenry's childhood bedroom.

"It's been a while since I've been up here," David said.

Months earlier, Jon had come home to Newport for a few days, just before he was to be discharged from Walter Reed to return to Fort Hood, Texas, for what he hoped would be a brief stop on his way back to Afghanistan, and had staged what his father later described as a purge in the large bedroom.

Jon had gone through desk drawers and his walk-in closet, methodically and purposefully, filling large trash bag after large trash bag with his childhood memories. Sports memorabilia, uniforms, trophies, medals—once-precious items had been tossed unceremoniously into the bags and hauled down the stairs to be thrown into the garbage. David had tried to reason with Jon that day and convince his son not to get rid of all the mementos that had meant so much in his childhood—one in which he had achieved so much by proving wrong those who doubted him because of his small stature. Jon had shown time and again that hard work, perseverance, discipline, and toughness could make up for a lack of size.

Jon, however, would not hear of it. He had seemed dead-set on putting his past behind him. He had already told his father during that trip home that he was heading back to Texas well before he was required to be there, leaving David to wonder if Jon wasn't in a hurry to put the whole IED incident behind him. The bedroom purge made his father think Jon didn't want anything more to do with his childhood, either. He kept telling his father he no longer needed all those items, and it was time to clean out the room. David later said the incident left him feeling hurt and fighting back tears—as though his son wanted to distance himself not only from the horrors of the IED blast in Afghanistan but also from his childhood and perhaps his family as well. Jon had seemed to want nothing to do with anyone or anything unless it involved him gaining closure, and the only way for him to achieve that was for the army to send him back to Afghanistan.

One year after that trip home, Jon had yet to return to Newport.

"I understand he's got a wife and a son now, and it's different when you've got your own family," his father said. "And I know he's a long way away, being in Texas, so it's a big trip to come home. But still, you have to wonder. Sometimes it feels like it's maybe not that important to him."

On this day, however, David McHenry got a pleasant surprise when he led his visitors into Jon's bedroom. A small smile began to crease across his face soon after he walked into the room and saw a few trophies sitting on a desk. The smile grew when he opened the door to the closet. Inside, still hanging on the clothes bar, were numerous items, including basketball jerseys, warm-up suits, and the like.

Jon's purge, it was becoming apparent, had not been a total, ruthless cleanout. He had kept a number of items, a number of links to his past and to the days when he first built a reputation as a tough, hardened warrior.

David took time to absorb each find, running his hands slowly across the items as he reminisced about their origins and recounted Jon's athletic exploits. Then, as he kept making his way around the room and found more and more treasures from the past, he came across a cardboard box. It was perhaps eighteen inches by fourteen inches, maybe six inches deep, and it was full of cards and letters. Some were get-well letters from the days and weeks after the IED blast. Some were from friends in Newport. Some were from across the country.

The box, David discovered, also contained several letters from back when Jon was still in school. There was one from a retired woman in nearby Duncannon who had seen Jon play basketball and became so enamored with his fearless, scrappy style of play that she had begun going to all of his games. David slowly pulled the letter from its envelope and began reading passages from the woman about how special Jon's talents were and how he clearly pushed himself to get the most out of his abilities. Looking up from the handwritten letter, David turned to his visitors and smiled. His son, as it turned out, hadn't completely purged his past.

———

Late in the summer of 2013, Jon McHenry was moving methodically closer to getting out of the army. The Med Board process was progressing, and all Jon was waiting on was a determination of his percentage of disability before the army could set a date for his release from the service branch.

Back in Newport, meantime, his father was looking for a new job after being laid off in the spring from AmeriGas, a Harrisburg natural gas company.

While pursuing several possibilities, including one that eventually landed him a job with a railroad as a conductor, David had plenty of time to reflect on his middle son's odyssey and how it had instantly changed the courses of several lives.

"Something like that just kind of takes over your life. It was truly amazing how the people—even today, I get teared up when I think about the support we had," he said. "And the care he got with Dr. Pai, I just wish all doctors were as caring as he was. I think that was an excellent experience, not only for Jon but for me."

"I'll tell you, people today still ask me, 'How's Jon? How's he doing?' But eventually, everything goes back to normal."

David paused.

"Except for the soldier."

And, perhaps, the soldier's loved ones.

David said that while rummaging through his house, he had recently run across a newspaper clipping about Jon from right after the IED blast, and he found that he had become quickly engrossed as he began to read it, fighting to control his emotions as the clipping washed up a sea of still-fresh emotional wounds.

"Even a year and a half, two years later, it still tears you up," he said. "You think about how lucky you are. So many of them don't come back. He's one lucky kid, that's for sure."

David paused again.

"One lucky man, I should say."

Staying by his son's side for months after his return from Afghanistan had helped strengthen their relationship. He recounted having given Jon a stern lecture after one of his son's carousing episodes in high school, and how Jon hadn't taken kindly to his father's words. Later, as Jon lay in a hospital bed recovering from his injuries, he found himself in a reflective mood one day. David described their conversation:

"I remember he said, 'Dad, remember us getting into it that time? Well, you were right.' I told him, 'I knew I was right, Jon, because I lived it. I've been there, done that.' He probably didn't realize that whatever he did, I did years earlier myself.'"

David shook his head and chuckled.

"Boy," he said, "I sure can't say that about everything Jon has been through now."

One subject they don't share much is what lies in the future for those who have suffered a significant TBI. David McHenry is well aware that there is evidence emerging that TBI patients can be more susceptible later in life to seizures, dementia, Lou Gehrig's disease, and other serious health problems.

"Right now he just focuses on the now, not the future," David said. "But it worries me. It worries me a lot. Especially dementia. Dementia runs in our family. I worry about it even with no TBI. Heck, I worry about it myself."

David had a grandparent who suffered from dementia, and his father was in the throes of the disease in 2013, appearing to get steadily worse each time David visited him.

"I look at where Jon is, how far he's come physically since he first got back in the US from Afghanistan, and it really is amazing," his father said. "But when you think about TBI and what it might lead to down the road, I just wish we knew more. I wish we knew more about what to look for, and I wish we knew what to do about it. But we don't. We really don't. I don't know what we can do about it. I don't think we can do anything about it.

"And as a parent, that's a pretty helpless feeling, because all I've ever wanted for Jon—all I've ever wanted for any of my children—is the best."

Jon McHenry said there was a reason that, unlike his father, he didn't worry too much about the possible long-term consequences of TBI, about what might happen to him down the road as he put more and more days, months, and years between himself and the IED blast.

"Just because I had a moderate TBI, which was how it was listed, that doesn't mean it's still moderate," he said. "I'd like to think it's in the past. It's just another thing that pushes me a little harder."

Jon said that since the IED blast, he had headaches "more frequently than I used to. But I don't let it keep me from doing what I want to do."

His only concessions to the TBI involved trying to keep his mind sharp. He tried to read as much as possible and watch game shows on television. Beyond that, his approach was to try to maintain a sense of normalcy in his life.

"It's definitely something that's in the back of my mind, sure," he said. "But beyond doing what I'm doing, I don't know what else to do. I mean, you can't stop living."

Jon said his approach to life as a TBI survivor was based on the fact that no two brain injuries are alike. As a result, everybody reacts in a different way to their injuries, and Jon's way was the only way he had ever reacted to adversity.

"They said I couldn't play on the basketball team when I was a freshman and weighed just 120 pounds," he said. "They said a five-foot-four freshman point guard wasn't big enough.

"I'm faster than you. I'll hustle more. I'll go around you. I'll dive for loose balls. You adapt. I've always adapted."

He took a deep breath and slowly exhaled.

"I'm sure I'll have my moments. But I'll get it done," he said. "I have to get it done."

———

While waiting for the Med Board process to play out, Jon McHenry finally was able to form a plan for his immediate future. He decided to take advantage of a generous GI Bill and work toward a college degree.

He had already accumulated nearly two dozen college credits through online courses and classes offered by the army. He applied to Wesley College, a 2,500-student school in Dover, Delaware, a drive of three-plus hours from Newport. Not only would Dover put him relatively close to home, but it also would place him in the same city as his older brother, Evan, an information technology project manager.

"This is the best thing for everyone, I think," Jon said. "I explained it to my dad. It's not firm that I'm going to live in Delaware forever, but it's a good spot to be now. This gets us closer to my family—everybody's all pretty close by. And Jay's got family in Manhattan, so we're not that far a drive from New York City."

The decision was the result of more than a year of considering a wide range of options, which included a decision to either stay in the army and pursue a career as an officer or to leave the military; going home to Pennsylvania and studying mortuary science, counseling, or some other field; and relocating to Arizona or Florida or staying in Texas to be close to the family of his friend and fallen comrade, Kurt Kern.

Once the army rejected his bid to return to Afghanistan, however, Jon had felt he could no longer in good conscience remain with the service branch. That being the case, the most prudent move was to get closer to home and to the people who loved and had supported him the most throughout his ordeal and get on with his life.

Going to school on the East Coast fit that bill.

"My next chapter is college," he said. "Once that was worked out, it was just a matter of figuring where I could get the most help. Evan can help me in Dover, and Wesley can help me get where I need to be. College is the next step for anything nowadays. I 'm not crazy about school and stuff, but I've got to grow up. I've got a kid. It's time to buckle down."

Another factor that eventually came into play, he said, was getting closer to home. Although he was especially appreciative of the bond he'd formed with Kurt Kern's family in Texas, he realized that getting back to or near Pennsylvania would be a better fit for his own family.

"My dad's always been there for me," he said. "There's never been a question about that. And I know he always will be."

The plans solidified on Saturday, August 13, 2013, when Jon got a letter in the mail from Wesley College informing him that he had been accepted for the January 2014 term in the school's K–12 physical education program. His father seemed relieved with the decision that would bring his son within easy driving distance of Newport and more relieved that the decision was the result of carefully considering a number of options over a significant span of time.

"Every other week, it was something different," David McHenry said. "I'm sure college is going to be a hard road. No doubt about it. He's got a family now.

"I imagine he's struggling a little bit to try to figure things out. But at least he's weighing things out now. He's looking at a little more than just the first thing that jumps out in front of him. And he's a hard worker. He's never let obstacles get in his way before, and I know he won't do that now, either. Jon's pretty strong. He's a tough customer."

That hard-working nature, as it turns out, came squarely into play when Jon chose Wesley. The college offers a number of teaching programs, and he decided to pursue a degree in physical education. Not only would that allow him to stay active physically, but he also could use the leadership qualities he had first discovered as a young athlete and pass them on to a new generation of youth, this time as a gym teacher.

There was another reason Jon wanted to get a degree in physical education. He was hopeful it would help him reconnect with a sport he loved, one that had helped develop the character and leadership he possessed at that stage in his life. He envisioned not only becoming a gym teacher but also parlaying that into a role as a basketball coach.

"I want to at least try it," he said. "Maybe it'll just be in middle school or something like that to start, but I think I can do it. I think I have some things I can bring to the job."

Make no mistake: Just because the army had turned him away in his bid to return to Afghanistan after initially saying he was physically fit to do so, and just because he had undergone subsequent surgery to make even more repairs on his badly fractured right leg, Jon McHenry had not abandoned his bid to show people he could make a comeback and prove to them that they should never discount his abilities or his heart.

The latest leg surgery had seemed to finally alleviate the significant pain that had been hampering Jon, and once again, he attacked his rehabilitation like a warrior. By late spring, he was running sub-eight-minute miles, this time with practically no post-run soreness, and by early summer, his workouts were approaching three miles in length. In addition, his right leg—which a few months earlier was too tender for him to try to jump off of and even more tender when he would try to land on it—could now withstand extended jump-rope sessions with no pain.

That set the stage for Sunday, July 7, when Jon and a couple of his buddies got together at Fort Hood for something that would have seemed at the very least improbable and perhaps impossible on the evening of December 27, 2011, when that IED in Afghanistan had ended three lives and forever changed three others.

It lasted, as Jon recalled, only about thirty minutes, and it wasn't the most physical contest ever. Yet for half an hour or so, the ball bounced again, the gym shoes squeaked again, some of the shots found nothing but net again, and some of the old trash talk surfaced again. Jon McHenry, sweating on a basketball court in Texas, found a measure of peace and comfort by completing his comeback in a most unlikely setting.

"It was a damn good feeling to pick up a ball again, to shoot a little bit and all that," he said. "I didn't blow by anybody or anything, but I can be a spot-up shooter. I can adapt. I've always been able to do that."

The significance of the occasion was not lost on him. Like so many others from small towns across America, this soldier had gone into the military, gone to war for his country, and been gravely wounded. He had worked tirelessly for months to recover and rehabilitate in order to earn a return trip to Afghanistan. He had done everything the army had asked of him, but he still had been turned away and told his efforts weren't good enough.

Now, however, all that hard work—all those hours in physical therapy, all the weightlifting sessions in the gym, and all the running workouts in which he pushed himself to the limit—had paid major dividends in a different way. Thirty minutes on the basketball court confirmed that, even though the army had let him down, he hadn't let himself down. He had his life back. He hadn't made it back to Afghanistan, but he could run again. He could jump again. He could create his own joy again on the basketball court.

Jon McHenry had faced the most horrific event in his life, and he adapted. Less than nineteen months later, he found a new normal in a place where he already had proven himself countless times: on a basketball court.

"That," he said, pausing as he searched for the right words, "was the first time…"

He didn't finish the thought.

He didn't have to.

CHAPTER THIRTY-FOUR

THE ART OF MEDICINE

While Jon McHenry sharpened his focus on the future as the summer of 2013 slipped into fall, his two comrades who survived the IED blast continued to fight their way back to health.

Michael Crawford remained in San Antonio, Texas, working hard in his rehabilitation as he tried to build a new normal.

One of the pictures he posted on his Facebook page was of him wearing his dress blues and using a walker, prompting a large number of supportive responses, including one from Kristi Korte, whose husband, Sgt. Noah M. Korte, had been one of the three men killed in the IED blast.

"So happy to see you doing so well," Korte's widow wrote, adding that she and her two young sons "think about you all every day."

Michael thanked her for her kind words, writing that he also thought about "the guys and all of that every day." He also said the "medals come at a price, and I'd give them all up in a heartbeat to be back to my old ways again!!!"

Capt. Luis Avila was still a patient at Walter Reed, where he continued to try to rebuild strength, put on weight, and learn to talk and walk again.

Jon had not spoken with Luis since their reunion in room 110 at McGuire in the late spring of 2012, and by late summer 2013 it had been roughly a year since Luis' wife, Claudia, had responded to any of Jon's attempts to contact her by telephone or via Facebook.

Burness Britt, meantime, remained at the Portsmouth Naval Hospital, waiting for the Med Board process to conclude so he could leave the Marine Corps and return to Georgetown, South Carolina. He planned to work as a driver for his father, who has a construction contracting business.

Jessica Britt was already back in Georgetown, having returned there after she and Burness split up in the late spring of 2012. Jessica was working as a massage therapist and looking into the possibility of going to college.

Dr. Bruce Wallace's wife, Helen, opted to take him out of McGuire's polytrauma unit in favor of a private rehabilitation facility in Blacksburg, Virginia, expressing hope that he could overcome the damage caused by his anoxic brain injury and be able to return—if not to work at Walter Reed, then at least to the couple's home in Bethesda, Maryland.

Marc Owens remained at Walter Reed, where he continued to labor away at the course work needed to complete his degree in hospital administration while he recovered from elbow and stomach surgery and kept going to physical therapy to adjust to his new artificial legs. The accident that had cost him his legs—and the subsequent recovery and rehabilitation—had become a long exercise in patience.

"I've been, I would say, more of a flexible person," Marc said. "I've learned to kind of roll with the punches."

Eric Petersen spent several months at his parents' home in the Philadelphia suburbs in the summer and fall of 2012. He was feted by his local school district and recognized on the field before a Philadelphia Eagles' home game in October. He then returned to Fort Riley, Kansas, to rejoin his unit. Petersen continued to regain weight and strength and spoke hopefully of attending Army Ranger training.

Marc Crawford was perhaps the most high-profile "graduate" of Richmond's polytrauma unit. He spent the late stages of 2013 at various specialized navy education programs on the East Coast, including Newport,

Rhode Island, and Dahlgren, Virginia, to help prepare him for his return to San Diego to take command in March 2014 of the USS Gridley, a guided missile destroyer staffed by roughly 280 sailors.

"It's the chance of a lifetime, and quite frankly, there was a time not too long ago when I didn't know if it would happen," Marc said. "The people at Richmond changed everything. They were amazing. I wouldn't be here if it weren't for them."

He was working out regularly and without limitations, and by December 2013, he had run six half-marathons since his TBI and was starting to talk about running a full marathon.

"I feel like I am close to being in the best shape I have been at in my life," he said, "so no complaints here. Physiologically, cognitively, it's very hard to discern a difference in me. Three years later, I have no challenges."

Marc kept sharing his story, telling several new people each week about his experiences.

"I look at it as a chance to give others a glimmer of hope," he said. "Good things still happen today. Miracles still happen."

David Rogers continued to chart a course of slow, steady improvement. His mother remained confident he would one day walk unaided, and she was hopeful he would one day talk without having to rely on his electronic keyboard. McGuire officials chose Lauri Rogers to deliver the keynote address when they held a ribbon-cutting gala on August 22, 2013, to celebrate the $8.5 million overhaul of the hospital's polytrauma unit. The renovations included such minute details as painting the entrances to each patient room different colors, a feature designed to help those with limited visual abilities who might not be able to read their room's number on the wall. Several patient rooms also had video cameras pointed at the beds to watch the movements of seizure patients, with an accompanying bank of monitors at the nearby nurses' station.

"This is the gem, the crown jewel in the VA at this point in terms of continuum of care," Dr. Shane McNamee, who was the unit's medical director when David Rogers arrived at Richmond, told a crowd of some 200 people who gathered in a unit built to take advantage of the latest technologies in rehabilitation medicine. In her remarks, however, Lauri Rogers made it clear she regards the true jewels of the unit as its staff. It was McNamee and the rest of the polytrauma team, she said, who took in her son when he was just "a curled ball of humanity" and used their human touch to help him recover to levels no one had predicted.

"Four years later," she said, "David is known by some as, 'The Miracle.' Throughout the inpatient and the outpatient rehab, his staff continued to care for David with encouragement and a relationship that exceeded that of a typical medical staff. They moved into our hearts as extended family—sometimes closer."

Those people, Rogers said, are not only making achievements in the often-frustrating world of brain-injury rehabilitation medicine, but their dedication charts a course for more improvements.

"As we run toward more victories in this important race, as we strive toward a prize that we may never fully grasp because of its vastness and limitations, let us remember that our goal is to get as close as possible," she said. "The prize of this race is a greater understanding of the human brain—the place where the human spirit dwells."

With the summer of 2013 passing into fall, David continued to expand on his daily routine of independence, waking before his parents and taking care of the family's dogs. By then, he was also preparing his own hearty breakfasts as well, loading up on protein to set the stage for hours of activities each day in which he would continue to push himself to get stronger and more agile.

On September 26, David returned to Peak Experiences, the indoor climbing center not far from the family's Midlothian home where he had first used a specially designed harness eleven months after his injury. This time, however, David was no longer such a prisoner to physical limitations. This time, on a beautiful fall day, David strapped his now-stunningly toned body into a regular harness and began his ascent, one in which he quickly demonstrated spiderlike abilities.

"Don't do it so fast," Lauri Rogers said below as her son practically scurried up the vertical face on his way to the top of the wall. "Do it slow."

If David heard her, he wasn't listening.

It was one of three visits he made that week to Peak Experiences.

———

On June 13, 2013, The US Department of Defense announced it was creating what it called the world's first brain tissue repository with the goal of helping foster better understanding of TBI in service members.

The hope was that the repository, established in Bethesda, Maryland, with a federal grant, would help researchers zero in on how head trauma might lead to brain damage that plays out over the course of years and decades after one or more TBIs. Specifically, researchers want to know more about possible links between TBI and chronic traumatic encephalopathy (CTE), a degenerative disorder in which tau protein accumulates in the brain. Tau protein can disturb brain function and appears to lead to symptoms seen in people who suffer repeated head trauma such as boxers and professional football players. Researchers have already established strong links between accumulated tau and Alzheimer's disease, and they are attempting to determine what role tau might play in other dementias and conditions, including PTSD.

"Little is known about the long-term effects of traumatic brain injury on military service members," said Dr. Daniel Perl, a neuropathologist and the director of the tissue repository. "By studying these tissues, along with access to clinical information associated with them, we hope to more rapidly address the biologic mechanisms by which head trauma leads to chronic traumatic encephalopathy."

Perl said researchers want to be able to more definitively answer such questions as what blast exposure does to the brain and whether different forms of brain injury experienced in the military lead to CTE. In recent years, various studies began to show links between people suffering one or more TBIs and a number of problems later in life, including Alzheimer's disease, Parkinson's disease, amyotrophic lateral sclerosis, and multiple sclerosis.

In addition, the National Football League was named in countless lawsuits filed by former players and their families who said there appeared to be a troubling pattern of repeated concussions suffered during playing careers and subsequent diagnoses of CTE, Alzheimer's disease, and other dementias. A number of family members of former players said the repeated concussions appeared to have played a role in suicides, and in several cases, the former players had shot themselves in the chest, allowing for their brains to be posthumously studied.

Perl said service members exposed to blasts "are coming home with troubling, persistent problems, and we don't know the nature of this, whether it's related to psychiatric responses from engagement in warfare or related to actual damage to the brain, as seen in football players. We hope to address these findings and develop approaches to detecting accumulated tau in the living individual as a means of diagnosing CTE during life—and, ultimately, create better therapies of ways to prevent the injury in the first place."

Dr. Ajit Pai applauded the establishment of the brain tissue repository as another important step in better understanding TBI and its long-term effects.

"This will help make strides in the right direction," Pai said. "All we have at this time is brain tissue from athletes and pro wrestlers. From all we know, blast injuries' effects on the brain are different from impact injuries. I hope this will give us some more insight."

However, Dr. Shane McNamee said, all the research done so far on brain injuries has not only produced some helpful information, but it also has served to remind us that we are in what McNamee called the dark ages of brain injury research and that we have a long, long way to go, and although brain injury research is struggling for definitive, course-changing answers, it's not keeping pace with modern military technologies.

"The simple truth," McNamee said, "is we have gotten better as human beings at warfare."

Pai concurred, saying research is "on the right track, but we've got to keep going, because we're always seeing new problems emerge. We're seeing a bunch of younger guys with memory problems already. That isn't dementia. That's memory problems associated with TBI. That's guys who have been repeatedly exposed to TBI."

Pai said he believes major discoveries will be made in brain injury research in the years and decades ahead and that significant strides will occur. However, he also said it might be unrealistic to expect any monumental breakthroughs to emerge on the immediate horizon.

"I think he's right," Pai said of McNamee. "I think we have a long way to go. But I also think it will happen in my lifetime—in the next five, ten, or fifteen years, I think we'll know so much more than we know now. I really think we're going to start to have some answers—or at least we're going to be able to discuss it in a less vague manner. But the brain is very complicated, and right now, answers are elusive. There's no easy fix out there."

"To me," McNamee said, "it's like we're still using flashlights in a cave— little penlights in a dark cave. There's still so much uncertainty, so much we don't know."

That cloud of uncertainty can be particularly challenging for a physician such as Pai, who had a strong grounding in medical school in spinal cord injuries.

"Often with spinal cord injuries, while you can't fix it, we at least know that when a certain area of the spinal cord is injured, you are going to see specific things and specific issues," Pai said. "But no two brain injuries are alike, and what you'll see in one person may not even be remotely similar in another. So while it's fascinating, it's also challenging—and it can be frustrating at times."

Pai continued to embrace the challenges of his job overseeing the polytrauma unit and had no plans to leave, but he also knew it would be natural to expect that, just as had occurred with McNamee, the unit's daily challenges and frustrations would likely take a toll on him at some point. At age thirty-four, Pai was already in his fourth year as the unit's medical director, and he spoke of eventually exploring possible options in teaching and administration.

McNamee, his predecessor, made it for more than four years as the unit's medical director, and after an additional four-plus years as the hospital's chief of PM&R, he was talking about looking for another new challenge, this time involving so-called informatics, the science of using computers for research.

McNamee even approached IBM officials in the summer of 2013 about the possibility of enlisting Watson, their heralded supercomputer, to take part in brain-injury research.

"I'm really just a geek when you get right down to it," McNamee said.

Part of his immediate future came into focus on August 10, 2013, when the White House announced that VCU was being awarded a $62 million grant—the largest federal grant in its history—to oversee a national research consortium studying TBIs and concussions. VCU's Dr. David Cifu, who had spent decades building a strong alliance with McGuire and the rest of the VA healthcare system, was named the principal investigator for the grant, and McNamee was among those named to work closely with him on the project.

No matter where McNamee and Pai end up, the polytrauma unit staff will continue to do what modern medicine offers: They will use the latest in electronic imaging equipment and the most up-to-date diagnostic tools; they will take advantage of the latest technologies in laboratory work, drug therapies, and rehabilitation equipment and methods; and they will work all of that into their care.

Pai's team at McGuire will also keep doing what helped distinguish them as what Lauri Rogers called "the flagship" of polytrauma care in the VA healthcare system. Quite simply, they will rely heavily on their people skills, their sense of caring, their sense of teamwork, and their diversity of expertise.

"There's somebody on the team who always brings something," Pai said. "And we're all growing. And when we're growing, we're able to help people."

Because their offices are right on the polytrauma unit with the patient rooms, the staff members often stop in to visit with the patients, and vice versa. When a doctor, nurse, therapist, or other staff member comes to see a patient, they don't stand in the doorway of the room and act as though they are in a hurry to move on to the next patient. They come in and stay for a while. They might even sit down in a chair and chat—or read to the patient or play video games with him or her.

"Most of the patients aren't here for just a few days," Pai said. "They can be here for months at a time. This becomes their home. So we want them to feel at home, and part of that means they should be comfortable. We want them to feel like family."

If that means Barbara Bauserman, the family education coordinator, steps out of her professional role and takes Cathy Powers to church with her, so be it.

If it means Pai gives patients and their caregivers his cell phone number because he thinks it might give everyone a little bit of peace of mind, so be it.

And if it means Pai and his staff don't rely exclusively on all the technology available to them, if it means that in addition to using the latest imaging equipment, the polytrauma unit staff also will take the time to sit on patients' beds and examine them, touch them, ask questions of them, and listen to the answers to make sure what the imaging equipment shows is also what the patients feel, then so be it.

There's far too little of that personal touch in modern medicine in Pai's opinion, and as far as he's concerned, there's no question that the reasons for the Richmond polytrauma unit's success, the reasons he and the rest of his staff get the positive results they do, are rooted in the staff's willingness to defy the trend and mix in as much hands-on healthcare as possible.

"I think we're on a slippery slope in medicine where we're doing procedures and studies to try to get more answers," Pai said. "But we're moving away from touching people. We're moving away from examining people, from listening to them, from truly involving them."

That compassionate way of care, that way of making patients feel like people instead of file numbers, has emerged in an unlikely place—amid a vast, often overloaded federal bureaucracy in a gritty neighborhood of Richmond, Virginia, at 1201 Broad Rock Boulevard, on the second floor of the McGuire VA Medical Center.

The VA established the five polytrauma centers around the United States to create a better system of care for the nation's military and veterans. It ended up getting an oasis in Richmond, where passionate and personalized medical care are the rule and not the exception, where the staff members will put their hands on you, sit with you, laugh with you, cry with you and for you, and be joyful for you when you leave.

"As healthcare providers, we are responsible—and we should be held re-sponsible—for doing things like that," Pai said, his voice rising as he leaned forward at the desk in his plain, cramped, windowless office.

"That should be the standard of care. And if it isn't, then we have to ask ourselves what we're doing. This is the art of medicine. Caring and compas-sion are part of that."

Made in the USA
Middletown, DE
07 July 2016